The Culture of Research

Insights from a 45-year practice in the design and execution of multicultural research

By Edward T. Rincón, Ph.D.

Copyright © 2020 Edward T. Rincón, Ph.D.

All rights reserved.

No content of this book whatsoever may be copied, excerpted, replicated or shared without permission from the author.

Published by Writer's Marq LLC

ISBN: 978-0-578-75825-1

DEDICATION

To my wife Lupita, my son Sergio and daughter Andrea. The countless hours that you spent listening patiently, debating and reviewing these ideas over the past three years are deeply appreciated and provided me the needed inspiration to complete this book.

Table of Contents

Acknowledgments i

Foreword iii

Advance Praise vii

Introduction 1

    Book Overview 2

Chapter 1: Multicultural Research — An Industry in Need of a Facelift 7

    The Wake-Up Call 7

    Curious Industry Indifference 8

    The Consequences 9

    A Love Affair with Positive Satisfaction Ratings 10

    Early Demise of The George Lopez Show 10

    The Texas Way 11

    Is Racial Profiling on the Decline? 11

    Coroners Taking Short-Cuts on Mortality Statistics 11

    The Absence of Cultural Intelligence 12

    Chapter Summary 16

Chapter 2: Planning the Multicultural Study 17

    The Need for a Roadmap: The Project Planning Checklist ... 17

    Project Planning Checklist 18

    Budget Concerns 19

    Chapter Summary 20

Chapter 3: Identifying Multicultural Persons 21

    Common Classification Errors 21

    Latino Identity Research 23

    The 2010 Census Questions on Hispanic Origin and Race ... 29

African American Identity Research ... 31
Asian American Identity Research ... 32
Chapter Summary ... 35

Chapter 4: Sampling Issues for Multicultural Populations ... 39
Understanding Basic Sampling Concepts ... 39
Probability vs. Non-Probability Samples ... 40
Sampling Frame Considerations ... 41
Sample Size Issues ... 47
Selecting a Sample List Vendor ... 49
Using Census Data to Kick Start the Sampling Plan ... 56
Sample Applications Using Census Data ... 59
Chapter Summary ... 66

Chapter 5: Adapting Research Instruments for Multicultural Populations ... 69
Knowledge of the Target Audience ... 69
Confusion About Language Behavior ... 71
Managing Translation of the Survey Instrument ... 72
Use of Offensive, Outdated Words or Phrases ... 74
Congruence of Survey Questions with External Sources ... 77
Deciding on the Length of the Survey Instrument ... 81
Translating Rating Scales ... 82
Visual Acuity ... 82
Literacy Rates ... 82
Use of Accent Marks ... 83
Skip Instructions ... 83
Adapting to International Communities ... 83
Pilot Testing the Adapted Survey Instrument ... 84
Chapter Summary ... 85

Chapter 6: Limitations of Traditional Data Collection Methods 89

Mail Surveys 90

Telephone Surveys 94

Online Surveys 103

Exit Polls and Intercepts 106

Use of Incentives 111

Chapter Summary 113

Chapter 7: Solutions for Common Data Analytic Problems ... 117

Missing Data on Key Study Variables 117

Too Many Interviews Conducted in English 118

Evidence of Response Sets 118

Descriptive vs. Multivariate Analyses 120

Confusion Regarding Margin of Error 122

Problematic Weighting Practices 123

Chapter Summary 125

Chapter 8: Mixed Mode Methods — An Intuitive Solution 127

The Logic of Mixed Mode Methods 128

Concerns About Mode Effects 133

Adjustment for Mode Effects 134

Race and Language Factors Overlooked in Mixed Mode Research 138

Review of Multi-Modal Studies with Multicultural Populations 142

Mixed Mode Case Studies 145

Mode Choices by Race-Ethnicity 147

Language Choices by Mode 149

Mode Profiles 150

How Do Multi-Modal, Multilingual Study Respondents Compare to Respondents in the American Community Survey? 151

Promising Research on Data Quality 154

Budget Planning for Multi-Modal, Multilingual Studies 155

Chapter Summary 158

Chapter 9: Focus Group Research — Special Problems 161

Our Qualitative Experience 162

Missed Opportunities 162

Project Management 167

Recruitment Issues and Incentives 167

Screening Criteria and Invitations 168

Location of Focus Group Facilities 170

Translation Support 170

Facility Hostessing 171

Moderating Groups 172

Reporting the Findings 174

Lessons from Qualitative Studies of Multicultural Consumers 175

Incorporation of Technology 178

Chapter Summary 179

Chapter 10: Procurement Practices That Undermine Research Quality 181

The Absence of a Research IQ 181

Evaluating Bidders 182

Evaluation of Proposals 183

Favored Survey Results 183

Intellectual Property Concerns 184

Contract Compliance 185

- Chapter Summary 185
- Chapter 11: Expanding Your Analytic Tools with GIS 189
  - GIS and Secondary Data Sources 189
  - Examples of GIS Applications 191
  - Race-Ethnic Distribution of Boston City Residents 192
  - Limited English-Speaking Latinos in the U.S. 194
  - Latino Food Expenditures in the U.S. 196
  - Environmental Hazards 198
  - Redlining by Coffee Shops 200
  - Crime 202
  - Public Housing and Social Services 204
  - Chapter Summary 206
- Chapter 12: Future Outlook for Multicultural Research 207
- About the Author 217
- Appendix 219
  - List of Selected U.S. Multicultural Research Firms 219
  - List of White Papers by Rincón & Associates 219
  - Viewpoints in Selected Publications 219
  - List of Blogposts by Rincón & Associates 220
  - List of Multicultural Marketing Publications with Some Attention to Research 221
  - News Source About Multicultural Marketing Trends and Events 222
- References 223

Acknowledgments

I would first like to thank the various individuals who reviewed the book and provided valuable insights regarding survey methodology, mixed mode methods, qualitative studies, statistical and sampling issues, and their relevance to multicultural studies. These individuals included Elten Briggs, Ph.D., Associate Professor and Chair Department of Marketing, The University of Texas at Arlington; Thomas M. Guterbock, Academic Director Center for Survey Research & Professor of Sociology, and Research Professor of Public Health Sciences, University of Virginia; Dr. Edith D. de Leeuw, MOA-Professor Emerita Methodology & Statistics, Utrecht University; Robert L. Santos, Vice President & Chief Methodologist at Urban Institute and President-Elect, American Statistical Association; and Pepper Miller, Recognized Black-American market researcher, author, thought leader and speaker.

In addition, much of the book's content was based on demographic information provided by the U.S. Census Bureau and surveys conducted by The Pew Research Center — two organizations that have always provided the research community the solid data, insights and expertise that guide the many surveys that we conduct each year. I am also appreciative of the student feedback I received from the classes I taught at four universities, including courses in statistics, survey research methods, Hispanic marketing, and mass communications research. These classes provided valuable insights regarding the learning that was missing in traditional college courses regarding multicultural content. I am also grateful for the grant provided by Deep Vellum Publishing to support the project expenses, the editing support by Melanie Saxton Media, and the formatting of the book by Holly Chervnsik with SuburbanBuzz.

Two additional individuals deserve recognition as well. Alex Nogales, former President of the National Hispanic Media Coalition, was instrumental in placing Rincon & Associates on the national stage when his organization engaged us to conduct research that challenged the methodology used by the Nielsen Television ratings for U.S. Hispanic audiences. Dr. Kevin Karlson, a divorce litigation consultant, introduced our company to the area of litigation support and use of statistics, surveys and other methodologies to decide the outcome of important legal issues.

Finally, my wife, Lupita C. Rincón, was extensively involved in reading and editing each book chapter, searching the web for relevant studies, and suggesting revisions.

Foreword

It has never been easy to produce high-quality survey research, but lately it seems to be getting more difficult. The survey research industry faces many challenges: declining trust in institutions, rapid changes in communication technologies and the laws and informal norms surrounding their use; the recent flood of robo-calls and rapacious consumer scams; as well as declining response rates and declining public confidence in polling results. Amidst these significant shifts, survey researchers must be able to address the increasing cultural and linguistic diversity of the nation's population.

It almost goes without saying that we are an increasingly diverse nation. Moreover, there are parts of the United States, including many of our largest cities and states, where racial and ethnic diversity is pronounced. Anyone seeking to learn about public sentiment in a diverse community or region, or about market potential for a product aimed at a broad cross-section of American consumers, can ill afford to ignore these facts.

This timely book is devoted to helping survey researchers deal more successfully with the multicultural challenge even as we deal with the other changes in our business and research environments. The book is chock-full of principled guidance and practical advice that is based both on current methodological research and on the author's practical experiences and lessons learned over many years of designing and delivering multicultural surveys.

In the face of the difficulties—and the cost—of carrying out probability-based sample surveys of the general population, many market researchers and research consumers in private firms have turned to the cheap and convenient expedience of relying on non-probability internet panels for most of their research. But large segments of our multicultural nation are shut out of these panel 'samples,' and no amount of post-survey weighting can reliably transform the skewed results into valid representation of the population of interest. This book points us in a different direction, seeking to awaken our Cultural Intelligence, appreciate the benefit of using multiple survey modes and sampling frames, and enable us to conduct multicultural research more effectively.

Let's face it: multicultural research is difficult to do. Cultural and linguistic differences affect response propensities and response rates across different survey modes. They affect the way people respond to various appeals and incentives, including monetary incentives. They affect the way people hear questions and evaluate answer choices. And of course, some groups are harder to locate and to sample than others. This book focuses primarily on African-Americans, Asians, and Hispanics, but the same patterns of difference—and corresponding survey difficulty—can be extended to other minority groups.

The goal of this book, then, is really to make the difficult easier. And the means of doing so is to make some difficult ideas easier to understand. Most methods texts are written by academics for academics (and for their grad students). This one is not. Ed Rincón has been around the multicultural research track a bunch of times. His is the voice of experience, and his approachable style and many examples always have a practical focus. He writes in carefully chosen terms that market researchers and business clients will find familiar.

But make no mistake, the insights he offers here are firmly grounded in the most relevant academic literature and the foundational conceptual frameworks of scientific survey methodology. Under the surface, this book is grounded in the Total Survey Error perspective, which tells us that any quality survey must adequately deal with different possible sources of survey error, including coverage error, sampling error, non-response error, measurement error, and post-survey adjustment error. It also echoes the recent academic work by survey experts such as Brad Edwards, the late Janet Harkness and others on multinational, multiregional and multicultural surveys and on hard-to-reach populations. All of this work emphasizes that success in meeting these challenges requires attention during every phase of the survey process, from sample design to questionnaire development to data collection, analysis and reporting. A glance at the table of contents of this book shows that Ed Rincón has taken the same perspective, elucidating the key issues at every phase of the survey project. In addition, Rincon's recommendations are informed by recent research on multi-mode surveys, including their benefits and their potential difficulties.

As this book makes evident, many (but not all) of the things required for successful multicultural research require more time, more effort, more specialized expertise, and more money. But improvements in survey quality are never free. The alternative is lousy results: data that are unreliable and likely unrepresentative of the target population. That would not be a felicitous bargain. For this reason, this book is especially important for those in private sector firms and government agencies who are tasked with commissioning and contracting for survey work. Going for the lowest bidder and the cheapest type of sample is not the right way to get reliable results in the multicultural environment we all must now work in. And just choosing a minority-owned firm does not in itself ensure that multicultural issues are going to be adequately addressed from start to finish in the project cycle.

So, enjoy this unique, wide-ranging handbook for multicultural survey success. I can promise that you'll find some gems in these pages that will make you a more effective practitioner, consumer or purchaser of survey research in our increasingly diverse environment.

Thomas M. Guterbock
Academic Director, Center for Survey Research
Professor of Sociology
Research Professor of Public Health Sciences
University of Virginia

Advance Praise

"*The Culture of Research* is an IMPORTANT 'how to' book for planning and executing the multicultural market research process. Author Edward Rincon's keen understanding of diverse consumer segments balances his spot on, no-holds-barred criticism of current multicultural research practices. He offers dozens of practical examples from his 40+ years of experience in multicultural research and reliable resources that will undoubtedly help readers conduct RELEVANT market research studies with the 'New America' while delivering EFFECTIVE outcomes for brands and organizations."

Pepper Miller
Recognized Black-American Market Researcher, Author, Thought Leader and Speaker
Author: *What's Black About It?* and *Black Still Matters in Marketing*

- - - - ◆ - - - -

"Great book. Liked it."

Prof Dr. Edith D. de Leeuw
MOA-professor Methodology & Statistics, Utrecht University

- - - - ◆ - - - -

"This timely book is devoted to helping survey researchers deal more successfully with the multicultural challenge even as we deal with the other changes in our business and research environments. The book is chock-full of principled guidance and practical advice that is based both on current methodological research and on the author's practical experiences and lessons learned over many years of designing and delivering multicultural surveys...Most methods texts are written by academics for academics (and for their grad students). This one is not. Ed Rincón has been around the multicultural research track a bunch of times. His is the voice of experience, and his approachable style and many examples always have a practical focus. He writes in carefully chosen terms that market researchers and business clients will find familiar...But make no mistake, the insights he offers here are firmly grounded in the most relevant academic literature and the foundational conceptual frameworks of scientific survey methodology."

Thomas M. Guterbock
Academic Director, Center for Survey Research
Professor of Sociology
Research Professor of Public Health Sciences
University of Virginia

- - - - ◆ - - - -

"This is a wonderful book for anyone involved in the process of multicultural research. Dr. Edward Rincón applies his wealth of knowledge and experience in the field to provide needed direction and words of caution. Readers of this text will avoid many of the common traps that arise when generating insight on ethnic minority consumers. Considering the dearth of sound educational material in the multicultural field, I am grateful I can now utilize *The Culture of Research* as a resource for my instruction."

Elten Briggs, Ph.D.
Associate Professor and Chair
Department of Marketing
The University of Texas at Arlington

Introduction

Having spent the past 45 years conducting multicultural research studies, I am delighted to finally take the time to share some of the lessons learned with stakeholders in the research industry — including practitioners, academics, buyers, and decision makers. I offer evidence and argue that a disturbing number of multicultural research studies that are conducted by private, public and academic organizations include recognized biases and indicators of questionable quality. Even more disturbing is the corresponding trend by procurement staff at these organizations who continue to fund these questionable studies by research vendors with little experience in multicultural communities. The term "multicultural" is used throughout the book as reference to three specific groups of U.S. residents: (a) Latinos or Hispanics, (b) Blacks or African Americans and (c) Asian or Asian Americans. Although the multicultural reference is often used by other analysts to include a broader list of non-white groups, my focus on these three specific groups was based on the reality that much of the available multicultural research literature has focused on these groups, and my past research experience was also more likely to include these groups.

Despite the dramatic demographic and technological changes that are taking place in the U.S., it seems illogical that research practitioners would continue to utilize outdated practices to engage survey respondents — such as one language or one mode of data collection — that are known to limit the demographic diversity of the U.S. population and the quality of the information collected. Our industry's increasing fascination with online survey methods to gauge public opinion appears to be driven more by the desire for efficiency and less by the need to include key demographic segments of the U.S. population, such as African Americans, Latinos and Asians.

It is my premise that the relative absence of knowledge about multicultural populations or "cultural IQ" among decision makers, buyers of research, and academics contributes to a collective indifference to the problems that have been commonplace in multicultural research studies. Hence, I take pleasure in sharing my experiences, along with the observations of other research practitioners, as a genuine effort to raise the bar in the quality of multicultural research.

Book Overview

I wrote this book with four distinct audiences in mind: research practitioners, decision makers, academic institutions and procurement staff. In the case of *research practitioners*, my own observations from the numerous industry research studies that I have reviewed over the past 45 years are that many include fundamental flaws in their design and execution that could have been avoided by understanding some basic concepts about multicultural persons. Secondly, *decision-makers* are typically more removed from the actual design and execution of research studies, but more involved with requests for proposals, budgets, and program decisions that must be made based on the results of a research study — which makes it even more important that decision makers understand the limitations of a study in order to avoid major errors in policy or program decisions. Simply reading executive summaries of research studies does not make for good decision making. Thirdly, my own experience with *procurement staff* is that their knowledge of research methods, statistics and multicultural issues is especially limited — a significant problem that often results in the award of research contracts to low bidders with sub-standard methodologies. Recognizing their limited knowledge and experience with research, I argue that procurement staff are given too much discretion in the evaluation and selection of research vendors who plan to study communities with a strong multicultural presence.

Lastly, *academic institutions* have a responsibility to train future students with more updated knowledge and skills to accurately measure the cognitive, affective and behavioral characteristics of *multicultural* persons. In my experience, academics do not seem to understand the concept that *global is not multicultural* — that is, students of research in different disciplines are being shortchanged when their academic departments focus their course content solely on global rather than U.S. multicultural consumers, and hire international faculty rather than U.S. Black, Latino or Asian faculty whose life experiences in the U.S. can add significant value to the classroom. At this writing, few academic institutions have shown leadership in offering multicultural courses and degrees to college students, although the Hispanic marketing program at Florida International University, under the direction of Dr. Felipe Korzenny, is the most mature and should serve as a model to other academic institutions that need direction in this area. Dr.

Introduction

Elten Briggs, Associate Professor of Marketing with The University of Texas at Arlington School of Business, teaches an undergraduate course on Multicultural Marketing that is unique in the Dallas/Fort Worth metro area and possibly the entire state of Texas. Academic departments across the U.S. are slowly introducing multicultural content into their degree programs, but their sense of urgency is not noticeable.

The focus of this book — raising the standards in multicultural research — is no accident. My past research and writings have often advocated for improving measurement systems that affect our collective quality of life, such as unfair college admissions testing, biased media rating systems like Arbitron and Nielsen ratings, and biased political polling. The inaccuracies of such measurement systems often have a negative impact on the lives of U.S. African Americans, Latinos and Asians, are not very transparent, and not well understood by the general public because the sources of bias are often disguised in technical language.

It is worth mentioning that this book is multi-disciplinary in its focus — that is, designed for research practitioners across different disciplines that share an interest in raising the standards for multicultural research including psychology, sociology, marketing and advertising, public relations, economics, politics, statistics, and demography.

In summary, I would consider this book a success if it encourages decision-makers, research practitioners, academics, students of research, and procurement staff to re-evaluate the traditional manner that research studies are funded and implemented, and to ask relevant questions about their appropriateness for culturally-diverse communities. My interest is not in reviewing the statistical and research concepts that are already covered in traditional textbooks and classes, but rather in discussing specific problems and challenges in multicultural research that traditional textbooks and classes are *likely to overlook*. To this end, I have dedicated attention to a review of existing research that specifically addresses multicultural issues as well as the experiences that I have personally accumulated over the past 45 years in the design and implementation of multicultural research studies.

Following is a chapter summary that describes the approach that I have chosen to share these experiences.

Chapter 1: Multicultural Research — An Industry in Need of a Facelift

Research practitioners have been reluctant to adapt their practices to the demographic and technological changes that are taking place in the U.S. I discuss some of the consequences of this apparent indifference to the quality of multicultural research and the potential influence of cultural IQ in the research industry.

Chapter 2: Planning the Multicultural Study

Like the physician who orders lab work of your body chemistry to supplement an evaluation of your physical condition, you also need to have discussions with your clients to understand the research objectives and limitations. The Project Planning Checklist provides a guide for asking the right questions in the planning stages of a multicultural study.

Chapter 3: Identifying Multicultural Persons

I discuss the common problems in using surnames, self-identification, birthplace, and language usage as well as recent innovations that can facilitate the task of identifying multicultural persons.

Chapter 4: Sampling Issues for Multicultural Populations

I discuss sources for enumerating the U.S. multicultural population (i.e., sampling frames), potential problems with these sources, and suggested methods for sampling multicultural persons.

Chapter 5: Adapting Research Instruments to Multicultural Populations

I discuss various aspects of designing the survey or interviewing instrument that can influence the quality of the data that is being collected, such as question wording and sequence, preferred mode (phone, mail, online, etc.), selection of the respondent, response format problems, problems with sensitive questions, translating the instrument, and enhancing respondent cooperation.

Chapter 6: Limitations of Traditional Data Collection Methods

I review the pros and cons of using different modes of data

collection in studies of multicultural populations — such as mail, telephone, online, and intercepts — and how to avoid common pitfalls when using these methods.

Chapter 7: Solutions to Common Data Analytic Problems

Despite the best planning, common analytic problems in multicultural research will emerge and require an immediate solution. I discuss several of the problems encountered in past multicultural studies and the solutions that allowed the analysis to continue, including such issues as missing values, language bias, response sets, weighting practices and confusion about margin of error.

Chapter 8: Mixed Mode Methods — An Intuitive Solution

To overcome some of the limitations associated with traditional data collection methods, I discuss the mixed-mode method approaches that utilize different modes of data collection to conduct a survey, problems related to adjusting for mode effects, its potential for minimizing coverage bias, and the relative absence of multicultural populations in such studies. I also review mode-related research from the American Community Survey and five case studies I have conducted with multicultural populations.

Chapter 9: Focus Group Research — Special Problems

Although there are various qualitative techniques that are used in the industry, I direct attention to focus group techniques, the particular problems that you are likely to experience in using this procedure with multicultural consumers, and the importance of facilities to improve their readiness.

Chapter 10: Procurement Practices That Undermine Research Quality

Experienced research practitioners are no strangers to the kinds of problems that can emerge when responding to a request for bids or proposals and how these problems are amplified in multicultural research studies. I discuss some industry practices and experiences with procurement programs that threaten the quality of multicultural research studies.

Chapter 11: Expanding Your Analytic Tools with GIS

There are numerous sources of secondary data that are provided by the federal government that can be utilized to address important questions about the quality of life of multicultural communities in the U.S. I discuss some of these sources and provide a few examples of GIS applications using these datasets.

Chapter 12: Future Outlook for Multicultural Research

In this chapter, I issue a wake-up call to all stakeholders in the multicultural industry to (a) encourage (or pressure) academic institutions and book publishers to diversify their content, writers and faculty, and (b) request that research trade organizations raise awareness of the common problems associated with multicultural studies. Lastly, I discuss model programs in the U.S. that are making great progress in educating the industry about multicultural consumers.

Note to Readers: Throughout the book, I use selected race-ethnic terms interchangeably, such as Hispanic and Latino, Black and African American and Asian or Asian American. Although partly a convenience to the writer, it is also an effort to utilize the race-ethnic labels that are commonly associated with the various studies cited throughout the book.

Chapter 1: Multicultural Research — An Industry in Need of a Facelift

The growth of the U.S. multicultural population — which principally includes African Americans, Latinos, and Asians in our discussion — has been closely monitored over the years and became center stage when the U.S. Census Bureau announced that their presence in 2010 had reached an incredible 102.6 million persons — a huge leap from their presence of 84.6 million persons in the 2000 Census.[1] Adding icing to the cake, the estimated buying power for these three segments — $1.4 trillion for Latinos, $1.2 trillion for Blacks, and $801 billion for Asians[2] — provided a strong incentive for advertisers to initiate or accelerate their multicultural campaigns.

The Wake-Up Call

As Figure 1 below illustrates, this growth was not just a temporary blip that was expected to disappear like a shooting star.

Figure 1: Projections of the U.S. Population by Race and Hispanic Origin, 2016 to 2060

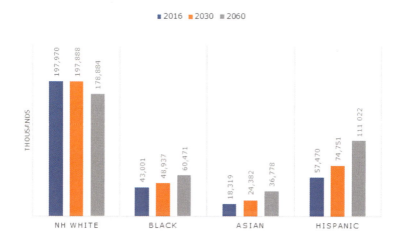

Source: U.S. Census Bureau Projections, March 2018.

Indeed, the latest Census Bureau projections tell us that the multicultural population is expected to grow from 119 million persons in 2016 to 148 million by the year 2030, and leapfrog to 208 million by the year 2060.[3] Pretty incredible by most standards of population growth. Yet another wake-up call that should have caught the attention of research practitioners is an announcement by the Census Bureau that the number of Chinese immigrants to the U.S. in 2013 had, for the first time in history, exceeded the number of immigrants from Mexico.[4]

Not everyone, however, has taken note of these wake-up calls or felt a sense of urgency about changing or adapting their practices to better understand and target this growing population segment — most notably the research industry.

Curious Industry Indifference

Indeed, the linguistic and cultural nuances that characterize multicultural populations have challenged a research industry that appears reluctant or perhaps unwilling to keep pace with the changing composition of the U.S. population. Latinos, Blacks and Asians are demographically and psychologically distinct from whites: they communicate differently, watch different media, and have unique attitudes and shopping behaviors. Is it realistic to expect research practitioners to capture the complexities of such diverse segments using traditional models of research and textbooks that are used in college? Perhaps not, since the majority of higher education institutions do not offer courses that provide research practitioners or students the skills needed to understand multicultural communities. Rather than improve their practices, however, research practitioners appear increasingly willing to make compromises that threaten the quality of multicultural research. Take note of these troubling trends:

- **Self-Serving Studies.** Desirous of better control over the conclusions reached by decision makers, ethnic media organizations are saturating the industry with their own research, which is often self-serving and rarely identifies any of the shortcomings of their own research.

- **Popularity of Online Surveys.** Online surveys have grown in popularity because they are economical and produce quick results. Because listings of email addresses are not readily available to select survey respondents, research practitioners are increasingly relying on panel companies that maintain large numbers of self-selected persons to complete online surveys. Unfortunately, many of these panel companies do a poor job of including multicultural persons, and their samples are known to produce biased statistical indicators for Black and Latino survey respondents. A few organizations are integrating probability samples of households as a method of recruiting panel members who complete online surveys — an approach that is more credible but distinctly more expensive than traditional panels.

- **Indifference by Academic Institutions.** Business, advertising, public relations and marketing classes at U.S. academic institutions have largely turned a deaf ear to the inclusion of multicultural faculty and curriculum. Instead, departments have distanced themselves by building their global faculty and curriculum, and graduating students who are ill prepared to fill the jobs requiring knowledge of multicultural consumers in the U.S.
- **Outsourcing to Foreign Countries.** Lacking their own multicultural talent, U.S. research practitioners are increasingly out-sourcing multicultural studies to research firms in foreign countries. Despite their lower costs, foreign shops come with their own set of problems: different language dialects and vocabulary; lack of familiarity with U.S. brands, geography, and institutions; and the tendency to become intolerant when misunderstood — problems that tend to alienate U.S. residents.
- **Evangelistic Advocacy.** Like religious zealots, some multicultural experts have dedicated their careers to convince Corporate America that marketing success is virtually guaranteed if they commit to a specific linguistic strategy, such as using only Spanish-language media to reach U.S. Latinos. Such narrow-minded advocacy can deceive marketers into thinking that such generalized advice can substitute for a well-designed study of a target audience.

The Consequences

The practical significance of such compromises can be far reaching and impacts many industries. In the short term, data quality problems become evident in the form of lower survey response rates, invalid or incomprehensible responses, presence of response sets (i.e., "yea-saying," extreme responding on scales), and higher levels of missing data. In the long term, such compromises can lead to erroneous decisions about the success or failure of a multicultural campaign, and the exclusion of multicultural persons from decisions that affect their quality of life. Are these concerns just imagined? Not really, as the following examples of actual studies vividly demonstrate.

A Love Affair with Positive Satisfaction Ratings

City leaders are often celebrating the positive satisfaction ratings of City services from annual surveys that they commission. The City of Dallas is no exception. A few eyebrows were raised recently when Dallas city leaders boasted about the positive ratings of City services that were reported in a 2016 community satisfaction survey, especially given the persistent problems with potholes, dogs attacking local residents, increasing homeless population, traffic congestion, police pension funds, and persistent poverty. What could explain this paradox? The answer is not hard to find if one bothers to review the tabulations in the appendix of the vendor's report: residents who were more likely to experience low quality City services — e.g., lower income, lower education, Spanish speakers — were significantly under-represented in the survey. Indeed, positive ratings can be achieved in more than one way.[5]

Early Demise of The George Lopez Show

When initially introduced, The George Lopez Show did not capture the Nielsen television ratings that were initially expected, especially among U.S. Latino audiences. To address this issue, the National Hispanic Media Coalition, with funding by ABC and CBS Television, engaged Rincón & Associates to conduct an independent study of Latino television audiences in five major U.S. metropolitan areas. Among other things, the study revealed that Latino audiences for The George Lopez Show were larger than originally estimated by the Nielsen ratings. How could this be? After all, Nielsen television ratings are supposedly the gold standard in the television industry. As explained by the study consultant, Nielsen's lower ratings for The George Lopez Show stemmed from the increased weight given to the ratings of foreign-born Latinos, which were not the primary audience for this show. Once the native and foreign-born weights were correctly applied in the independent Rincón study, the true picture emerged with larger audiences than reported by the Nielsen ratings, and The George Lopez Show survived.[6]

The Texas Way

In the state of Texas, nearly four in ten residents are Hispanic, and our past research confirms that two-thirds of these residents prefer to communicate in Spanish when provided a choice. With high-speed rail on the horizon, the Texas Transportation Institute (affiliated with Texas A&M) commissioned a study on high-speed rail that was required to capture a "representative" sample of Texas residents. Rather than capturing the required 38 percent of survey respondents that were Hispanic, only 20 percent of the study respondents included Hispanics, and most of these respondents completed the interview in English. Despite guidance by a committee of academic experts, the survey vendor was apparently allowed to provide minimal Spanish-language support — thus excluding these taxpayers from sharing their opinions about a transportation system that they will be expected to support with their tax dollars. Interestingly, the same survey vendor was awarded a second contract to conduct a survey using the same flawed methodology.

Is Racial Profiling on the Decline?

A recent analysis of traffic stops made by the Texas Highway Patrol revealed that racial profiling of Hispanics was on the decline, although critics suspected that the Department of Public Safety was deliberately misclassifying Texas drivers that they stopped in order to lower the state's racial profiling statistics.[7] Further analysis, however, revealed that the DPS troopers were assigning the race category based on the physical characteristics of the drivers, rather than simply asking each driver to identify themselves by race or ethnicity. The classification of Hispanic drivers as "white" was systematically reducing the racial profiling statistics reported by the state.[8]

Coroners Taking Short-Cuts on Mortality Statistics

Research practitioners are not the only ones who become accustomed to aggregating Asian respondents into one group, perhaps out of convenience, indifference to the consequences, or just to increase the sample size for analytic purposes. It turns out that state coroners have been doing the same thing for many years, making it difficult to report the causes of death for the different Asian subgroups[9] which are known to vary.

Although there are many more examples of similar practices in diverse industries that we could discuss, suffice it to say that decisions regarding multicultural programs and campaigns are compromised when the standards for quality research are lowered.

The Absence of Cultural Intelligence

It seems incredible that such compromises are being made in contemporary times, even under the guidance of experts from reputable institutions. Although the reasons that explain these compromises can be many, my own research and teaching experience points to three possible explanations. First, research practitioners and industry decision-makers often lack fundamental knowledge about multicultural populations — or "cultural intelligence" — as some theorists have called it.[10] Secondly, some institutions are simply indifferent to issues that systematically exclude key segments of the communities that they serve. Thirdly, the U.S. population remains racially segregated (see Figure 2) in terms of residential patterns, while increased segregation continues in places where we worship, where we study, our news sources, and how we socialize. This trend matters greatly since it significantly limits our collective understanding and experience with culturally diverse groups.

Figure 2: Residential Segregation, 2020

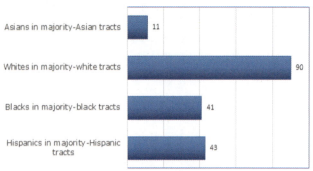

% from each group living in census tracts where the majority of residents are from their racial/ethnic group

Asians in majority-Asian tracts	11
Whites in majority-white tracts	90
Blacks in majority-black tracts	41
Hispanics in majority-Hispanic tracts	43

Note: Based on total population, including adults and children. Asians, whites and blacks are single-race, non-Hispanic. Hispanics are of any race.
Source: Pew Research Center tabulations of 2010 Decennial Census SF1 data.

Cultural intelligence, mentioned earlier, is not a new concept and has been the subject of inquiry by several past investigators. For example, organizational psychologists have explained that cultural intelligence means understanding the impact of an individual's cultural background on their behavior, which is *essential* for effective business[11] and have developed the CQ scale to measure different aspects of cultural intelligence. The Black Intelligence Test of Cultural Homogeneity (B.I.T.C.H)[12] was introduced in 2006 to demonstrate how traditional intelligence tests were culturally biased as a consequence of the language used by test developers. It primarily measured knowledge of words and phrases that were commonly used by U.S. Blacks. Along the same lines, The Chitling Intelligence Test[13] was introduced in 1971 and measured different aspects of Black culture, such as language usage, music, history, decision-making, and significant figures. In his book Multicultural Intelligence (2009),[14] author David R. Morse explains that companies, like people, also have an MQ or multicultural intelligence, and he developed a battery of questions to measure MQ. Morse explains that he can calculate a company's MQ by evaluating the following five factors:

- The percentage of employees who own a passport and have visited a foreign country in the last three years
- The percentage of the management team that is non-white or gay
- The number of employees that speak a language in addition to English
- Whether the company offers diversity training
- Whether the company has a multicultural advertising agency

Like the CQ discussed earlier, Morse's MQ assumes that a higher score means that the company is likely to be more effective in addressing the needs of multicultural consumers. While the factors appear intuitive, the MQ does not measure the level of knowledge that a company's employees may have about multicultural consumers. Nonetheless, the MQ offers promise in guiding organizations to recognize their shortcomings related to multicultural consumers and potential courses of action.

Does cultural knowledge or awareness influence a person's behavior? Two studies seem to indicate that there is a definite connection. One recent study explored the trend in pain management wherein whites were more likely than Blacks to be prescribed strong pain medications for equivalent treatments.[15] Researchers at the University of Virginia quizzed white medical students and residents to learn how many believed inaccurate statements about biological differences between the two races — such as "Black people's blood coagulates more quickly," "Blacks' skin is thicker than whites'," and "Blacks' nerve endings are less sensitive than whites.'" Although they expected some endorsement of these statements, the investigators were surprised that so many in the group with medical training endorsed such beliefs. It was discovered that those who held false beliefs often rated Black patients' pain lower than that of white patients and made less appropriate recommendations for the treatment of their pain.

Yet another news article described an unusual training program at the Cambridge police academy on the appropriate use of pepper spray when apprehending Mexican American suspects.[16] Police academy trainers were instructing new cadets to use stronger doses of pepper spray on Mexican American suspects. Officer Gutoski, the department training officer, explained their rationale in rather un-scientific terms: "Mexicans grow up eating too much spicy food, and because they spend so much time picking hot peppers in the fields...so with Cajuns, Mexican-Americans, Pakistani, Indian...what happens is that pepper spray is effective for a much shorter time." Even more unnerving is the explanation by departmental spokesman, Frank Pasquarello, that "Officer Gutoski was repeating information that's shared all the time among officers in informal training sessions on the use of pepper spray." These two studies suggest that we should be very concerned about the knowledge and beliefs that practitioners in general have about culturally diverse groups and how this knowledge or beliefs can influence their behavior. Indeed, this research points to the real possibility that decisions made by research practitioners may also be based on inaccurate knowledge or beliefs about African Americans, Latinos and Asians.

Out of simple curiosity to understand the level of familiarity with basic facts about U.S. Latinos, I introduced the Test of Latino Culture©[17] — a 20-item multiple choice test that measures knowledge of U.S. Latino culture in six areas:

- Ethnic identity
- Demographic characteristics, trends

- Language behavior
- Culture
- Immigration issues and trends
- Research insights

The Test of Latino Culture© was completed online in 2012 by a non-scientific sample of 434 respondents, which included undergraduate and graduate students at three academic institutions (3 Texas, 1 Florida) as well as various industry professionals in marketing and advertising who had visited the test link provided on the Advertising Age website.[18] In designing this test, I was interested in exploring the extent to which college students and industry professionals knew selected fundamental facts about the U.S. Latino population — facts that were well publicized by U.S. media and that, in my experience, should be known by persons who are involved or plan to have involvement with Latinos in some manner, that is, via a job, a community project, or a research study. I hypothesized that Latino respondents would score better on the test than non-Latinos, based on their presumed greater exposure and experience with Latino culture. In a nutshell, the study revealed that:

- **Overall knowledge of U.S. Latinos was definitely lacking.** Only 54 percent of the 20 items were answered correctly by the total respondents. The items that were most likely to be answered incorrectly related to language behavior, immigration issues, and demographic trends.

- **Latino test-takers did not have a decided edge over non-Latino test takers.** The average raw score of 11.2 for Latinos and 10.4 for non-Latinos suggests that Hispanics did not have the "cultural edge" expected from their cultural origin or experiences.

- **More education was an asset.** Respondents with bachelor's degrees or higher revealed higher average scores (11.5) than those without a bachelor's degree (9.0).

How much importance should one associate with the results of the Test of Latino Culture©? Perhaps only limited importance since the sample of respondents was not chosen at random and not generalizable beyond these respondents. The study results, however, do raise some interesting questions. For example, should the buyers and users of research studies be concerned about the knowledge that research practitioners have about Latinos? The answer to this question, in my opinion, is an emphatic "yes" and this is my reasoning. A limited knowledge of Latinos, African Americans and Asians can be problematic at a time when their presence in the U.S. continues to grow, as societal segregation deepens, and decisions continue to be made about their quality of life.

Should we simply *assume* that these decisions are being made based on accurate and current information about multicultural persons? And is it safe to assume that a person's cultural origin or language proficiency pre-qualifies them to advise others on multicultural issues or strategies? Both of these assumptions are shaky. For many situations, a person's knowledge of multicultural persons can be just as important as other skills in assuring a positive outcome in an advertising campaign, a job or research study. Perhaps it is time to introduce some standards of knowledge regarding multicultural persons, especially as it concerns decision makers and research practitioners who have responsibility for planning, execution and reporting such studies.

Chapter Summary

This chapter focused on an interesting paradox. Despite the massive demographic and cultural changes that are taking place in the U.S., our research industry is adapting slowly to these changes, and it was proposed that the absence of "cultural IQ" may be a potential explanation for this industry inertia. Of course, other structural barriers were noted, including academic inertia, increasing segregation, and procurement practices. In the next chapter, I discuss the importance of a road map or checklist as a suggested practice for addressing important design and executional elements in the planning of a multicultural study.

Chapter 2: Planning the Multicultural Study

When traveling to an unknown destination, common sense suggests that you might want a road map to ensure that you arrive at your destination with few delays or detours. And you would certainly want a driver or tour guide who is accustomed to taking road trips. Unfortunately, multicultural research studies are often conducted without the benefit of a road map or an experienced investigator, resulting in flawed data, questionable conclusions and cost overruns.

The Need for a Roadmap: The Project Planning Checklist

The Project Planning Checklist in this chapter includes a series of questions that a research buyer or purchasing agent should discuss with a research vendor to help guide the study design and implementation — a particularly important step for multicultural research studies that are usually more complex and require special resources and expertise. Although many of the items on this checklist could apply to any research study, it is also the case that several of the items will become more salient in a multicultural research study and require added resources and creative thinking to resolve.

A formal request for proposals is the traditional method for research buyers or purchasing agents to identify their research needs, although less formal approaches could include a telephone call or email invitation. In my experience, research buyers often lack technical knowledge about research design and practices, often incorrectly specify or omit technical criteria, allocate insufficient funds for the study, set up unrealistic timelines, and lack experience with multicultural research studies. I discuss more issues related to procurement in a later chapter. For now, let's assume that you are not dealing with a sophisticated research buyer, and that it will be your responsibility to gather information that will be essential in planning a multicultural study. Even sophisticated research buyers often lack knowledge and experience with multicultural research and may depend on you for guidance.

Project Planning Checklist

Although the objectives and methodology for a research study will be unique, following are some general questions that my past experience has shown will require your attention in the design and implementation of a multicultural research study:

- What is the study goal and specific objectives? Specifically, what are the questions that the research is expected to address? Without specific research questions, the study may appear to be a fishing expedition with no clear direction — making it difficult to create a credible research plan.
- What is the timeline for the study? What are the key deliverables that are expected, and the dates that they are expected?
- What is the geographic area of interest — city, county, metropolitan area, state, national, area of dominant influence (ADI), or something else?
- Who is included in the target audience? That is, what are the characteristics of the persons to be included in the study in terms of age, gender, race, ethnicity, nativity, education, income, language abilities or other relevant attributes? What cultural factors are likely to influence participation in the study — such as religious beliefs, family values, authority figures, or sensitive topics?
- If the study requires a *quantitative approach* (i.e., surveys, structured interviews):
    - What is known about the sample design? Will a probability or non-probability sample be required? What is the sampling frame and expected sample size? Will the complexity of the sample design require the expertise of a sampling statistician?
    - What mode(s) of data collection is planned — telephone, online, mail, in-person interviews, or mixed-modes? What resources are available to accommodate these modes of data collection, i.e., staffing, software, facilities, out-sourcing, etc.? Will remote interviewers be required?
    - What is the expected length of the interview? Are you planning a pilot study to evaluate the questionnaire?

- What languages will need to be supported?
- Will visual exhibits need to be evaluated by the research participants? Will these exhibits be presented in English or native languages?
- Will incentives be needed to improve response rates? Are proposed incentives sufficient and relevant to engage different multicultural groups?
- What is the budget that has been allocated for the proposed study?

• If the study is *qualitative* (focus groups, ethnographic, in-depth interviews), these additional questions will require attention:
  - What products or services are being evaluated?
  - What exhibits will be evaluated?
  - Will a professional focus group facility be needed, or are other venues being considered, such as a hotel or community center?
  - Will recording of the sessions require video, audio or DVD recording?
  - Is travel distance to the facility a barrier? Will online focus groups work better?
  - Will incentives be needed to encourage participation in the study? If so, which types of incentives would be more effective for the target audience?

Of course, the Project Planning Checklist is not an exhaustive listing of the questions that will need to be addressed in planning your multicultural study, but it should serve as a good starting point to stimulate thinking in areas that need attention, especially if your research team does not include a research practitioner with significant experience in conducting multicultural research or collectively lacks sufficient knowledge about multicultural populations.

Budget Concerns

The budget allocated to the study may not be disclosed to the research provider because it is a competitive bidding process, or perhaps because the research buyer prefers to first review the budgets submitted by each of the vendors. Not knowing the allocated budget can be problematic since multicultural research studies are generally more expensive to implement than studies of the general population and include additional financial risk. Research practitioners with limited experience in conducting multicultural studies will often submit budgets that are much lower or higher than vendors with more experience with multicultural research studies. Once the questions in the Project Planning Checklist have been addressed, however, you should be in a much better position to prepare a realistic proposal and budget for the multicultural research study. On the other hand, if the research buyer has not provided sufficient information to address the various questions in the Project Planning Checklist, you may be assuming a larger risk in the implementation of the study that you can afford to take. If you decide to conduct the study with insufficient information, however, greater reliance will be placed on your own knowledge, experience and company resources to get the job done.

Chapter Summary

This chapter was relatively brief but nonetheless important in underscoring the importance of using a project checklist to guide the design and execution of a multicultural study, especially when the study sponsors lack experience in conducting such studies. The less that is known about the study specifications and implementation, the greater financial risk that will be assumed by the study investigator who will usually be expected to know more than the study sponsors.

In the following chapter, I discuss some of the challenges that you are likely to encounter in identifying the multicultural populations in a study that you are planning, how other researchers have dealt with these issues, and some practical advice for resolving these issues.

Chapter 3: Identifying Multicultural Persons

It would seem like the easiest task in the planning of a multicultural research study: identifying African American, Latino or Asian respondents. After all, organizations like the U.S. Census Bureau have been doing this task for decades and reporting their results to members of Congress; federal, state, and local agencies; the media; and commercial enterprises. These standard race and ethnic classification questions are updated periodically, well publicized, and carefully documented by the Census Bureau and its various agencies. Despite the availability of this information, too many research practitioners continue to use ethnic identification or classification procedures that are inaccurate or outdated, leading to incorrect conclusions in studies of multicultural populations. When African Americans, Hispanics and Asians are over-counted, under-counted or classified as "other" in such studies, the consequences are felt in the many programs or policies that affect their quality of life --- including employment trends, setting of minority goals in public contracts, healthcare, college admissions decisions, award of scholarships, housing and loan discrimination, and public education outcomes — just to name a few.

Common Classification Errors

Before discussing some of the relevant research in this area, allow me to share a couple of anecdotes that illustrate the consequences of misusing race and ethnic labels:

The Guessing Game. I'm in a supermarket with my wife, paying the cashier for groceries, when we notice a person with a clipboard who is gazing at us. I asked the individual what she was doing, and she explained that she was recording customer attributes, such as race and other characteristics. Perplexed by this, I asked "Why don't you just ask me about my racial background?" To which the observer responded: "Because I was instructed to record my best guess about the race based on how people look." After a good laugh, my wife and I left the store, wondering which racial-ethnic group she had selected since we have often been mistaken as Italian, Greek or Middle Eastern while living in different parts of the U.S. We both self-identify as Latino or Hispanic, but over the years have also used such labels as Mexican, Mexican American, and Chicano. Looks can be deceiving.

Labels that Disconnect. In reviewing a mail survey used in a high-speed rail study of Texas residents, I noticed that the form included a limited number of race-ethnic options for respondents to select: White, Black, Hispanic, Asian and Other Race. These race-ethnic labels are commonly used in U.S. surveys but can pose problems for ethnic respondents. For example, what is likely to happen if an African American respondent does not like the term "Black?" What about the Cuban respondent that dislikes the term "Hispanic?" And what about the person from China or India that does not identify with the term "Asian?" These disconnects can result in a refusal or "other race" response that can render a survey less useful when analyzing key indicators or trends by race or ethnic background.

Just American. Yet another reason that the race and ethnic information is often lost in surveys is the tendency for U.S. residents to state that they are "just American." Although it may be convenient for an interviewer or analyst to classify these persons into the "other race" category, it overlooks the possibility that further probing on a respondent's parental ancestry may yield some clues about the relevant race-ethnic origin of the respondent.

You Look Latino or Black. Texas highway patrol officers were recently accused of deliberately lowering racial profiling statistics by reporting lower rates for Blacks and Latinos. It turns out that rather than asking drivers to identify their race or ethnicity, DPS officers were simply classifying ethnic drivers on their physical characteristics[19] and making errors that lowered the racial profiling statistics.

Loss of Asian mortality rates. Prior to 2003, birth and death records for U.S. Asian subgroups were not available, allowing morticians to aggregate all persons that appeared to be Asian into one group, which contributed to the loss of key information about their leading causes of death for distinct Asian subgroups.[20]

Although just a sampling of the race-ethnic identification

issues that I have observed over the past years, these scenarios illustrate some of the challenges that research practitioners are likely to face, sometimes with less than ideal information, when classifying people into race and ethnic categories.

Interestingly, the challenges and recommended practices for identifying and classifying populations by race and ethnicity have been documented for many years, especially as it concerns the Latino population. Some research practitioners apparently do not understand the implications of using ambiguous or outdated race-ethnic labels in their studies, especially in the estimation of critical behaviors that are influenced by race or ethnicity. Perhaps past research courses in college have not devoted adequate attention to this topic. More recent studies, however, provide us guidance on the race-ethnic identity preferences of U.S. African Americans and Asians. Let's review these studies and how they can help us improve the manner that multicultural persons are identified and classified.

Latino Identity Research

About 26 years ago, a couple of health research practitioners provided much needed advice regarding the best methods for identifying or classifying Hispanics in research studies. In a book titled *Research with Hispanic Populations*,[21] Marín and Marín did a thorough job of reviewing the literature regarding the usefulness of using five techniques for identifying Hispanic-origin populations in the U.S. Although no attempt was made by these researchers to evaluate the appropriateness of methods for classifying Asian or Black populations, some of their insights are relevant to these groups as well. The following table summarizes

> **Relying on Surnames: A Legal Matter**
>
> In a Dallas County murder trial that engaged me as an expert witness, the defense attorney had requested a change of venue because he felt that a fair trial was not possible for his Hispanic client. Why? Because the share of Hispanics in the jury pool was likely to be substantially different from the Hispanic share of the county's population. I was asked to conduct a statistical analysis to address this issue; however, the race-ethnic information recorded by the court for jury pool members was considered unreliable for the analysis because it was inconsistently recorded. A surname was the only information available to estimate the likely ethnicity of the jury pool members. But is the surname method sufficiently accurate to reach a reliable conclusion in this legal situation?

the general conclusions reached by these early pioneers in identifying Hispanic-origin persons.

Table 1: Pros and Cons of Methods for Identifying Hispanic Origin Persons

Method	Pros	Cons
Surname	Easy to use when a list of Spanish surnames is available, commonly used to select a sample of respondents from a list	1. One-third of those claiming Hispanic origin do not have a Spanish surname 2. One-third who have Spanish surnames do not consider themselves to be Hispanic 3. Spanish names may be acquired through intermarriage and adoptions
Ancestry	Most reliable indicator, focus on place of birth of respondent, parents and grandparents	Could miss a Hispanic person whose ancestry goes beyond three generations
Spanish-language usage	Observable behavior and valid indicator	1. Proficiency varies widely by generation 2. Non-Hispanics speak Spanish as well
Self-identification	Broader enumeration of the targeted population	1. Can change over time 2. Labels may be disliked 3. Unreliable

According to Marín and Marín, the surname method was a common and straightforward way for identifying Hispanic origin persons, especially when selecting respondents from a list with unknown ethnic data. As the investigators explained, the Census Bureau produced a list of Spanish surnames commonly used in the Southwest that the research community could use to identify Hispanic origin persons. Not everyone, however, was familiar with the Census Bureau's surname list, and various other surname lists with unknown accuracy have been used by research practitioners. While easy to use, such surname lists still miss Hispanic origin persons *without* a Spanish surname and include persons who have a Spanish surname but do not identify as Hispanic origin. Some sampling frames that use RDD (random digit dialed) listings do not provide surnames.

By contrast, the ancestry method was considered by Marín and Marín as a solid indicator of Hispanic origin when the generation of parents and grandparents was available — not something that is usually included in surveys. And while the use of the Spanish language is common among Hispanic origin persons, it can also include non-Hispanics who use Spanish. The self-identification method, while more subjective than the other methods, provided the best enumeration of Hispanic origin persons; however, it's accuracy depended on the extent to which respondents liked or disliked the labels provided, such as "Hispanic," "Latino," "Spanish origin," "Chicano," "Mexican American," and others. In addition, self-identification varies over time due to intermarriage, assimilation, and adoptions. A recent analysis by Pew Research Center, for example, revealed that intermarriage rates between persons of different race-ethnic groups varied widely.[22] (See box.) Based on their analysis of the research regarding the use of these methods, Marín and Marín recommended the following guidelines for research practitioners:

> **Intermarriage rates between persons of different race-ethnic groups vary widely:**
> - Asians (29%)
> - Hispanics (29%)
> - Blacks (18%)
> - Whites (11%)
>
> Pew Research, 2017

- Hispanic ethnicity should be established by asking respondents if they identify as "Hispanic" or "Latino;"
- Spanish surname lists should be avoided;
- Present the Office of Management and Budget's description of Hispanic to respondents and ask them if they fit the description;
- A more comprehensive and reliable definition of "Hispanic" should be developed by producing an index that takes into account birthplace of self and parents, self-identification, and ancestry.

These recommendations provided research practitioners timely advice regarding best practices for identifying Hispanic origin persons, although each came with their noted limitations. Since the Marín and Marín recommendations were first published, additional developments and research have extended and re-defined some of the recommendations introduced by Marín and Marín. The U.S. Census Bureau, for example, continues to use the self-identification method for their decennial census and other periodic surveys because this method provides the best enumeration of the U.S. Hispanic population in comparison to the other methods.

While Marín and Marín discouraged the *use of Spanish-surname lists* for identifying Hispanic origin persons, a recent innovation in ethnic identification methods by Ethnic Technologies, Inc. shows that accuracy can be improved by incorporating first name, last name, and geographic residence in identifying the most likely race-ethnicity of an individual.[23] I had the opportunity to use their E-Tech ethnic identification method in a national study of multicultural consumers whose race-ethnic information was not available. I found a high degree of correlation between their system's assigned race-ethnic classification and the survey responses by African American, Hispanic and Asian respondents to a question about their race and ethnicity. In a recent study using geo-coding and surnames to estimate race and ethnicity, the investigators concluded that the combined approach can yield positive predictive values of 80 percent, thereby offering a viable means for assigning race and ethnicity for the purpose of examining disparities in care until self-reported data can be systematically collected.[24] While not perfect, the method shows much promise and provides research practitioners a needed tool for planning their data collection language strategies.

The third recommendation regarding a respondent's acceptance of the OMB's description of a Hispanic origin person seems like a time-consuming task, but actually makes sense: not everyone understands the meaning of the terms "Hispanic," "Latino," or "Asian" — especially foreign-born persons who are not accustomed to using these labels in their countries of origin. This confusion applies as well to other common U.S. race-ethnic labels like "white" and "black" that are commonly used in surveys. In my own research practice, an interviewer who encounters a likely Hispanic respondent that does not self-identify as "Hispanic" or "Latino" is expected to read examples of the 22 Spanish-speaking countries that the Census Bureau defines for this category (see Table 2 on the following page for these Census Bureau categories). This tactic minimizes confusion surrounding these pan-ethnic terms and typically results in the respondent selecting a specific ethnic label (i.e., Hispanic or Latino), thereby improving accuracy by reducing the number of refusals or no answer responses. As discussed in a subsequent chapter, similar ethnic origin descriptions are being proposed for the new Census race question to clarify the meaning of the race categories.

Identifying Multicultural Persons

Table 2: Hispanic/Latino Origin Groups Defined by American Community Survey 2018

Hispanic/Latino Origin Groups
Mexican
Puerto Rican
Cuban
Dominican
Central American
Costa Rican
Guatemalan
Honduran
Nicaraguan
Panamanian
Salvadoran
Other Central American
South American
Argentinean
Bolivian
Chilean
Colombian
Ecuadorian
Paraguayan
Peruvian
Uruguayan
Venezuelan
Other South American

Source: www.data.census.gov Table 0300I

The fourth recommendation suggesting the use of a more reliable and comprehensive index of Hispanic origin can be very helpful to more precisely confirm an individual's Hispanic origin. However, research practitioners seldom collect each of the items included in the proposed index: self-identification, birthplaces of self and parents, and ancestry. The important point to keep in mind, nonetheless, is that it makes good sense to include one or more of these items in a survey so that you may be able to "impute" or estimate a person's race or ethnicity from other relevant attributes in the event that the race or ethnic information is missing. I have had to "impute" a person's race or ethnic origin in many surveys when re-contacting the individual was not possible or other options had been exhausted.

More recent studies have expanded our knowledge about the ethnic identity preferences of U.S. Latinos. For example, a national survey of U.S. Latinos conducted in 2012 by the Pew Hispanic Center[25] revealed:

- Most Hispanics (51%) preferred to use their family's country of origin over pan-ethnic terms like Hispanic or Latino.

- One-quarter (24%) used the terms "Hispanic" or "Latino" while over two in ten (21%) used the term "American" most often.

- Of those who preferred a pan-ethnic term, "Hispanic" was preferred over "Latino" by more than a two-to-one margin — 33% versus 14%.

- The foreign-born are more likely to prefer their country of origin (63%), while the preferences of the native born were mixed: country of origin (37%, Hispanic or Latino (19%), and American (40%).

While the Pew research points to a stronger preference among U.S. Latinos for a country of origin identity, a recent review of studies by Latino Decisions comparing national origin and pan-ethnic identities suggests that the two are not mutually exclusive — that is, Latinos may choose a pan-ethnic identity in some contexts and a national origin in others.[26] Referred to as "linked fate," the concept explains the cohesiveness of Latinos and African Americans over time because their life chances are perceived to rest on the overall success of their respective groups. I have recently observed the use of the term "Latinx" appearing in blogs and other writings, which represents a gender-neutral term that is sometimes preferred over more gender specific terms like Latino or Latina. Care should be exercised if one chooses to use the term Latinx in a survey question since it could create confusion among respondents who are not familiar with the term, or prefer to identify with other more commonly used terms. In surveys of Hispanics that I have conducted in recent years, the Latinx term has rarely been mentioned as a response to the race or Hispanic origin question. As a general rule of thumb, the survey practitioner should (a) utilize the categories from the source that will be used for comparing the survey responses — such as the American Community Survey — especially if post-stratification weights will be based on that source, and (b) gauge acceptance in the target community for these labels from pilot studies or focus groups with ethnic community members.

The findings by Pew Hispanic Center and Latino Decisions underscore the importance of including both country of origin and pan-ethnic terms in a study. However, the research practitioner should keep in mind that these identity preferences will vary across the geographic areas under investigation and other factors that are peculiar to each community, such as politics and history. Before discussing some of the ethnic identification findings for African Americans and Asians, let's take a look at how the Census Bureau measured Hispanic origin and race in the 2010 Census questionnaire.

The 2010 Census Questions on Hispanic Origin and Race

From my past 45 years of experience in the research industry, I have concluded that many research practitioners are either indifferent or unaware of important design elements of questions that accurately measure race and ethnicity. This perception is based on the many surveys that I have personally reviewed that included questions on race and ethnicity that used limited options, vague or offensive terminology, redundant options, and outdated concepts. As a starting point, let's review how the Census Bureau measures these two important characteristics. Figure 3 presents the format of the Hispanic origin (Q8) and race (Q9) questions that were used in the 2010 Census questionnaire. The first thing that we notice is an explanation that precedes Question 8 that distinguishes between Hispanic origin (an ethnicity) and race, and encourages the respondent to answer both questions. Secondly, Question 8 asks the respondent about their Hispanic, Latino or Spanish origin and provides examples of

Figure 3: 2010 Census Questions on Hispanic Origin and Race

→ NOTE: Please answer BOTH Question 8 about Hispanic origin and Question 9 about race. For this census, Hispanic origins are not races.

8. Is Person 1 of Hispanic, Latino, or Spanish origin?
   - ☐ No, not of Hispanic, Latino, or Spanish origin
   - ☐ Yes, Mexican, Mexican Am., Chicano
   - ☐ Yes, Puerto Rican
   - ☐ Yes, Cuban
   - ☐ Yes, another Hispanic, Latino, or Spanish origin — *Print origin, for example, Argentinean, Colombian, Dominican, Nicaraguan, Salvadoran, Spaniard, and so on.*

9. What is Person 1's race? *Mark ☒ one or more boxes.*
   - ☐ White
   - ☐ Black, African Am., or Negro
   - ☐ American Indian or Alaska Native — *Print name of enrolled or principal tribe.*

   - ☐ Asian Indian   ☐ Japanese   ☐ Native Hawaiian
   - ☐ Chinese   ☐ Korean   ☐ Guamanian or Chamorro
   - ☐ Filipino   ☐ Vietnamese   ☐ Samoan
   - ☐ Other Asian — *Print race, for example, Hmong, Laotian, Thai, Pakistani, Cambodian, and so on.*   ☐ Other Pacific Islander — *Print race, for example, Fijian, Tongan, and so on.*

   - ☐ Some other race — *Print race.*

which groups are included in the Hispanic origin category. Question 9 then asks the respondent to identify their race and provides the standard race options along with specific Asian and Pacific Islander categories. The Black population is provided three options to self-identify — Black, African American or Negro — although the Negro option has been dropped because it is outdated and offensive to some respondents and does not change the count of the Black population. The Asian categories, like the Hispanic ones, are important to adequately capture the different subgroups that could be missed by reliance on a single "Asian" label. While the Hispanic or Spanish origin question has done a good job of enumerating the Hispanic population, the race question has not largely because Hispanics do not identify with the race categories presented, especially the foreign born who are not accustomed to using such terminology in their home countries. The Census Bureau is considering including the Hispanic category in a combined race question since its research shows that it provides a better enumeration of the Hispanic population and leads to fewer missing responses.[27] More recent announcements by the Census Bureau, however, state that the categories will remain similar to the 2010 questionnaire.[28]

African American Identity Research

Relatively less research has been dedicated to the race identity preferences of the Black or African American population in the U.S., perhaps because there has been more consistency in the race categories utilized by research practitioners and the categories have been largely accepted by African Americans. As mentioned earlier, however, the term "Negro" has been phased out because it is offensive to some members of this segment and its removal does not change the number of African Americans that are counted by the Census Bureau. Differences in the preference between the "Black" and "African American" labels, however, have been documented and it is important that the research practitioner understand the consequences of using one or the other label.

In their book *What's Black About It?*,[29] authors Miller and Kemp reviewed several research studies that addressed the race identity preferences of U.S. Blacks and found that, for all practical purposes, the terms "Black" or "African American" make little difference in the way that African Americans want to be addressed. The Gallup Organization[30] has tracked identity preferences among U.S. Blacks since 1991 and the most recent poll in 2007 revealed that the preferences depend upon whether respondents are provided an option for "no preference" or "does not matter." When not provided a "no preference" option, the latest poll showed an even split between the "Black" (48%) and "African American" (49%) response options. However, when "no preference" or "does not matter" was provided among the response options, over six in ten respondents (61%) chose this option, while relatively fewer respondents chose the "African

American" (24%) or "Black" (24%) labels. From the qualitative research experiences that the Hunter-Miller Group has had with African Americans across the U.S., Ms. Miller adds these insights:

> We learned that when many African Americans use the term 'Black' with each other, it is associated with intimacy and familiarity. However, when the race is referenced publicly or formally by both African Americans and non-African Americans, many prefer the term 'African American.' (p.8)

In yet another recent publication entitled "In Plain Sight: The Black Consumer Opportunity,"[31] the editors explained that while African Americans represent 89 percent of the U.S. Black population, this segment also includes Black Hispanics, Caribbean and African, European and Canadian immigrants — many who feel that the term "African American" does not accurately reflect their cultural background. They concluded, however, that either term was currently acceptable and often used interchangeably.

A more recent discussion of this topic in USA Today shows that the topic of racial identity is more complicated.[32] The influx of foreign-born Blacks into the U.S. has re-energized the debate about the meaning of 'African American' — does it include only individuals with descent from the slave trade, or does it include those born in Somalia and Barbados? Black immigrants value the African American label and culture but are reluctant to dilute their distinct cultures. Moreover, some Black immigrants are also reluctant to identify as African American due to the negative stereotypes of U.S.-born Blacks.

My own research experience mirrors the general conclusions reached by these studies and leads to the general recommendation that *both labels* — African American and Black — should be included in questions related to racial background as added insurance that the question will be more inclusive of the diverse groups that it represents. However, the increasing presence of Black immigrants in some communities points to the need to broaden the standard definition to include Blacks from other countries of origin.

Asian American Identity Research

Research studies that target the U.S. Asian population face some unique challenges in classifying the various Asian subgroups. Research practitioners have generally used the term

"Asian" as a catch-all category for persons from commonly recognized Asian countries such as China, Japan, Vietnam, Thailand, and others. Geographically speaking, however, the continent of Asia also includes other countries that are not traditionally thought of as "Asian" such as Saudi Arabia, India, Israel, Kuwait, Pakistan, and Iran. Persons from these countries have little in common linguistically or culturally and hence, not comfortable identifying themselves as "Asian." Table 3 on the following page presents each of the Asian groups that are included in the American Community Survey 2018 5-Year File, which are similar to the Census 2010 questionnaire.

Fortunately, a recent national study entitled "The Rise of Asian Americans" conducted by the Pew Research Center[33] provides research practitioners concrete direction on the race identity preferences of U.S. Asians. The study was conducted in English and seven Asian languages with 3,511 Asian Americans. Regarding race identity, the study revealed the following about the respondents:

- Only 19% most often described themselves as "Asian American" or "Asian."
- A majority (62%) most often described themselves by their country of origin, such as Chinese, Korean or Vietnamese.
- Just 14% called themselves "American," a choice that was higher among U.S.-born Asians (28%).

Thus, the research practitioner should always include options that represent the countries of origin when using the term "Asian" in a question about their racial background. Although space and time limitations may prohibit a full display of all the relevant countries, a short list should include the Asian countries that are more frequently represented in the targeted geographic area.

A recent analysis in the epidemiological arena should serve as a lesson to survey practitioners about the potential problems that can emerge when Asian identity is treated carelessly in research studies. In their historical review of the practices in handling Asian respondents in epidemiological studies,[34] the authors stated that few studies had examined the leading causes of mortality among Asian American subgroups because few states collected Asian subgroup information on death records. Before 2003, only seven states were required to report specific Asian racial-ethnic subgroups (California, Hawaii, Illinois, New Jersey,

New York, Texas). In addition, coroners were more likely to make

Table 3: Asian Origin Groups Defined by American Community Survey, 2018

ASIAN ORIGIN GROUPS
Asian Indian
Bangladeshi
Bhutanese
Burmese
Cambodian
Chinese (except Taiwanese)
Filipino
Hmong
Indonesian
Japanese
Korean
Laotian
Malaysian
Nepalese
Pakistani
Sri Lankan
Taiwanese
Thai
Vietnamese
Other Asian, specified
Other Asian, not specified

Source: www.data.census.gov / Table B02015

race-ethnic classification errors for Asian Americans (13%) than Hispanics (7%), and less than 1 percent for others. Moreover, National health surveys (i.e., Framingham Heart Study, Cancer Prevention Study, Behavioral Risk Factor Surveillance Survey) did not report data for Asian American subgroups. As a result, misleading and erroneous conclusions were often made due to the omission of Asian respondents resulting from small sample sizes, or the aggregation of data that masked important differences among the Asian subgroups. For example:

- Asian Indians have greater coronary heart disease risk than Chinese persons when compared to non-Hispanic whites;
- Japanese have greater risk for incident cancers while Asian Indians have the lowest risk;
- Liver cancer mortality rates are higher for Vietnamese, Koreans and Chinese when compared to other Asian American subgroups and non-Hispanic whites.
- Colorectal cancer rates are particularly higher for Japanese and exceed the rates for non-Hispanic whites and all other Asian subgroups.

The study investigators also discussed the results of recent pharmacogenomics studies that document how some Asian American subgroups respond differently to a variety of drug treatments, including chemotherapy, anti-coagulants, anti-platelets, and anticonvulsants. At least in the medical arena, the study investigators clearly illustrate that carelessness or indifference to the use of Asian subgroup identities can have significant consequences.

An additional commentary seems warranted about the use of the "white" label as a racial category. Anecdotal observations suggest that the term "white" is not universally accepted by survey respondents whose ethnic background would typically include Swedish, English, German, Russian, Polish, Greek, Italian, Albanian, Ukrainian, and French. The term "Anglo" or "Anglo American" is also used in some surveys in reference to whites as well as the term "Caucasian," which is not recommended because it can also include Latinos. It might be a good idea to speak with residents of the target community to explore which race and ethnic labels are commonly used by local residents and which labels should be avoided.

Chapter Summary

Granted, you now have some useful information from several studies to guide the process of identifying Hispanic, African American and Asian respondents for a research study.

Considering the results of these research studies along with my own research experience, I would suggest the following guidelines:

- Understand your target audience. Plan to study the demographic characteristics of the community using the most current Census data, including the size of specific multicultural segments, the share of foreign-born persons, and other attributes that could influence response rates or participation in your study.

- Avoid offensive terms. What's offensive? Conduct a pilot test of your potential study respondents in all relevant languages or query local civic leaders or community organizations to identify potentially offensive race or ethnic labels and ensure that they are not included in your research instruments. Experienced interviewers can serve as an early alert system in recognizing offensive terms.

- Standard terms. If you plan to compare your study data to Census Bureau or other external sources of population data, you should include survey questions and response categories that are consistent with the question format of these sources. This is especially important if you plan to use the race question formats for post-stratification weighting (discussed in a later chapter) in a survey.

- Provide more than one race or ethnic option. Use race or ethnic response options that are more, not less, inclusive. For example, use both Hispanic and Latino as choices and describe the countries of origin that they represent. For Asians, use Asian and Asian American but also describe the countries that they represent. For further clarification, county of origin should also be provided along with race labels so that respondents can better understand the origins of people included in such race labels as "white" and "Black."

- Ancestry. Make it a practice of including a question about the ancestry of the respondent's parents, which can be used to impute or estimate race or ethnic origin if the respondent refuses to self-identify their race or ethnicity using the options that you have provided.

- Caucasian. The term "Caucasian" is often included along with "white" in questions about race as if the two terms have the same meaning. "Caucasian," however, also refers to Hispanic-origin persons and should be avoided in questions about race.

- Careful translations. Exercise caution when translating race-ethnic labels into another language, and carefully check these translated labels with members of the target audience that understand the language. Remember that the race and ethnic classification system used in the U.S. is not readily understood by recent immigrants who may be accustomed to other forms of classifying or enumerating the population in their countries of origin.

Now that you have some options for identifying multicultural persons, the following chapter will focus on important considerations related to the sampling of multicultural populations for the study you are planning.

Chapter 4: Sampling Issues for Multicultural Populations

As discussed in the Project Planning Checklist (Chapter 2), prior to collecting data on your multicultural research study, the data collection team will need a finalized sampling plan or sample design to guide the data collection activities.

Understanding Basic Sampling Concepts

The sampling plan should include a detailed explanation of the sampling frame or list that will be used to select the study respondents; the sampling scheme for selecting different groups of respondents or stratification of defined segments; the expected incidence and sample size requirements; and the expected sampling accuracy. Are you familiar with these sampling concepts? If not, I would recommend that you expand your basic sampling IQ by reading one of the following textbooks:

- Gary T. Henry, *Practical Sampling*, Applied Social Research Methods Series, Volume 21, 1990 Sage Publications.
- Bill Williams, *A Sampler on Sampling*, 1978, John Wiley & Sons.

I do not have the space in this chapter to discuss the different sampling designs which may be the most appropriate for a specific study. However, after reading the recommended books, or perhaps attending a seminar on sampling techniques, you should acquire an understanding of basic sampling concepts. While this suggestion will not transform you into a sampling expert, you should be better prepared to communicate with a sampling statistician and understand how to follow their advice in implementing the sample design for the multicultural study that you are planning. Sampling experts are not easy to find, expensive, and not always familiar with the concepts and terminology associated with multicultural populations; therefore, make the best use of this resource by raising your knowledge of basic sampling concepts. For the moment, let's discuss some of the sampling considerations that will require your attention as you finalize a sampling plan.

Probability vs. Non-Probability Samples

Perhaps one of the most important decisions that you will need to make for your multicultural study is whether you will select your sample randomly (probability sample) or non-randomly (non-probability sample). Of course, there may be occasions where the size of the population universe is so small — say a few hundred persons or households — that it makes sense to include all members of this universe, and no sample is needed. In most cases, however, you will likely be confronted with a large population universe from which you will need to select a sample of units to conduct a survey within the time and budget constraints that you have for the study. The important thing to remember is that the sample must be selected randomly if you (a) plan to generalize the survey findings to the population universe, (b) need an estimate of the sample's accuracy, and (c) desire some reasonable expectation that the sample demographic characteristics will be representative of the population from which it was drawn.

There are situations where it makes sense to use a non-probability sample. The use of non-probability samples has been increasing, especially in the medical industry where sampling frames and listings do not exist for hidden populations, such as drug users, males having sex with males, migrants, and other groups that live under the radar. However, debates continue about the quality of the survey data produced when using non-probability samples. Advocates of non-probability samples argue that telephone surveys using probability samples do not provide quality data due to their low response rates. Recent studies comparing the quality and bias of probability and non-probability samples have concluded that probability samples — even with low response rates — introduce less bias than studies using non-probability panel samples.[35]

In yet another analysis regarding the data quality of probability vs. non-probability online surveys,[36] researchers compared the results of nine online surveys using non-probability samples with one online survey using a probability sample. Importantly, the results revealed that the best estimates of key demographics were associated with one of the non-probability samples which used a special methodology to produce a more representative and more accurate national sample. More important to our conversation, however, was the finding that all of the non-probability samples produced large, biased estimates of key benchmark variables for both Hispanics and Blacks, leading to the conclusion that online *non-probability samples* are at risk of drawing erroneous conclusions about the effects associated with race and ethnicity. For now, I would recommend not using non-probability samples in multicultural studies.

Sampling Frame Considerations

The sampling frame is generally defined as an exhaustive listing of the elements of a defined universe that are under study. Some examples of a sampling frame would be:

- All the students enrolled in a university
- All occupied households in the U.S.
- All customers visiting a shopping mall on a given day
- All hospitals in a particular state

To be useful to the research practitioner who is planning a multicultural study, a listing of all units in a sampling frame would need to be accessible, appear only once in the listing, have its contents organized in such a manner that allows the selection of any unit in the sampling frame, and include relevant information on race and ethnicity to select multicultural persons. A carefully prepared Project Planning Checklist should provide the starting point for defining the most appropriate sampling frame for the multicultural study that you are planning. Your choice of a sampling frame will depend on the questions that you are trying to address with the research study and the desired coverage of the target audience. Let's discuss some common sampling frames and their appropriateness for the multicultural study that you may be planning.

1. Households with a valid postal address are usually provided by a direct mail shop or other vendors with access to postal data. Addressed-based samples (ABS) usually provide the best coverage of a geographic area, especially if it is updated on a monthly basis using the change-of-address file from the U.S. Post Office. The value of an ABS sample is greatly improved if the list provider also includes reliable indicators of race or ethnic origin, country of origin, and other demographic attributes that facilitate the identification and selection of multicultural persons or households. In my experience, an estimated 15 percent of U.S. householders move on a monthly basis, although the move rate varies considerably by geographic area and type of dwelling. A recent report by the Census Bureau tells us that renters are considerably more likely (21.7%) to move than homeowners (5.5%).[37] Overall, the move rate was higher for Blacks (13.1%) and Asians (12.1%), followed by Hispanics (11.7%) and non-Hispanic whites (10.0%). Since multicultural persons are more likely to be renters, you should plan to order more sample records to compensate for a higher likelihood of outdated or bad addresses. Dataman Group Direct[38] is one direct mail shop that has provided satisfactory addressed-based samples in many of my past multicultural studies. Possibly the most important advantage provided by a household sampling frame is that it provides nearly 100 percent penetration of all occupied U.S. households, allowing the use of a probability sampling design with the best coverage of key demographic subgroups. Additionally, the cost of addressed-based samples is low in comparison to other sampling frame listings, their records are usually updated on a monthly basis, and older respondents are often more engaged with a mail questionnaire. Two key disadvantages to keep in mind, however, are the higher move rates of multicultural households and inaccurate racial-ethnic classification strategies, which can undermine the quality of your survey experience.

2. Telephone households present more challenges to the research practitioner in terms of defining the best sampling frame since choices need to be made between RDD (random digit dialed), landline, and wireless numbers. Some of the more established shops that provide telephone samples include Scientific Telephone Samples, Research Now-SSI, and Genesys by Marketing Systems Group. There is a high potential for coverage bias when using telephone households as a sampling frame, especially if relying only on landline telephones. As discussed later in Chapter 6, the research practitioner will need to devote careful attention to the inclusion of landline and wireless telephones in the sampling plan since they can lead to different outcomes in terms of the inclusion of different multicultural respondents. Indeed, response rates to telephone surveys have declined substantially from 36 percent in 1997 to 6 percent in 2018[39]

> **Robocalls are very problematic**
>
> During Jan. 2014 to May 2018, the Federal Trade Commission litigated against one telemarketer who made an average of 883 million unlawful robocalls per year to U.S. residents — nuisance calls that lower response rates to legitimate surveys.
> Federal Trade Commission, www.ftc.gov

— leading to concerns that data quality and respondent representativeness, referred to as "non-response error" — were being undermined at such low response rates. However, several studies addressing this issue have shown that low-response rate telephone surveys are still able to capture representative samples of respondents and that data quality is comparable to surveys with higher response rates.[40, 41, 42] Thus, the telephone sampling frame continues to be utilized in the survey industry despite its known limitations, and has maintained its usefulness by the careful integration of wireless numbers into the sampling frame — a strategy that provides greater access to frequent users of wireless phones such as African Americans, Latinos and Asians. Traditional approaches used in telephone surveys that do not incorporate wireless numbers, however, are less likely to adequately represent multicultural persons. RDD landline samples, in particular, do a poor job of capturing Blacks and Latinos, while wireless numbers are decidedly more effective in reaching these groups. The decline in telephone response rates, coupled with TCPA requirements for manually dialing wireless numbers, have led to increased costs per completed interviews — a factor which has discouraged the use of the telephone methodology. Other contributing factors to lower telephone response rates include technological barriers such as do not call lists, call blocking, caller ID and the relative absence of bilingual interviewers in many telephone survey centers.

Outsourcing telephone survey work to international research shops has become more popular in recent years, although it introduces new problems related to interviewers that have not mastered U.S.-appropriate language accents, a lack of familiarity with U.S. brand names and institutions, and social skills that may clash on occasion. Caution should be exercised when considering outsourcing as a solution.

3. An online panel consists of a group of research participants who have agreed to provide information to a panel company at specified intervals over an extended period of time. Members of a panel are asked to provide information about themselves and family members, such as household information, demographics, consumer behavior and lifestyles. Panel members are usually paid some type of incentive to complete an online survey, such as a gift, a coupon to a retailer or some type of commodity. The popularity of online panels for conducting survey research has increased in recent years, especially as the cost of traditional surveys has increased, internet usage has expanded, and response rates to telephone surveys have declined.

In past years, online panels were not readily embraced by industry professionals and perceived as a non-scientific, "quick and dirty" solution for clients with smaller budgets, limited timelines and lower standards. To address these perceptions, some panel companies initiated the use of a probability, addressed-based sample (ABS) of households in the targeted geographic areas to recruit respondents for participation in a panel. In some cases, panel members were provided internet access and a computer if these were not already available in the selected household. By introducing probability sampling into the panel creation process, the scientific credibility of the online panels was enhanced, resulting in reduced coverage bias and improved demographic representation. Cost efficiencies were also realized since all panel members could now complete the surveys online without the need for a costly data collection effort. Nonetheless, the cost per completed interview (CPI) for ABS-based panel surveys can be high, in my opinion, and more affordable for organizations with large budgets. Some of the leading online panel companies include the following:

- Research Now — https://www.surveysampling.com/
- Knowledge Network — http://www.knowledgenetworks.com/GANP/
- YouGov — https://today.yougov.com/find-solutions/omnibus/

I had the opportunity to conduct an online survey of U.S. Latino millennials and used a panel to complete 1,000 interviews. Despite the recognized limitations in representing immigrants, the lower income, and non-English speakers, the panel approach worked well because the study targeted younger, English-language dominant millennials who were more educated — a good fit with the panel member demographics. To summarize, the decision to use an online panel for conducting an online survey of African Americans, Latinos or Asians should include a careful consideration of the panel provider's reputation, the demographic characteristics of its panel members, and the need for probability sampling. This decision should not be based solely on the available budget. If the study requires scientific credibility and minimal coverage bias, I recommend using a high-quality panel that has been recruited through ABS household sampling.

4. On-Site Locations. When time is an issue or a listing is not readily available to randomly selected respondents, it is a common practice to utilize different venues to collect survey data, such as malls, airports, retail stores or other locations where members of your target audience can be found. In such venues, respondents are intercepted in person, complete an interview or self-administered questionnaire, and receive an incentive for their participation in the study. Probability samples of respondents are not easy to achieve in such venues since researchers usually have less control in selecting persons in public places. The adequacy of such venues for intercepting multicultural respondents varies considerably, and you should plan to conduct some preliminary checks on the racial-ethnic composition of visitors to that venue before finalizing plans to use it as an intercept location for completing surveys with particular multicultural population segments. Some shopping malls will provide a demographic profile of mall visitors that would be very helpful to the research practitioner in planning a data collection strategy. For a study of multicultural consumers, it is essential to determine the days and times of the week that these shoppers are most likely to visit the mall. The practice of using shopping malls to intercept visitors may be waning as more malls across the U.S. are closing. According to one source, there are an estimated 1,100 malls in the U.S. with one quarter of them at risk of closing over the next five years.[43] The same source estimated that 8,600 stores could close in 2017, many of them brand name anchor outlets. When it comes to shopping malls as a research venue, proceed with caution.

5. Reaching Hidden Populations. In some industries, the target audience is especially difficult to find, such as injection drug users, men having sex with men, musicians, prostitutes or migrants. Standard sampling methods do not adequately capture these groups; therefore, a specialized sampling procedure known as respondent-driven sampling (RDS) was developed for this purpose.[44] RDS is a procedure that combines "snowball sampling" (wherein individuals refer those they know) with statistical adjustments that compensate for the non-random selection of respondents. Although often used in the medical industry, RDS is becoming more popular in the social sciences as well.[45]

To generate an RDS sample, the research practitioner starts by selecting a small number of initial participants ("seeds") from the target population who are asked — and compensated financially —to recruit their contacts in the population. The sampling continues with current sample members recruiting the next wave of sample members, continuing until the desired sample size is achieved. Participants are usually allowed to recruit up to three other contacts in order to ensure that the completion targets are achieved. If you are faced with a multicultural study that involves hard-to-reach segments, such as migrants, you might consider using RDS. However, you should plan to read extensively on this complex procedure and perhaps engage an expert on RDS to help you plan and execute the study.

6. Social Media as a Sampling Frame. The large number of individuals that utilize social media makes it an attractive medium for conducting online surveys as demonstrated by one creative research study using Facebook.[46] Finding a non-probability sample acceptable, the investigator utilized a snowball sampling technique to select the respondents. The study began with a small sample from the target subpopulation and then extended the sample by asking those individuals to suggest others for the study. Within five days, 2,700 individuals had completed the online survey at an "incredibly cheap" cost which further resulted in an adequate demographic representation of respondents. The study investigator strongly recommended Facebook as an ideal tool for studies with low budgets and willing to utilize snowball sampling instead of probability sampling procedures. An important limitation, however, is that social media companies will not make available to the research practitioner a listing of their subscribers, which precludes the selection of a probability sample.

A more recent study that focused on the use of Facebook for recruiting research participants, however, provides a less encouraging picture.[47] Facebook was used to recruit two distinct groups of participants — Filipino Americans and type 2 diabetics — to complete an online survey regarding consumer health information technology. While the study investigators reported 87 completions for the first group and 70 completions for the second group, respectively, both recruitment efforts produced mixed results regarding the representativeness by gender, race and ethnicity. The investigators concluded that Facebook may be more appropriate for recruitment in qualitative research, but not for obtaining large samples that would be needed in quantitative studies.

Does this mean that social media should be used as source for conducting surveys of multicultural persons? Perhaps, especially if you have a limited budget and the desire for scientific credibility is not important. However, Latinos, African Americans and Asians are frequent users of social media and use it for many of their lifestyle activities, suggesting that it would be more useful for recruitment of participants in qualitative studies that are not designed to generalize their results to a larger population.

Sample Size Issues

The calculation of a sample size for a multicultural study presents several challenges to the research practitioner, especially when the research team's experience with multicultural studies and knowledge of sampling concepts are limited. Assuming a simple random sample of a population, it is fairly easy to use a common sample size formula to estimate the number of interviews needed assuming a particular confidence interval, confidence level and an estimated proportion of cases. For example:

$$n = \frac{Z^2 * (p) * (1-p)}{e^2}$$

Where,
    e = margin of error or confidence interval
    p = estimated proportion or incidence of cases
        (0.5 used for example)
    Z-score = 1.96 for 95% confidence Level
    n = sample size needed

Thus, assuming a confidence level of 95 percent, a confidence interval of .05 and an estimated proportion of 0.5, the estimated number of completed interviews needed would be 384. Of course, this formula does not tell us how many sample records will be needed to complete 384 interviews, which is one reason that a good estimate of the incidence rate would be desirable. For example, if the incidence rate (see box) was assumed to be .10, then dividing the 384 interviews by .10 would equal 3,840 records needed. However, the number of records needed would be 7,680 if the incidence rate was .05.

> **What is the incidence rate?**
>
> A basic computation of incidence rate is derived by dividing the number of qualified respondents by the total number of respondents that were contacted.

It is a common practice for discussions to take place concerning the incidence that is associated with a particular study — incidence being defined as the percentage of the sample that is qualified to complete the study after the screening criteria has been met. In my experience, the incidence rates shared by potential clients have rarely been accurate, and often not supported by any objective information. When concrete information is not available on incidence rates from past studies, it might be a good idea to calculate a preliminary estimate of incidence by using the chain ratio method. For example, let's assume the following information for a study of Asians in one geographic area was retrieved from the most recent American Community Survey:

- Total number of Asians: 100,000
- Percent of Asian adults: 80%
- Percent Asian homeowners: 60%
- Percent Asian households with incomes over $50,000: 20%

To estimate the theoretical incidence rate of Asian adult homeowners with household incomes over $50,000 annually, multiply each of the three percentages together (i.e., .80 x .60 x .20 = 9.6%). By multiplying the incidence rate by the total number of Asian adults (100,000), the resulting number of Asians persons meeting this criterion is 9,600. Further adjustments would need to be made, of course, for other factors that would impact the percentage of Asian adults that actually complete the survey, such as refusals, dropouts, and bad contact information. Incidence estimates can sometimes be just wild guesses that need to be verified before finalizing a budget for a study. If you remain doubtful about the accuracy of an incidence rate provided by a client, then offer to conduct a pilot test of 30 to 50 interviews so that you can determine the actual incidence rate and number of completed interviews per hour before finalizing a budget. If a pilot test is not feasible, then it might be wiser for you to quote an hourly rate for your interviewing time and bill your client for the total number of interviewing hours required to complete the study — regardless of what the incidence rate happens to be. Once you accumulate enough experience in conducting multicultural studies, you will be able to estimate an incidence rate based on verifiable Census data and your own experience, and these incidence rates will be quite different for African American, Latino, and Asian studies. A sampling expert, however, should have the last word on sample size, design and the number of records needed to complete the study.

Selecting a Sample List Vendor

Regardless of whether you will be targeting persons or households in the sampling universe, you will need to identify a vendor who will provide you access to a listing of the desired universe of your target audience, keeping in mind that you are targeting *multicultural* persons and your study specifications may be more challenging to meet. Following are some key factors that you should consider in selecting the appropriate sample list vendor:

- **Reputation.** Ask for references from colleagues in professional networks to verify their experience with a particular list vendor. Established list vendors should be pleased to provide you client references as well. Getting recommendations from professional colleagues with the relevant multicultural experience would be ideal.

- **Updates.** How often are their records updated? Monthly, yearly or less often? Multicultural consumers are more likely to be renters and immigrants who move residences often, so more frequent updates are preferred. Older listings will likely lead to more non-contacts from returned mail, disconnected telephones, and bounced online invitations.

- **Method of Classifying Multicultural Persons.** As discussed in Chapter 3, there are different methods for classifying multicultural persons. Vendors who provide listings of persons or households may provide information related to race and ethnicity, but in most cases this information is not derived by asking a person this question but rather by using a person's surname, first name, or geographic residence — sometimes all of these are used to derive a race-ethnic classification with varying degrees of success. As I discussed in a previous chapter, the E-Tech product by Ethnic Technologies does a good job of identifying the likely race or ethnic origin of a person based on their first name, surname and geographic residence. Their race-ethnic identifier product was used in a national study of multicultural consumers that we conducted that lacked race-ethnic information and was thus very useful in planning a linguistic strategy for the data collection process that targeted five distinct language groups. Information about E-Tech and other related services can be viewed at this address: https://www.ethnictechnologies.com/

- **Coverage.** To what extent does the vendor's listing include your desired target audience? Which segments does it exclude? This is especially important because multicultural persons are often excluded or misclassified in vendor listings, especially if the study is focused on a local market. Try to get a demographic profile that provides counts of all records in the vendor's listing by race-ethnicity, country of origin, gender, household income and tenure. You may discover that the listing is biased toward a particular demographic subgroup. Online panels, for example, do not capture multicultural persons very well, especially immigrants, while they do a better job of including English-speaking, higher income, and more educated persons. If a list vendor cannot provide information on who is included or excluded in their database, I suggest that you not use them.

- **Size of Sampling Frame and Method of Data Collection.** The size of the sampling frame will vary considerably depending on whether you are conducting a telephone, mail or online survey. In general, you can expect a much larger frame for an addressed-based sample (ABS) of residential households for any geographic area. However, you are likely to experience significant coverage bias in using a telephone-base sample that depends on landline connections since the penetration of landline telephones has dropped considerably in recent years. Using RDD (random digit-dialed) samples does not resolve this problem since it introduces considerably more non-working telephone numbers into the sampling frame. More contemporary approaches used by telephone studies includes about 75 percent cell numbers and 25 percent landlines — a strategy that is strongly supported by the Pew Research Center because it provides improved representation of persons across ethnicity, age, and income levels.[48] An important observation related to RDD samples is that traditional RDD methods only work with number blocks that are assigned to landline service, and do not include cell telephone numbers.[49] Sample vendors now offer enhanced wireless support that offers cell telephones that are active and working; however, additional fees are involved. Once you receive the sample list that you ordered from the selected vendor, you will need to conduct a few audit checks of the list prior to sending it to your data collection center. The first step is to import the sample list into SPSS or some other data analysis program and run a frequency tabulation of key demographics in the sample list, such as race-ethnicity, country or origin, geography (state, metros, countries, cities, zip codes, census tracts), and others. Carefully check the distribution of these variables against the specifications from your sample design and plan to identify any anomalies (see sample map on page 191). If you have provided the list vendor instructions for stratifying the sample by a geographic area (i.e., city, county, zip code, metro area), you must take the time to check the distribution of the records selected to ensure that the sample list conforms to your sample design specifications. This is your opportunity to let the listing vendor know whether the sample that you ordered meets your specifications. Once verified, reputable listing vendors will quickly make the necessary corrections and send you a replacement sample list.

In my experience, following are some of the problems that I have encountered in using vendor listings of multicultural samples:

Insufficient Numbers. On occasion, I have been unable to complete the minimum number of interviews required for a multicultural group, especially when using the telephone method. In one urban area with large numbers of multicultural households, I was unable to complete the requested number of telephone interviews because I under-estimated the final incidence that resulted from the application of all of the client's screening criteria and the number of telephone households available — a problem that could have been anticipated with a more careful review of current Census data. Although various factors can pose a barrier, the number of telephone households — landline or wireless — that are available in any geographic area is not infinite. According to the Pew Research Center,[50] response rates to telephone surveys have declined from 36 percent in 1997 to 6 percent in 2018, and likely to decline further as increasing numbers of research vendors fail to provide the linguistic resources to interview multicultural respondents in languages other than English. It is a good idea to be very conservative in the number of sample records that you request for a multicultural study, taking into account population data from the most recent Census, the screening criteria for a study, and past experience. As mentioned earlier, multicultural persons are more likely to be renters and move more often than homeowners, so you may need to order more sample to compensate for this reality.

Multiple Families in Households. The increase in multi-generational households in the U.S. leads to another set of concerns. Multigenerational households are defined as those that include two or more adult generations, or that include grandparents and grandchildren. Asian and Hispanic persons are more likely than whites to live in multigenerational family households.[51] First, with multiple adults living in one household, it is important to employ a strategy for randomly selecting an adult for the appropriate family unit. Secondly, unless you specify to the listing vendor that you want only one record selected per household, your sample is likely to include multiple records with a different person's name using the same address — a real problem for probability samples. Duplication needs to be checked carefully at the household address level.

Inaccurate Race-Ethnic Coding. The formulas used by list providers to estimate the race-ethnic identity of multicultural populations or households varies considerably in their accuracy if one compares the derived race-ethnic category with the race-ethnic category that a respondent chooses to describe themselves in a survey. The accuracy rate, in my experience, ranges from 50 to 80 percent and tends to be more accurate for Hispanic and Asian persons whose surnames and geographic residences are more recognizable. It makes sense to ask the list vendor to describe the method used for classifying persons by race-ethnicity or country of origin. A Spanish-surname file created by the Census Bureau many years ago is one approach to use, although the surnames derived were based more on Latinos living in southwestern states where Mexican-origin persons are concentrated, and tend to exclude Spanish surnames that are more common in other geographic areas of the U.S. I would have more confidence, however, knowing that the list vendor used the ethnic identifier system used by Ethnic

Technologies, described at https://www.ethnictechnologies.com.

Unreliable Segmentation Information. Aside from the typical contact information provided by the listing vendor, additional information is sometimes offered that allows the research practitioner to fine tune their sampling strategy by categorizing or segmenting multicultural persons into language usage or acculturation groups. Language groups are usually created by asking respondents to describe their language usage at home in terms of whether it is mostly English, mostly Spanish or bilingual. This simplistic measure is problematic in several ways. My past research experience confirms that Latinos tend to over or underestimate their language abilities on self-reported measures.[52] Moreover, self-reported language measures are generally too vague and non-specific to be useful. For example, rather than ask a person which language they use more often at home, it would be more valid to inquire about their language usage in different contexts: reading, writing, speaking, and listening — and it matters a great deal if one is talking to a child, teen, or adult whose language skills often influence the language used by an individual. You are taking a broad leap of faith in using simplistic measures of home language usage.

An acculturation scale is another type of segmentation tool that may be developed by the research practitioner from questions included in a survey, or the scale may be provided by some listing companies to classify persons into low, medium, and high levels of acculturation — presumably to understand the influence of culture on behavior and the extent to which a person has "adapted" to the mainstream environment. These scales vary considerably in their complexity, and are typically comprised of such attributes as nativity, home language usage, and media usage. Figure 4 on the following page presents The Short Acculturation Scale, which was developed[53] to classify Hispanics into acculturation groups by obtaining responses to questions related to usual language for reading and speaking, language usually spoken at home, language in which one usually thinks, and the language usually spoken with friends. The responses are scored, and ranges are proposed to classify persons into low and high acculturation groups.

Figure 4: Short Acculturation Scale

A. English Version

In general, what language do you read and speak?
- Only Spanish 1
- Spanish better than English 2
- Both equally 3
- English better than Spanish 4
- Only English 5

What language do you usually speak at home?
- Only Spanish 1
- Spanish better than English 2
- Both equally 3
- English better than Spanish 4
- Only English 5

In which language do you usually think?
- Only Spanish 1
- Spanish better than English 2
- Both equally 3
- English better than Spanish 4
- Only English 5

What language do you usually speak with your friends?
- Only Spanish 1
- Spanish better than English 2
- Both equally 3
- English better than Spanish 4
- Only English 5

B. Spanish Version

¿Por lo general, qué idioma(s) lee y habla usted?
- Sólo Español 1
- Más Español qué Inglés 2
- Ambos por igual 3
- Más Inglés qué Español 4
- Sólo Inglés 5

¿Por lo general, qué idioma(s) habla en su casa?
- Sólo Español 1
- Más Español qué Inglés 2
- Ambos por igual 3
- Más Inglés qué Español 4
- Sólo Inglés 5

¿Por lo general, en qué idioma(s) piensa?
- Sólo Español 1
- Más Español qué Inglés 2
- Ambos por igual 3
- Más Inglés qué Español 4
- Sólo Inglés 5

¿Por lo general, qué idioma(s) habla con sus amigos?
- Sólo Español 1
- Más Español qué Inglés 2
- Ambos por igual 3
- Más Inglés qué Español 4
- Sólo Inglés 5

Scoring instructions: To score, the respondents' answers can be averaged across the four items and the score used as an interval scale, where the scores closer to five indicate high levels of acculturation while those closer to one indicate little acculturation. Alternatively, the respondents' average scores can be split at 2.99 to create a nominal variable. In this case, a score below 2.99 can be considered to reflect low acculturation (less acculturated respondents) while scores above 2.99 would correspond to the more acculturated respondents.

There are many types of acculturation scales that have been developed for diverse race-ethnic groups as revealed by two literature reviews on such scales.[54, 55] Acculturation scale developers, however, have been inconsistent in providing users key psychometric information about these scales — such as their factor structure, reliability and validity — to support their usage in multicultural studies.

I have not used acculturation scales very often in past

multicultural studies for two reasons. First, many studies have demonstrated a relationship between level of acculturation and various behaviors, which in turn have led to various types of conclusions and proposed interventions. For example, a person with a low level of acculturation would likely be foreign-born, show limited English proficiency, watch mostly native-language media, and shop at supermarkets that offer a range of recognizable brands for products that fit their cultural lifestyle. A more highly acculturated person, however, would show contrasting behavior: native born, more proficiency in English, view mostly English-language media, and perhaps shop at supermarkets that offer mainstream brands as well as brands for culturally-relevant products that continue to be consumed. While both low and high acculturated persons may show distinctive demographic attributes and behaviors, the usefulness of this information in terms of marketing or advertising tactics is limited in my opinion (see side box for further discussion on this topic). Nonetheless, you may find an existing acculturation scale that helps you classify and understand multicultural consumer behavior in general. It is my view, however, that your client will probably seek an analysis that is more tailored to their specific product or service.

> **Demographic vs. Psychographic Segmentation**
>
> Most demographic characteristics, such as gender and race-ethnicity, are static attributes that do not change. In addition, within any specific demographic subgroup, one can expect to find psychological variation that tells us more about the relationship of a respondent to a particular behavior. In one study of paint usage, we developed a psychographic scale that measured DIY (do-it-yourself) attitudes and behaviors related to paint products, which allowed us to define three clusters or groups of Latinos related to paint usage. This strategy allows one to develop a more specific positioning strategy that can target Latinos who share relevant product or service-related attributes, regardless of their demographic attributes. As we all know, advertisers develop positioning strategies and appreciate having this type of information available.

Customer-provided lists. Such lists may initially seem like a blessing but can be problematic. It is easy to assume that a customer list provided by a client will include current information if the client maintains and uses a customer list to communicate with their customers. Organizations have different practices when it comes to updating customer information and you will suffer the consequences if you do not thoroughly check a customer list prior to conducting a survey. In my experience with customer lists, I have encountered records with incomplete information, outdated telephone or email addresses, inaccurate or missing race-ethnicity status, and duplicate records. In a telephone survey of vendors that we conducted for a government entity, the sample of business firms was not "cleaned" prior to implementing the study — that is, checked for disconnected numbers or removal of non-qualified non-profit organizations. Additional sample was required to complete the study, interviewing costs were increased, and the timeline had to be extended. With customer-provided lists, plan to take extra time to check the quality of the sample provided.

Using Census Data to Kick Start the Sampling Plan

Regardless of which geographic areas or multicultural groups have been defined in the Project Planning Checklist, a good place to start planning your sampling needs is the U.S. Census Bureau's Explore Census Data website which is accessible at the following internet address: https://data.census.gov/cedsci. There are several reasons why I recommend this starting point:

- The Census Bureau is the most comprehensive and objective source of demographic information for the U.S. and its territories;
- It includes detailed information at different levels of geography;
- It is well documented and used as a trusted source by all levels of government and commercial enterprises; and
- Unless you require a customized report, most of the data is available at no cost to you — your tax dollars have already paid for it.

You or some member of your research team needs to become very familiar with Census Bureau geographic and demographic terminology, and their numerous data files. The U.S. Census Bureau conducts a decennial census every decade that includes all U.S. households, while a sample of households are interviewed each year in the American Community Survey. The following three tables, extracted from a Census Bureau webinar,[56] presents important information about the American

Community Survey that is useful for anyone planning a multicultural study. For example, Table 4 below presents the numerous subjects that are included in the ACS including social, demographic and housing characteristics.

Table 4: Subjects Included in the ACS

POPULATION		HOUSING
SOCIAL Ancestry Citizenship Disability Educational Attainment Fertility Grandparents Language Marital Status Migration School Enrollment Veterans	**DEMOGRAPHIC** Age Hispanic Origin Race Relationship Sex **ECONOMIC** Class of Worker Commuting Employment Status Food Stamps (SNAP) Health Insurance Hours/Week, Weeks/Year Income Industry & Occupation	Computer & Internet Use Costs (Mortgage, Taxes, Insurance) Heating Fuel Home Value Occupancy Plumbing/Kitchen Facilities Structure Tenure (Own/Rent) Utilities Vehicles Year Built/ Year Moved In

Table 5 below presents the release dates for each of the three ACS data products (i.e., 1-year, 3-year, 5-year estimates) and the minimum population size, or threshold, for the geographic areas included.

Table 5: Release Schedule for ACS Data

The American Community Survey
Availability of 2018 Data Products

Estimated Population of Geographic Area	1-Year Estimates	1-Year Supplemental Estimates	5-Year Estimates
65,000 or more	X	X	X
20,000 to 64,999		X	X
Less than 20,000			X
Release Date	September 26, 2019	February 6, 2020	December 19, 2019

Table 6 on the following page describes the types of geographic areas included in the ACS, the total number of geographic units included for each geographic area, and the percentage of the geographic areas covered for each data product.

Table 6: Major Geographic Areas and Type of ACS Estimates Received

Type of geographic area	Total number of areas	Percent of total areas receiving...		
		1-year, 3-year, & 5-year estimates	3-year & 5-year estimates only	5-year estimates only
States and District of Columbia	51	100.0	0.0	0.0
Congressional districts	435	100.0	0.0	0.0
Public Use Microdata Areas*	2,071	99.9	0.1	0.0
Metropolitan statistical areas	363	99.4	0.6	0.0
Micropolitan statistical areas	576	24.3	71.2	4.5
Counties and county equivalents	3,141	25.0	32.8	42.2
Urban areas	3,607	10.4	12.9	76.7
School districts (elementary, secondary, and unified)	14,120	6.6	17.0	76.4
American Indian areas, Alaska Native areas, and Hawaiian homelands	607	2.5	3.5	94.1
Places (cities, towns, and census designated places)	25,081	2.0	6.2	91.8
Townships and villages (minor civil divisions)	21,171	0.9	3.8	95.3
ZIP Code tabulation areas	32,154	0.0	0.0	100.0
Census tracts	65,442	0.0	0.0	100.0
Census block groups	208,801	0.0	0.0	100.0

*When originally designed, each PUMA contained a population of about 100,000. Over time, some of these PUMAs have gained or lost population. However, due to the population displacement in the greater New Orleans areas caused by Hurricane Katrina in 2005, Louisiana PUMAs 1801, 1802, and 1805 no longer meet the 65,000-population threshold for 1-year estimates. With reference to Public Use Microdata Sample (PUMS) data, records for these PUMAs were combined to ensure ACS PUMS data for Louisiana remain complete and additive.

Source: U.S. Census Bureau, 2008. This tabulation is restricted to geographic areas in the United States. It was based on the population sizes of geographic areas from the July 1, 2007, Census Bureau Population Estimates and geographic boundaries as of January 1, 2007. Because of the potential for changes in population size and geographic boundaries, the actual number of areas receiving 1-year, 3-year, and 5-year estimates may differ from the numbers in this table.

Figure 5 illustrates the hierarchy of the geographic units covered by the American Community Survey. It is important to keep this hierarchy in mind as you retrieve the data tables from the Census website.

Figure 5: ACS Geographic Hierarchy

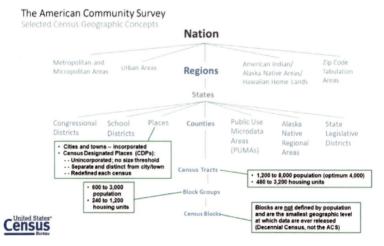

For any level of geography — U.S., state, metropolitan area, county, or place — you should plan to retrieve the following important information to develop the sampling plan for your multicultural study:

- Number of all persons
- Age
- Gender
- Race and Hispanic origin
- Detailed Hispanic and Asian subgroups
- Nativity (native vs. foreign-born)
- Citizenship status
- Marital status
- Economic: household income, median household income, aggregate household income, number/percent in poverty, and tenure (homeowner vs. renter)
- Household composition: family and non-family households, multigenerational households
- English-language proficiency

To give you an idea of how useful ACS data can be in planning a multicultural study, I would like to discuss four client experiences where I utilized some of the items listed above.

Sample Applications Using Census Data

Client 1: The client wanted to know how important it was to provide Spanish-language support for a study of Texas Latinos.

To address this concern, I examined ACS Table 05003I (see Figure 6 on following page) which shows the number of persons who are native-born and foreign-born by age group. In the absence of other information, the nativity table allows you to explore a linguistic strategy for any geographic area included in the ACS. That is, the higher the proportion of foreign-born Latinos, the greater their reliance on Spanish. Conversely, the higher the proportion of native-born Latinos, the greater their reliance on English. I have confirmed this relationship over hundreds of studies that I have conducted over the past 45 years, and it holds true for Asians as well. Table B05003I also displays further information about Texas Latinos, including their gender, age, and citizenship status. By summing the counts for persons 18 years and over to include males and females, you can obtain the count of native born (4,367,129) and foreign-born (2,956,418) Texas Latino adults. Thus, of the 7,323,547 million Latino adults in Texas, 59.6 percent were native born and 40.4 percent were foreign born. With such a large presence of foreign-born Latino adults, one might conclude that Spanish-language support should be included in the planned study.

Figure 6: ACS Table B05003I

	Texas
	Estimate
⌄ Total:	10,921,556
⌄ Male:	5,497,449
⌄ Under 18 years:	1,832,172
Native	1,735,470
⌄ Foreign born:	96,702
Naturalized U.S. citizen	9,919
Not a U.S. citizen	86,783
⌄ 18 years and over:	3,665,277
Native	2,158,557
⌄ Foreign born:	1,506,720
Naturalized U.S. citizen	417,701
Not a U.S. citizen	1,089,019
⌄ Female:	5,424,107
⌄ Under 18 years:	1,765,837
Native	1,673,339
⌄ Foreign born:	92,498
Naturalized U.S. citizen	10,112
Not a U.S. citizen	82,386
⌄ 18 years and over:	3,658,270
Native	2,208,572
⌄ Foreign born:	1,449,698
Naturalized U.S. citizen	458,899
Not a U.S. citizen	990,799

Client 2: This client was concerned about the specific linguistic approach to take in the translation of a survey for Texas Latinos and Asians since many different types of Latinos and Asians resided in the state — that is, which type of Latino or Asian subgroup should receive more weight in the translation process?

To address the Latino language issue, I retrieved Table B03001 from the ACS (see Figure 7 below) that shows the counts of the various Latino subgroups residing in Texas. The table tells us that Texas is home to 11.2 million Latinos, and that 9.5 million of these persons, or 85 percent, are of Mexican origin. Thus, "Mexican" Spanish should be given more consideration in the translation process.

Figure 7: ACS Table B03001

	Texas Estimate
∨ Total:	28,701,845
Not Hispanic or Latino	17,333,001
∨ Hispanic or Latino:	11,368,844
Mexican	9,659,802
Puerto Rican	214,765
Cuban	93,713
Dominican (Dominican Republic)	24,409
∨ Central American:	696,270
Costa Rican	11,841
Guatemalan	108,501
Honduran	175,601
Nicaraguan	26,375
Panamanian	19,366
Salvadoran	351,209
Other Central American	3,377
∨ South American:	221,287
Argentinean	16,059
Bolivian	5,866
Chilean	8,716
Colombian	84,283
Ecuadorian	14,674
Paraguayan	398
Peruvian	30,748
Uruguayan	2,804
Venezuelan	56,804
Other South American	935
∧ Other Hispanic or Latino:	458,598

Similarly, Table B02015 (see Figure 8 on the following page) regarding the Texas Asian population suggests that more weight in the translation process should focus on Chinese, Filipino and Vietnamese residents. While Asian Indians also have a large presence in Texas, previous research suggests that they are more comfortable communicating in English.[57]

Figure 8: ACS Table B02015

	Texas Estimate
∨ Total:	1,430,857
Asian Indian	452,598
Bangladeshi	13,442
Bhutanese	960
Burmese	22,429
Cambodian	9,993
Chinese, except Taiwanese	215,366
Filipino	146,320
Hmong	2,280
Indonesian	7,547
Japanese	24,311
Korean	80,649
Laotian	18,102
Malaysian	2,590
Mongolian	841
Nepalese	20,684
Okinawan	41
Pakistani	67,368
Sri Lankan	5,781
Taiwanese	17,731
Thai	14,116
Vietnamese	267,996
Other Asian, specified	501
Other Asian, not specified	17,161
Two or more Asian	22,050

Sampling Issues for Multicultural Populations

Client 3: This client wanted to identify the Texas counties that included Latino households with the greatest buying power.

Although the American Community Survey does not provide a specific measure of buying power, a crude measure of buying power is provided in the aggregate household income indicator which measures the income earned by all working members of a household. When summed across all households in a geographic area, the aggregate household income allows you to identify the geographic areas with the highest and lowest "buying power." Table 7 below displays the top 20 Texas counties ranked by Latino aggregate household income. The data was retrieved from Table B19025I in the American Community Survey 2018 5-Year Estimates. The 5-year file was used for this table because it included all the 254 counties in Texas, whereas the 1-year file includes only a sample of these counties.

Table 7: Top 20 Latino Texas Counties, Ranked by Aggregate Household Income, 2018

Rank	County	Aggregate Household Income
1	Harris County, Texas	$34,251,707,500
2	Bexar County, Texas	$20,533,797,700
3	Dallas County, Texas	$15,996,881,700
4	El Paso County, Texas	$11,339,681,200
5	Hidalgo County, Texas	$10,994,731,900
6	Tarrant County, Texas	$9,826,602,200
7	Travis County, Texas	$8,148,654,500
8	Cameron County, Texas	$5,042,351,400
9	Nueces County, Texas	$4,726,166,100
10	Fort Bend County, Texas	$4,355,349,200
11	Webb County, Texas	$4,031,114,700
12	Denton County, Texas	$3,217,089,100
13	Collin County, Texas	$3,187,017,400

Table 7: Top 20 Latino Texas Counties, Ranked by Aggregate Household Income, 2018 (continued)

Rank	County	Aggregate Household Income
14	Williamson County, Texas	$2,647,267,500
15	Montgomery County, Texas	$2,517,151,900
16	Brazoria County, Texas	$2,307,390,300
17	Ector County, Texas	$2,004,374,800
18	Lubbock County, Texas	$1,723,122,800
19	Midland County, Texas	$1,637,960,200
20	Galveston County, Texas	$1,579,846,800

Source: American Community Survey 2018 5-Year Estimates

From this table, a survey practitioner would find it easy to select the counties with the highest Latino buying power as a starting point for their sampling plan.

Client 4: This client requested a study of U.S. Black consumers that was representative of major U.S. markets.

As a starting point, I retrieved all the U.S. metropolitan areas from the American Community Survey 2018 5-year estimate file, Table B02001 and rank ordered them by the total population of Black persons. Table 8 below presents the top 20 metropolitan areas for Black persons that was used as a starting point for selecting the study sample.

Table 8: Top 20 Black Metropolitan Areas in U.S., Ranked by Population, 2018

Rank	Metropolitan Area	Persons
1	New York-Newark-Jersey City, NY-NJ-PA Metro Area	3,131,986
2	Atlanta-Sandy Springs-Roswell, GA Metro Area	1,928,984
3	Chicago-Naperville-Elgin, IL-IN-WI Metro Area	1,560,816

Table 8: Top 20 Black Metropolitan Areas in U.S., Ranked by Population, 2018 (continued)

Rank	Metropolitan Area	Persons
4	Washington-Arlington-Alexandria, DC-VA-MD-WV Metro Area	1,521,416
5	Philadelphia-Camden-Wilmington, PA-NJ-DE-MD Metro Area	1,233,368
6	Miami-Fort Lauderdale-West Palm Beach, FL Metro Area	1,223,979
7	Houston-The Woodlands-Sugar Land, TX Metro Area	1,143,282
8	Dallas-Fort Worth-Arlington, TX Metro Area	1,105,876
9	Detroit-Warren-Dearborn, MI Metro Area	955,994
10	Los Angeles-Long Beach-Anaheim, CA Metro Area	845,917
11	Baltimore-Columbia-Towson, MD Metro Area	803,038
12	Memphis, TN-MS-AR Metro Area	627,480
13	Charlotte-Concord-Gastonia, NC-SC Metro Area	546,419
14	Virginia Beach-Norfolk-Newport News, VA-NC Metro Area	515,493
15	St. Louis, MO-IL Metro Area	511,016
16	New Orleans-Metairie, LA Metro Area	436,942
17	Cleveland-Elyria, OH Metro Area	403,848
18	Richmond, VA Metro Area	377,295
19	Orlando-Kissimmee-Sanford, FL Metro Area	376,660
20	Boston-Cambridge-Newton, MA-NH Metro Area	357,027

Source: American Community Survey 2018 5-Year Estimates

On occasion, I have also used the network of state data centers to obtain additional demographic information, such as annual population estimates and projections for states, metro areas, and counties. Following is the link to the Census Bureau's State Data Center Program that identifies all of its members: https://www.census.gov/about/partners/sdc/member-network.html

Of course, there are various third-party commercial sources that you could utilize to obtain similar demographic information, such as Claritas (https://www.claritas.com). While convenient and easier to use, these services usually require a fee and may not provide some of the Census indicators identified above. Many of these third-party sources incorporate Census Bureau data into their own population estimates.

Chapter Summary

This chapter covered a range of information that I consider essential knowledge in the sampling of multicultural persons. The key ideas to consider going forward are:

- Get a good understanding of basic sampling concepts and seek out a sampling expert to address the complexities of sample design;
- Although there may be barriers to implementing probability sampling in a particular study, you should incorporate probability sampling if you plan to generalize from a study sample to the universe from which the sample was drawn and an estimate of sampling error is needed;
- Use caution in selecting a sampling frame and a list vendor, utilizing recommendations by professional colleagues with experience in sampling multicultural populations;
- Learn to be skeptical of client-provided incidence indicators for planning a multicultural study, and place more confidence in a good pilot study or Census data for estimating potential incidence;
- Become familiar with the common problems discussed in this chapter that you are likely to encounter when using sampling list vendors, and learn to question the methods that they use to classify their listing records by race, ethnicity, country of origin, language behavior and

Sampling Issues for Multicultural Populations

acculturation level; and

- Utilize the wealth of information provided by the Census Bureau to plan important elements of a multicultural study, focusing on the most current data available.

In the following chapter, we will consider the various challenges that you are likely to face in the adaptation and translation of survey instruments in studies of multicultural populations.

Chapter 5: Adapting Research Instruments for Multicultural Populations

In this section, I do not spend time on the general steps involved in designing survey instruments since there are numerous publications devoted to this topic, and college-level courses generally utilize such publications. If you need a refresher on designing survey instruments or just starting to learn about this area, I recommend the following publications:

- Stanley L. Payne. *The Art of Asking Questions*. Princeton University Press, 1951.

- Seymour Sudman and Norman M. Bradburn. *Asking Questions: A Practical Guide to Questionnaire Design*. Jossey-Bass Inc, 1982.

- Don A. Dillman, Jolene D. Smith, and Leah Melani Christian. *Internet, Mail, and Mixed-Mode Surveys: The Tailored Design Method*. Third Edition, John Wiley & Sons, Inc. 2009.

Instead of talking about the basic design of survey instruments, I devote attention to the problems and challenges that you are likely to encounter in using traditionally designed survey instruments with multicultural populations. In my experience, these problems can be classified into the following categories: knowledge of the target audience, language behavior, translations, topic sensitivity, congruence of questions with external sources, survey length, scale formats, font size and accents, navigational aids, and selection of colors.

Knowledge of the Target Audience

The information that you may have collected in the Project Planning Checklist (see Chapter 2) should serve as a good guide in planning the adaptation and translation of the survey instrument. For example, the first thing that you need to determine is whether you need a translated version of the survey instrument. A careful analysis of selected demographic characteristics of a community using the most recent version of the American Community Survey is the place to go for this preliminary but important assessment. The following link takes you to the U.S. Census Bureau website *Explore Census Data* that provides access to the American Community Survey and various other files collected periodically by the U.S. Census Bureau. (https://data.census.gov/cedsci/)

The Census tables that you should retrieve and analyze carefully include race and Hispanic origin, specific Latino or Asian origin subgroups, the proportion of native vs. foreign-born residents, and language usage. The race and Hispanic origin information will provide counts for the total population, Latinos and Asians — the two groups that are most likely to need a survey instrument in a language other than English. The relative size of the foreign-born population will confirm the degree to which a native-language survey instrument is needed — that is, a definite need is indicated if the proportion of foreign-born residents is 30 percent or higher for either Latinos or Asians. ACS Table B03001 (Figure 7) shows specific Latino origin subgroups which will guide you on whether the translated instrument should align its vocabulary and idioms more closely with a specific Latino subgroup like Mexicans, Puerto Ricans, Cuban or other subgroups. Similarly, Table B02015 in the ACS of specific Asian origin subgroups can be used to determine the need for a native-language instrument in Chinese, Korean, Vietnamese or some other Asian language. A useful language question provided by the American Community Survey captures the English-language proficiency of the population. Unfortunately, proficiency in speaking a language other than English is not captured by the ACS. The English-language proficiency information can be used as another indicator of the extent to which respondents in a specific community are not able to speak sufficiently well in English. For example, if a large proportion of the population (i.e., 30 percent or more) indicates that they speak English "not well" or "not at all," this should signal to the survey practitioner that a non-English questionnaire is needed in the study for a self-administered survey, or underscore the need for bilingual support in a telephone or face-to-face interview.

In preparation for the 2020 Census, the Census Bureau identified the key language needs of the U.S. population by six Census Regional Office Areas based on the languages spoken by 1,000 or more limited English-speaking households. Table 9 below presents this information.[58]

Adapting Research Instruments for Multicultural Populations

Table 9: Language Needs for Census Regional Office Areas.

Language Needs for Census Regions
Based on languages spoken by 1,000 or more limited-English-speaking households (2016 ACS 5-year estimates)

Census Regional Office Areas					
Atlanta	Chicago	Denver	Los Angeles	New York	Philadelphia
Spanish	Spanish	Spanish	Spanish	Spanish	Spanish
Haitian Creole	Chinese	Vietnamese	Chinese	Chinese	Chinese
Chinese	Polish	Chinese	Korean	Russian	Korean
Vietnamese	Arabic	Korean	Vietnamese	Portuguese	Vietnamese
French	Russian	Arabic	Tagalog	Korean	Russian

Note: All the listed languages are among the 12 non-English languages being supported online and by phone.

The table provides a useful guide for the type of language support that might be required in different regions of the U.S.

Confusion About Language Behavior

In their efforts to understand the language preference of a target audience, research practitioners often confuse the language functions that are relevant for the mode of data collection to be used. For example, it makes little sense to know how well a segment of the population speaks English if the respondent will be required to read a paper or online survey. A respondent's ability to speak a language is clearly more relevant for telephone or personal interviews, while a respondent's ability to read in a specific language is more relevant for paper or online surveys. Two fairly unproductive methods that research practitioners use to assess language preference includes (a) asking how well a person "communicates" in a language — which tells you nothing about the language function involved, or (b) asking a person which language they speak most often at home, which may also be limited in its usefulness since the language spoken at home by Latinos or Asians will vary considerably by the age and language preference of other members of the household. Older members of the household, especially if they are foreign born, will usually prefer to speak in their native language, while most native-born members will usually prefer to speak in English.

Children will generally prefer to speak in English, especially if they are native born. Further complicating the language issue for research practitioners is the tendency for immigrants to over-estimate their English-language proficiency, and a similar tendency for native-born Latinos and Asians to over-estimate their native-language proficiency. In each case, the respondent is motivated by social desirability to demonstrate how well they have retained command of their native language, or how proficient they have become in learning English. Inexperienced interviewers are not always trained to recognize these language nuances and may complete an invalid interview with a respondent who has only a fragile understanding of the interviewing language.[59]

By comparison, the language needs of U.S. Asians have received relatively less attention in the research literature than the language needs of U.S. Latinos. Nonetheless, several studies illustrate that U.S. Asians are responsive to surveys, especially when the appropriate linguistic options are provided. For example, an online survey of first-generation U.S. Asian Indians by New American Dimensions and interTrend Communications[60] found that the Asian classification was perceived negatively and regarded as an attempt to overlook their distinct culture origin. Although the respondents were most comfortable with the English language, over 90 percent of the respondents were proficient in their native language which helped to maintain a connection to the Indian culture. A second study of 1,003 Filipino subscribers to The Filipino Channel, conducted by telephone, revealed that the majority of the interviews were conducted in Tagalog even though English was also offered as an option.[61] A more recent study of U.S. Asians was conducted by Pew Research[62] which included telephone interviews of 3,511 Asian respondents, i.e., Filipino, Chinese, Korean, Vietnamese, and Muslims. The study provided a wealth of information about each Asian subgroup and should serve as a methodological model for the survey industry.

Managing Translation of the Survey Instrument

Once a decision has been made to translate a survey instrument into a language other than English, a research practitioner may have several options at their disposal, such as using a staff member or interviewer that has knowledge of the language involved; hiring an external translator or translation shop; or using translation software that is readily available online or other formats. This decision carries considerable responsibility for the research practitioner who cannot afford to use a translated survey instrument that deviates much from the English-language version. The translation of survey instruments can be a complicated process, especially if the multicultural study requires multiple languages. Don't make the mistake of assuming that an employee or interviewer that works on your research team has sufficient knowledge and experience to translate a document just because they happen to be Latino or Asian. If an employee studied their native language formally in school, the chances of an adequate translation increases, and if translating documents has been a part of their past employment, then one can feel more confident. You should understand that native-born Latinos in the U.S. rarely study Spanish formally and will likely have a fragile grasp of formal Spanish, while foreign-born Latinos living in the U.S. can have good to excellent speaking skills but may or may not have formal training in reading or writing Spanish. Your best bet is to spend the extra dollars for a professional or certified translator to translate your survey instrument into a language other than English. The work of any translator — professional or not — still requires a good pilot or usability test to check the ability of the target audience to understand the translated survey instrument. To further your understanding of the detailed procedures related to the translation and adaptation of survey instruments for cross-cultural surveys, I suggest that you start by reading the following publications:

- *Guidelines for Best Practices in Cross-Cultural Surveys*. The Survey Research Center, Institute for Social Research, University of Michigan, 2011. (Chapters 7 and 8)
- *Research with Hispanic Populations*. Gerardo Marín and Barbara VanOss Marín, Applied Social Research Methods Series, Volume 23, Sage Publications, 1991. (Chapters 4 and 5)

The Guidelines publication is a lengthy one (725 pages) that will require some time and patience for the reader to fully appreciate and focuses primarily on cross-cultural research with international populations. This book appears to be written for the research practitioner that is planning a study in international markets using a survey instrument that needs to be adapted to the needs of persons living in each country. The Marín & Marín book, while 32 years since its initial publication, nevertheless provides a detailed discussion about the several methods used to translate a document for Hispanic populations, but relies considerably on the authors' experience in conducting health-related studies in the U.S. Both publications should have a place in your multicultural research library.

The Guidelines publication evaluates various industry practices and strongly recommends the team or committee approach, which involves a group of people working together where translators independently produce the translations; committee members review the translations with the translators; and one or more adjudicators decide if the translation is ready to move to detailed pretesting and when the translation is considered finalized and ready for fielding. To the extent that an organization has the financial and staff resources to follow these detailed steps in the survey translation process, it makes sense to follow the team approach, especially when conducting surveys of linguistically diverse populations. However, survey practitioners that have minimal resources to follow the team approach to survey translation should at least ensure that knowledgeable staff or professionals are involved in the process, and that members of the target audience are included in the pre-testing phase. One survey industry professional also suggests that translators should understand issues related to survey methodology, such as writing good questions and constructing questionnaires that flow well.[63]

The importance of evaluating a translated survey was illustrated in a recent usability study of the Chinese version of the 2020 Census questionnaire.[64] The online survey in Chinese was presented to Chinese respondents who could read and write in Chinese but had limited English-language proficiency. The investigators discovered several problems with the translated questionnaire, including problems related to sentence structure or verb tense, grammar, lack of context, name order, validation rules, and navigation instructions. The study underscored the important point that translators are not the last word on translated surveys, which should always be evaluated prior to fielding a study.

Use of Offensive, Outdated Words or Phrases

As some research practitioners may have already discovered, there are various words, phrases and labels that are likely to offend multicultural research respondents. In Chapter 3, we discussed the various methods that have been used in the past to identify and classify the race or ethnicity of multicultural persons, although research practitioners have been slow to adopt the recommended best practices. For example, the term "Negro" is outdated and offensive to African Americans. Latino immigrants sometimes reject the pan-ethnic terms "Latino" or "Hispanic," preferring instead to identify with their country of origin. Similarly, Asian immigrants generally prefer to identify with their country of origin, while some Asian Indians prefer to identify as Indo-American, Indian or their specific country of origin.

> **Politics and Language**
>
> During one U.S. study of Vietnamese adults, our Vietnamese telephone supervisor observed terminology in the translated instrument that was reflective of a "communist" vocabulary. To avoid of-fending potential respondents, we opted to replace these terms with more neutral words or phrases.

The use of offensive or outdated words, phrases or labels undermines data quality and eventually leads to higher refusal rates, more missing data, or under-counting and over-counting of race-ethnic groups. Unless absolutely necessary, questions about a person's legal status in the U.S. should be avoided in a survey instrument because it creates a "chilling effect" that is likely to result in a terminated interview. In the same context, the use of the word "investigación" could set off some alarm bells in a study of immigrants in the U.S.

As shown by Figure 9 below, the American Community Survey 2018 questionnaire includes a question on citizenship status, which may be less threatening to respondents than asking about their legal status, although citizenship questions can also be perceived as threatening during a period of time where considerable hostility is directed toward immigrants.

Figure 9: ACS 2018 Citizenship Question

Is this person a citizen of the United States?
- ☐ Yes, born in the United States → SKIP to question 10a
- ☐ Yes, born in Puerto Rico, Guam, the U.S. Virgin Islands, or Northern Marianas
- ☐ Yes, born abroad of U.S. citizen parent or parents
- ☐ Yes, U.S. citizen by naturalization – Print year of naturalization
- ☐ No, not a U.S. citizen

The Department of Justice announced their decision to include a question on citizenship in the 2020 Census questionnaire, which industry observers warned would depress participation of immigrants who fear that the government could use the information against them.[65] Although a federal judge ruled against inclusion of the citizenship question in the 2020 Census and the U.S. Supreme Court recently decided to exclude the question about citizenship in the 2020 census,[66] a recent survey of the American public revealed that 56 percent incorrectly believed that a citizenship question would appear in the 2020 Census.[67] Coupled with the rise of anti-immigrant rhetoric and elevated immigration enforcement under the Trump administration, the path to a historic undercount of non-citizens in the 2020 Census is already being realized. In the first test-run of the 2020 Census in Providence County, Rhode Island, it is already apparent that many non-citizens are refusing to take part in the census test for fear that their information, and that of mixed families, will be shared with the federal government.[68] Several other studies have also confirmed the fear and anxiety surrounding the citizenship question in the 2020 Census, which includes immigrants and citizens who fear for the safety of immigrant family members and friends.[69, 70]

In their continuing campaign to diminish the count of immigrants in the 2020 Census, the Trump administration recently announced the deployment of elite Border Patrol agents to sanctuary cities that have refused to support ICE staff in the apprehension and incarceration of undocumented immigrants.[71] To justify this deployment, Trump explained that the agents will assist in apprehending the "dangerous illegal criminals" that are being harbored by sanctuary cities — which is a pretext for this campaign since numerous past studies have confirmed that immigrants — both legal and undocumented — show significantly *lower crime rates* than native-born Americans.[72]

A large census undercount threatens the allocation of federal funding for the nation's communities, which totals about $800 billion a year. Given the anti-immigrant policies being promoted in the current political environment, survey practitioners should brace for the likelihood of higher refusal rates by immigrants on all surveys. As a consequence of the formidable legal advocacy that challenged the inclusion of the citizenship question, the New York Times recently reported that the Trump administration had abandoned its quest to add the citizenship question to the 2020 census, a week after being block by the Supreme Court.[73] This outcome was a significant sigh of relief for Census Bureau staff and survey practitioners throughout the U.S. Given the current political environment, survey practitioners should plan to expand their current resources to address expected declines in the survey response rates in multicultural communities with large concentrations of immigrants.

There are potentially a wide range of sensitive topics that should be evaluated carefully during pilot testing to determine if the respondent reveals extreme sensitivity to these topics, such as incidence of abusive or deviant behavior in families, criminal history, mental illness or health, and others. On one recent occasion, I received a mail survey from a healthcare provider that included a question about the incidence of violence toward children in the household. Among the series of questions included, the survey asked if I believed that any child in our household had ever been sexually abused, physically abused, or psychologically abused. I was stunned that such a question would be included in the questionnaire since a response that affirmed the presence of such violence against children would need to be reported to local authorities — an observation that I verified with a family attorney. Indeed, research practitioners must be cautious and advise clients when the inclusion of a question is likely to be offensive or raise potential ethical or legal issues.

Congruence of Survey Questions with External Sources

Survey instruments generally include a set of demographic and socioeconomic questions that serve an important role in describing the sample of study respondents and how well the sample characteristics match the universe of persons from which the sample was drawn. These questions typically include such measures as race or ethnicity, gender, nativity, language usage, tenure, household income, educational attainment, and others. As I will discuss in a subsequent section related to data analysis and weighting, research practitioners do not always use questions and response categories that match the external sources of information that they plan to use to make such comparisons and for post-stratification weighting that may be required. For example, the following format is commonly used in surveys to measure race and ethnicity:

Which of the following categories best describe your race or ethnic background? Would you say that it is white, African American or Black, Latino or Hispanic, Asian or some other race-ethnic group?
__White
__African American, Black
__Latino, Hispanic
__Asian
__Other race or ethnic group (PLEASE SPECIFY: _____)

If the research practitioner wishes to compare the survey responses to this race-ethnic question with data from the American Community Survey, they will probably experience a problem because the response categories do not match the categories used below in the Hispanic and race questions in the 2018 ACS (see Figure 10 below):

Figure 10: ACS 2018 Hispanic Origin and Race Questions

→ NOTE: Please answer BOTH Question 5 about Hispanic origin and Question 6 about race. For this survey, Hispanic origins are not races

5 Is Person 1 of Hispanic, Latino, or Spanish origin?
☐ No, not of Hispanic, Latino, or Spanish origin
☐ Yes, Mexican, Mexican Am., Chicano
☐ Yes, Puerto Rican
☐ Yes, Cuban
☐ Yes, another Hispanic, Latino, or Spanish origin – *Print origin, for example, Argentinean, Colombian, Dominican, Nicaraguan, Salvadoran, Spaniard, and so on.* ⇲

6 What is Person 1's race? *Mark (X) one or more boxes.*
☐ White
☐ Black or African Am.
☐ American Indian or Alaska Native — *Print name of enrolled or principal tribe.*

☐ Asian Indian   ☐ Japanese   ☐ Native Hawaiian
☐ Chinese   ☐ Korean   ☐ Guamanian or Chamorro
☐ Filipino   ☐ Vietnamese   ☐ Samoan
☐ Other Asian – *Print race, for example, Hmong, Laotian, Thai, Pakistani, Cambodian, and so on.* ⇲   ☐ Other Pacific Islander – *Print race, for example, Fijian, Tongan, and so on.* ⇲

☐ Some other race – *Print race.* ⇲

Since the race-ethnic question in this hypothetical survey includes a "Hispanic" option, it assumes that Hispanic is a distinct race category when it is actually an ethnic category. The ACS questionnaire recognizes this distinction by first asking the respondent to self-identify as Hispanic or Latino origin, then asking a second question about their race. Using the two questions in ACS, an analyst is thus able to define all Blacks, whites, and Asians who are NOT of Latino or Hispanic origin and those who self-identify as Hispanics regardless of their preference for race. These distinctions may not be important to all analysts but should be important to those who want to know the extent to which a survey sample reflects the race-ethnic attributes of persons residing in a particular community or universe. Interestingly, it is common to hear research practitioners explain the under-representation of certain race-ethnic groups as resulting from a respondent's lack of interest, negative attitudes toward surveys, or just indifference to the sharing of opinions. While some of these explanations may be true, it is equally plausible that researcher practitioners who use incorrect or outdated race-ethnic categories may be discouraging survey participation. Consequently, rather than improving the quality of their data collection procedures, the under-representation of multicultural persons in surveys is sometimes resolved by applying post-stratification weights — no matter how large the disparity between the survey data and the ACS data. As will be discussed in a subsequent chapter on data analysis and weighting, post-stratification weighting should not be used as a remedy for poor data collection procedures. If one is starting a study that includes a multicultural segment of the population, research practitioners should first complete the Project Planning Checklist to determine if they have the resources required to complete a high-quality study. If important resources are missing, then it is better to subcontract some of the research tasks to other qualified research practitioners with the right resources and experiences. Or just turn the work down and refer the whole study to a more qualified firm. The client will appreciate your honesty and candidness.

Figure 11 on the following page presents the proposed format of the 2020 Census Hispanic origin and race questions, which is similar to the format used in the 2010 Census.

Figure 11: Race and Origin Questions for 2020 Census

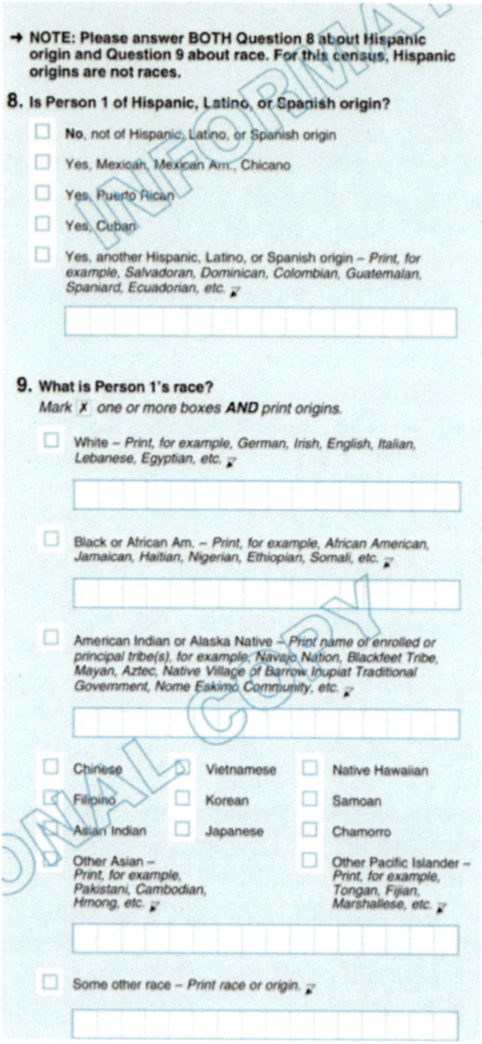

→ **NOTE: Please answer BOTH Question 8 about Hispanic origin and Question 9 about race. For this census, Hispanic origins are not races.**

8. Is Person 1 of Hispanic, Latino, or Spanish origin?

- ☐ **No**, not of Hispanic, Latino, or Spanish origin
- ☐ Yes, Mexican, Mexican Am., Chicano
- ☐ Yes, Puerto Rican
- ☐ Yes, Cuban
- ☐ Yes, another Hispanic, Latino, or Spanish origin – *Print, for example, Salvadoran, Dominican, Colombian, Guatemalan, Spaniard, Ecuadorian, etc.*

9. What is Person 1's race?
Mark ✗ *one or more boxes* ***AND*** *print origins.*

- ☐ White – *Print, for example, German, Irish, English, Italian, Lebanese, Egyptian, etc.*
- ☐ Black or African Am. – *Print, for example, African American, Jamaican, Haitian, Nigerian, Ethiopian, Somali, etc.*
- ☐ American Indian or Alaska Native – *Print name of enrolled or principal tribe(s), for example, Navajo Nation, Blackfeet Tribe, Mayan, Aztec, Native Village of Barrow Inupiat Traditional Government, Nome Eskimo Community, etc.*
- ☐ Chinese ☐ Vietnamese ☐ Native Hawaiian
- ☐ Filipino ☐ Korean ☐ Samoan
- ☐ Asian Indian ☐ Japanese ☐ Chamorro
- ☐ Other Asian – *Print, for example, Pakistani, Cambodian, Hmong, etc.*
- ☐ Other Pacific Islander – *Print, for example, Tongan, Fijian, Marshallese, etc.*
- ☐ Some other race – *Print race or origin.*

It bears repeating that the inclusion of specific "categories" next to each race label (e.g. WHITE: German, Italian, Irish, Polish, English, French) can be very beneficial to respondents who are not accustomed to the race labels commonly used in U.S. surveys — a practice that I would strongly encourage survey practitioners to adopt to minimize measurement error. In addition, using specific Asian countries of origin makes more sense since country of origin is often preferred by U.S. Asian survey respondents instead of the term "Asian" or "Asian

American." To ensure that the appropriate race or ethnic labels are utilized in a survey, a survey practitioner should take the extra step to understand the labels that are more commonly used by members of the target community as well as the labels that are considered outdated or offensive.

Deciding on the Length of the Survey Instrument

Let's begin by accepting the fact that there is no "ideal length" for a survey instrument, although there may be some general truisms that come from industry experience. A 10-minute survey may appear long to someone that is in a hurry, while a 20-minute survey may not seem long if the respondent is enjoying the experience. In my own experience, I try to keep the length of telephone surveys between 10 and 15 minutes. Online surveys, on the other hand, are generally easier to complete and often include incentives — two reasons that you might encourage you to design a longer survey. By contrast, mail surveys are not as easy to navigate, especially if they include skip instructions that are vague or confusing. The reality is that the ideal length of a survey instrument will ultimately depend on the audience that you are targeting, the complexity of the questions, and the mode used for collecting the survey responses. Keep in mind that the factors that influence survey length may not be similar for Latinos, Blacks and Asians. A translated version of a survey will often be longer than an English-language version of the same survey instrument; however, less time may be required to complete the native-language questionnaire since a respondent that selects this option will likely find it easier to understand and complete — assuming it was properly translated and tested. Also keep in mind that the inclusion of open-ended questions in multicultural surveys presents challenges in several areas. First, special training will be needed in all languages to ensure that interviewers capture quality responses.

Secondly, interviewers should be required to record *verbatim* responses in the language of the interview; otherwise, you will end up with fragmented responses because interviewers are usually not trained to be translators. Lastly, a trained coder will need to content code the verbatim responses in the relevant languages. In mixed mode surveys, the "length" of the survey is defined differently and varies by mode: a self-administered survey (mail or online) may take 10 minutes to complete, but the telephone mode may add another 5 to 10 minutes due to the interviewer-respondent interactions — a factor that needs to be considered in the budgeting process since a client will not want to shorten the questionnaire because the telephone interview requires more time to complete. In one national study that included multicultural respondents, the mail and online versions of the survey required about 15-20 minutes to complete but the telephone mode required from 45 to 60 minutes to complete — a disparity that added significantly to the study budget.

Translating Rating Scales

The translation of rating scales — such as Likert scale or semantic differential — often present problems when trying to achieve a literal translation. The end result of translating strongly agree, agree, neither agree nor disagree, disagree or strongly disagree into non-English languages can be problematic because the meaning is sometimes lost in the translation. And it becomes very redundant for telephone interviewers to read Likert scales across a series of statements. To avoid translation problems with rating scales in their global polling, The Gallup Organization relies more on dichotomous yes/no response options in place of scalar question formats. Rather than translate questions or response options, Korzenny and Korzenny[74] propose that a question and its response options should not be translated, but rather designed from scratch in the native language as long as its conceptual equivalence is maintained with the English-language version.

Visual Acuity

African Americans and Latino adults are more likely than whites and Asians to have visual acuity problems (discussed in more detail in Chapter 7).[75] Font sizes of 12 points should be a minimum in paper and online surveys in order to enhance reading ability and comprehension.

Literacy Rates

African Americans and Latino adults also have lower literacy rates than whites and Asians, suggesting that the reading difficulty level of most survey instruments should not be higher than necessary.[76] It is also interesting to note that several studies have observed that minority groups in general read at a grade level that is significantly lower than their reported years of education[77] — a possible consequence of attending lower quality schools.

Use of Accent Marks

Many languages require the use of accent or diacritical marks for proper reading comprehension. In my experience, however, I have observed many native language survey instruments without the required accent marks or diacritical marks. My own conclusion is that the research practitioner was uninformed about the need for accent marks or decided to take the easy way out and choose a software translation solution or a close friend or employee who lacked the required skills. Importantly, the software platform that will be used for a telephone or online survey must be able to display these accent or diacritical marks. If valid responses are desired from multicultural populations, avoid the low-cost solutions and use only the best tools and talent for your translated documents.

Skip Instructions

Most self-administered surveys require instructions that direct the respondent to a particular location or question in the survey instrument. These skip instructions are usually automated in online and telephone surveys, but usually printed in mail surveys. Because mail surveys require the respondent to take control of the navigation, the use of skip instructions should be kept to a minimum or removed completely. If skip instructions are misunderstood, respondents can omit key questions or sections of a survey or complete the wrong ones. Such was the finding of one study evaluating an English and Spanish-language mail survey for the PRAMS (Pregnancy Risk Assessment Monitoring System) which found that less educated and older respondents were less likely to successfully follow skip instructions, while the placement of skip instructions influenced the number of missing values.[78] The American Community Survey Is a good model to follow in designing a mail survey with skip instructions.

Adapting to International Communities

On occasion, the adaptation of survey instruments may require a deliberate modification of a question or questionnaire in order to create a new question or questionnaire that provides a better fit to the needs of a new population, location, language or mode as is commonplace in international studies.[79] Some common examples where adaptation is often required include units of measurement (i.e., temperature, currency, distance), description of local symptoms of a given disease, the direction that languages are read, color symbolism, language simplification based on educational level, timing of holidays, work schedules, and worship times.

Pilot Testing the Adapted Survey Instrument

Much has been mentioned throughout this section about the importance of conducting a pilot test to check question comprehension, timing, instructions, and navigational issues. The importance of the pilot study results cannot be over-stated since much is at stake for the study progress and budget. In the *Cross-Cultural Survey Guidelines* by the Institute for Survey Research,[80] eleven approaches for conducting a pilot test are discussed, including such approaches as field tests, interviewer or respondent debriefings, behavior coding, focus groups, cognitive laboratory methods, usability testing and others. You are encouraged to consult the chapter on Pre-Testing in this publication for further information regarding these eleven approaches to pilot testing. In my own research practice, I have typically used the field testing and focus group approaches to conduct pilot studies.

For a field pilot test of a telephone survey instrument, I will select a sample of 30 to 50 respondents that represent the target audience and have a team of telephone interviewers complete the pilot test. These completed pilot surveys are then analyzed in detail in order to identify problems with the quality of the responses, data anomalies, offensive language, high number of refusals on questions, or other undesirable issues. For telephone interviews, interviewer feedback is also incorporated into the evaluation process as well as monitoring of the interview by a bilingual supervisor. Once corrections are made, the survey instrument is translated into the appropriate languages, and the pilot testing is repeated with a different language-appropriate sample.

For pilot testing mail survey instruments, I strongly recommend a semi-structured focus group format with follow-up discussions. From my experience, the following simple steps will increase the likelihood that survey respondents will be able to understand the questions, record their responses correctly, and appropriately follow any directions — all important elements in obtaining valid responses and reducing measurement error:

Step 1: Recruit a sample of participants that represent your target audience and invite them to participate in a focus group to improve the readability of a survey instrument. You should plan on conducting at least two focus groups with 8-10 participants per group in order to accommodate languages other than English.

Step 2: A trained moderator should distribute a copy of the survey instrument to each of the participants along with pencils and a red ink pen. The participants are instructed to complete the survey independently without asking for any assistance from the moderator or other participants. While completing the survey, the participants are also instructed to use the red ink pen to circle or underline words, phrases, or instructions that are confusing, offensive, or vague. No discussion is taking place during this time and participants are free to take the time needed to complete the survey, although the length of time that they spend taking the survey should also be recorded.

Step 3: Once the surveys have been completed by the participants, the moderator opens up the discussion by focusing on each section of the survey in the sequence presented. Specific feedback is requested for each item in the survey instrument that was red-lined with the expectation that the discussion will also identify potential solutions.

Step 4: Lastly, the moderator prepares a summary report of the pilot study results, presents this report to the client, and recommends the appropriate changes to the survey instrument.

This method of pilot testing has proven highly effective in past survey projects and could also be utilized in evaluating online surveys as long as respondents are being observed by survey staff while completing the survey.

Chapter Summary

Adapting and translating survey instruments is a time-consuming and challenging task for survey practitioners, which is probably one reason that so many surveys in the U.S. are conducted primarily in English. However, this task is essential in studies that involve linguistically and culturally diverse populations. This chapter reviewed several tactics for facilitating this process, including the following points:

- Avoid the guesswork in evaluating the need for a native-language questionnaire by checking the relevant Census

Bureau tables that provide relevant information about English-language proficiency, language usage, race, ethnicity, nativity and country of origin. English-only surveys should only be justified in a very homogenous community of native-born persons with good proficiency in the English language;

- Use professionals, preferably a team or committee approach, to translate your survey instruments to avoid potential problems when using untrained staff, and ensure that the translated documented is evaluated by a pilot or usability study before field work is initiated;

- Make it a practice to design key demographic questions — such as race, ethnicity, and income — to reflect the formats used by the Census Bureau or other external sources that you plan to use for comparison purposes or post-stratification weighting;

- The ideal length of the survey will depend on the mode utilized (i.e., mail, telephone, online), reading difficulty, clarity of instructions, and other factors related to the respondent's literacy level and proficiency in the survey language; make it a practice to include only the most essential questions in the survey since respondent fatigue and frustration will lead to drop-offs and budget overruns.

- Various other recommendations for adapting the survey instrument included the design of a rating scale in-language instead of translating it; using larger fonts to accommodate respondents with visual acuity problems; simplifying the reading difficulty level of the survey instrument; using accent and diacritical marks in translated instruments; minimizing the use of skip or filter instructions; encouraging respondents to provide their best guess on economic or other sensitive questions; and recognizing the need for other methods of adaptation for recent immigrants in terms of units of measurement (i.e., temperature, currency, distance), disease symptoms, color symbolism, and timing of holidays, work schedules or worship times.

- Ultimately, what matters most in ensuring that you have a valid survey instrument is not simply the evaluation by research professionals or the translator, but the survey experience of the target respondents.

In the next chapter, we turn our attention to understanding the limitations of traditional data collection methods.

Chapter 6: Limitations of Traditional Data Collection Methods

Previous chapters have discussed the challenges one is likely to encounter in sampling multicultural populations as well as the adaptation of survey instruments. This chapter focuses on the special issues or challenges that you are likely to encounter during the planning and execution of the data collection activities. At this point in the process, it is assumed that the research practitioner has completed the appropriate pilot or usability study to avoid any major mistakes during the data collection activities. If a pilot or usability study has not been conducted, be prepared for some surprises during the data collection phase. In this chapter, I discuss some of the lessons learned in using traditional data collection modes in multicultural studies, including mail surveys, telephone surveys, online surveys and panels, exit polls and intercept interviews. Attention is also devoted to the use of weights when adjusting survey data, and the use of incentives to improve response rates.

Readers who have not studied some of the fundamental concepts regarding data collection procedures are encouraged to read one of the following books:

- *Telephone Survey Methods: Sampling, Selection and Supervision*, Second Edition (1993) by Paul J. Lavrakas.[81]

- *Internet, Mail and Mixed-Mode Surveys: The Total Design Method*, Third Edition (2009) by Dillman, D.A., Smith, J.D., and Christian, L.M.[82]

The Dillman et al. book provides a detailed and comprehensive discussion of the key steps in designing and implementing internet, mail and mixed-mode surveys, while the Lavrakas book focuses only on telephone surveys. Although 16 years separates the publication of these two books, a race-neutral and language-neutral approach is apparent in both publications owing to the minimal attention devoted to the methodological problems in conducting surveys with racially and linguistically diverse populations. Consequently, my discussion focuses attention on the situations where traditional survey data collection practices may require additional resources to study multicultural populations.

Mail Surveys

Perhaps the primary reason that a research practitioner would want to use a mail survey is that it provides nearly 100 percent penetration of a defined population of persons or households with mailing addresses. This is an attractive motivator because it facilitates the selection of a probability sample and calculation of sampling error — an important element of scientific research. This superior sample coverage is difficult to achieve with telephone or online samples. As pointed out by Dillman et al.,[83] people are already accustomed to completing forms without the use of technology, while others may be uncomfortable with attachments that accompany emails. Moreover, obtaining a sample of household addresses is relatively easier and less expensive than other types of samples.

There are two major downsides, however, to mail surveys: the steps required to achieve a good response rate, and the cost of printing and postage.

For example, the Total Design Method developed by Don Dillman recommends a system of multiple contacts as follows:

- A prenotice letter
- A questionnaire mailing with a cover letter
- A thank you postcard
- A replacement questionnaire
- A final contact made by a different mode of delivery

Coupled with a pre-paid token incentive and various other important design features, mail survey response rates ranging from 20 to 81 percent have been achieved from several experiments of various populations, including college students and Northeast residents. Before you get too excited about conducting a mail survey, however, consider the fact that most of these studies made no mention of including multicultural populations or languages other than English. Additionally, the costs involved in conducting a mail survey with multiple contacts received minimal attention by the book authors, Dillman et al. Assuming a first-class postage rate of $0.55, one mailing of 20,000 mail pieces would cost $11,000. The postage cost alone would increment rapidly with each additional contact that is made to respondents. In one national survey I completed a few years ago, we mailed approximately 200,000 survey packages that would currently cost about $110,000 just for one mailing.

Limitations of Traditional Data Collection Methods

Multiple mailings may also include additional costs for printing and fulfillment. One would also need to consider the timeline that would be required to accommodate these multiple contacts. Thus, a survey practitioner considering a mail survey would be wise to focus attention on the budget required to achieve an adequate response rate within the required timeline and consider its potential benefits over other modes for the target audience.

One of the first things that you will need to develop is a good working relationship with a printing and fulfillment company that has significant experience and capabilities with mail survey projects, and preferably one that has completed large-scale, multi-modal and multilingual surveys. Everyone may have a good printing and fulfillment shop, but not all printers understand the complexities of working with large-scale surveys that utilize unique passcodes, multiple languages, booklet-style surveys, fulfillment teams and tight timelines. Following are some of the lessons I have learned from past mail survey projects:

Early Planning. The Project Planning Checklist that you may have completed earlier with your client should provide sufficient detail to get the mail survey details finalized; however, you will likely need to schedule another one or two follow-up meetings to understand the communities that will be targeted in the study.

Timeline. Always allow at least 20 percent more time to complete the mailing than previously planned. Multicultural persons are likely to be renters who move more frequently, which causes delays in mail delivery and increases the amount of undeliverable mail. The complexities of coordinating multiple languages in a mail survey usually slows the process in order to assure a quality fulfillment.

Survey Package. The outside appearance of survey packages is often unappealing and may look just like all the other junk mail that arrives in U.S. mailboxes. To avoid having your survey package go directly to the trash can, you can follow the Total Design Method approach of giving the envelope a traditional look that does not make it stand out from traditional mail; however, the appeal of this traditional look may or may not have relevance to multicultural respondents. In my experience, you need to give the respondent a reason not to trash the package before looking inside the package. Start by ensuring an attractive package design with engaging phrases in the relevant languages to raise some curiosity. Mention of a sweepstakes or other incentive is also engaging when placed on the front side of the envelope.

Inside the survey package, you should include a cover letter, the questionnaire in booklet form, and a stamped self-addressed return envelope. A window should clearly show the contact name and address. Instead of adding the common phrase "Or other resident in household," recent research[84] tells us that survey response rates are provided a lift when a phrase is used that describes a potential subgroup affiliation that is being targeted in the household, such as "Cooking Enthusiast," "Environmental Lover," or "Foodie."

Cover letter. Ensure a cover letter is attached to the first page of the survey booklet so that the information the cover letter contains is returned with the completed questionnaire. The letter should be easy to understand and use a font size of 12 points or larger. Some type of unique identification number should be utilized to track the survey, help in identifying and removing duplicates, and preventing entry by non-qualified persons. If you decide to only mail an English-language survey instrument, your client should add a statement that instructs the respondent to call an 800 number if they want a non-English questionnaire. This instruction for requesting a survey booklet in another language, however, should NOT be printed just in English since it may not be understood by a respondent who cannot read English very well.

Survey Booklets in Relevant Languages. Should you wait for survey respondents to request a questionnaire in another language? My emphatic response is "no." Many federal surveys in the U.S. are providing language options other than English; however, my own observations suggest that most mail surveys in the commercial world are sent only in English. Sending an English-only survey may seem to be more cost-effective to the naïve research practitioner. However, when you recognize the fact that 60 to 70 percent of Latino and Asian immigrants prefer to communicate in their native language when provided the choice, it makes more sense to include a native-language questionnaire along with an English-language questionnaire in order to improve response rates. The extra cost of including a native-language questionnaire in the same survey package is minimal, while the postage paid will not change up to a certain number of ounces per package. The main reason it is better to initially include both language versions of the questionnaire is that you have provided Latinos or Asians a choice of the interviewing language. My past experience demonstrates that 50 to 70 percent of the mail questionnaires will be completed in the native language when both versions are provided to Latino or Asian respondents. Like the bilingual telephone interviewer that tells the respondent that they can communicate in English or the native language, including a native-language questionnaire together with an English-language questionnaire establishes much needed rapport with the respondent. The higher response rate that you are likely to achieve and the time saved by not requiring a formal request for a non-English survey will be very beneficial to the study. When possible, non-English speaking respondents should not be given the extra burden of having to contact a research center to request a non-English language questionnaire.

First-Class or Cheaper Postage? It is always a tough decision — whether to pay the lowest postage rate or first class for a mail survey. Of course, this ultimately depends on your postage budget, the timeline, and end-of-project accounting. Once you have all your survey package inserts available, a quick trip to the U.S. Post Office will provide you a cost estimate for mailing the survey package using either first class or standard rate delivery. If mailing to local market addresses, standard rate will likely be enough to have the item delivered within one week. However, a national campaign may require 2 to 3 weeks for delivery using standard rate postage. Aside from a slower delivery time, standard rate postage means that the item will not be returned to you if it is considered undeliverable by the U.S. Post Office. If you are producing a disposition report for a client, not knowing how many mail pieces were undeliverable could be important in calculating a final survey response rate. With first-class postage, all undeliverable mail will be returned to you over a period of several months from the first mail launch date.

In summary, a mail survey option can be a good choice for your multicultural study, but it will require a considerable amount of homework by the research practitioner since current knowledge about the effectiveness of mail surveys with multicultural populations is limited. A well-executed pilot study may be the best tool to help in confirming the mail survey data collection strategy that will work best for a multicultural study.

In the section that follows, I discuss the telephone survey method and the challenges that it presents in studies of multicultural populations.

Telephone Surveys

The Project Planning Checklist should give you a preliminary assessment of the resources available to conduct a telephone-based study of multicultural populations. There are many reasons a research practitioner may choose a telephone-based study over other modes: a quick turn-around time, less dependence on respondent literacy level, more control over skip logic and presentation of questions, real-time reports on survey progress, and ability to integrate various telephone teams into one study using a common online portal. Despite these benefits, there are various reasons to be cautious in using a telephone-based approach, especially in multicultural studies. These observations are based on my past 45 years of industry experience in conducting telephone surveys and observation of industry trends as well.

Changes in Telephone Industry. Over the past decade, Pew Research has documented the staggering decline in response rates to telephone-based studies — from 36% in 1997 to 6 percent in 2018[85] — due in part to an increase in technology options like call blocking and caller ID, and the proliferation of nuisance calls. These trends inspired adoption in 1991 of the Telephone Consumer Protection Act (TCPA) which restricts telephone solicitations and limits the use of automatic dialing systems, artificial or prerecorded voice messages, SMS text messages, and fax machines. Moreover, autodialing systems cannot be used to call wireless numbers without consumer consent. Coupled with the declining response rates, the TCPA penalties have understandably discouraged the use of telephone-based studies, increased costs due to the requirement for manually dialing wireless numbers and shifted attention to other modes of data collection.[86, 87]

Inadequate Staffing Resources. With the exception of a few noteworthy companies, the vast majority of U.S. survey research shops do not have adequate levels of interviewing staff to conduct multicultural research studies by telephone, relying instead on monolingual interviewers with backup interviewers on standby for non-English languages, or outsourcing non-English surveys to foreign language shops. Reliance on monolingual interviewers with backup interviewers for non-English languages is not an effective strategy[88] since it introduces delays in the completion of interviews and leads to lower response rates. Bilingual interviewers, on the other hand, can immediately make the appropriate language switch when necessary and complete the interview. The outsourcing solution to foreign-language shops is also problematic for three reasons: (a) interviewers may have proficiency in a language like Spanish or Chinese, but their accents may be very pronounced and distracting to U.S. residents; (b) interviewers may be unfamiliar with U.S. brand names, institutions, and lifestyles; (c) interviewer social skills are quite different and appear overly rude at times, and (d) sponsoring clients often do not have the native language resources to monitor the interviews that are being conducted by foreign-language shops, thus bypassing a key quality control responsibility. Figure 12 below clearly illustrates that when Hispanic and Asian adults are provided the choice of the interviewing language, they are most likely to choose their native-language option, especially if they are foreign born.[89] The use of English-language monolingual interviewers would likely lead to more refusal rates in such studies.

Figure 12: Language Choices by Hispanic and Asian Adults in Telephone Survey

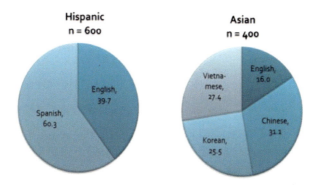

Source: Dallas/Ft. Worth Multicultural Study, Rincón & Associates, 2008

Hire and Train Your Own Multicultural Team. All things being equal, you will be in a better position to control the quality of your multicultural study if you hire and train your own interviewers. By using a series of proficiency tests of reading and speaking skills, each job candidate should be able to demonstrate their reading and speaking proficiency in the relevant languages. Some writing skills would also be helpful for the recording of responses to open-ended questions. In conversations with research vendors, I have found they are sometimes reluctant to expand their language support because they lack the internal staffing resources to recruit and train interviewers in different languages, and further rationalize that they rarely get requests for native-language interviewing. My response to this line of reasoning is that you need to start by hiring multilingual staff, not just monolingual English speakers, at all levels of the research organization. A quick review of current Census data will provide an assessment of the most dominant languages in your specific market. Once a research vendor hires the right staff to cover the relevant languages, they need to communicate to the research industry that they now have key multicultural capabilities in place.

Translating On-the-Fly. There have been several occasions where our interviewing team was engaged to support a general market research shop by conducting telephone interviews with the "Hispanic sample." With such engagements, I always ask the client if they are providing both an English and Spanish-language questionnaire to program into our interviewing software program. Their response has sometimes stunned me: "Just have your bilingual interviewers translate the Spanish-language interview on-the-fly. Aren't they Spanish speakers?" I never hesitate to remind clients that written questionnaires are always provided to our interviewers in the relevant languages because they are not trained translators, and not being compensated for that task. Moreover, the practice of "translating-on-the-fly" violates the fundamental need to standardize interviewing procedures to ensure reliability in the measurement process.

Call Scheduling. Scheduling the days of the week and hours of the day to make telephone calls requires a careful understanding of your target audience and should not be driven primarily by the availability of your interviewing team. Based on various studies of multicultural persons at varying income levels, I have learned that middle to upper-income multicultural persons are extremely difficult to engage via a telephone interview, while the lower-income segment is more cooperative. Elderly residents are generally more available during the day and very responsive to telephone interviewing calls, but less responsive during the evening hours. Younger adults and teens have busier schedules and difficult to find at home, but more accessible using wireless numbers. The best interviewing production days continue to be Monday through Friday, while Saturdays have grown less productive over the years. We generally respect Sunday as a day of worship and refrain from making telephone calls and recognize that worship schedules can vary in multicultural communities. The number of call attempts one makes to each household may depend on the standard defined by a client or research organization; but experience may quickly change how many times you call one household before being identified as a nuisance call. Interviewing shops facing tight timelines sometimes make the mistake of burning through telephone sample during a limited number of days, a practice made easy by the use of predictive dialers. This is a costly and inefficient practice that can result in skewed samples, such as over-inclusion of the elderly, homemakers, and the unemployed. Scheduling calls over various days and hours — mornings, afternoons and evening hours — will yield the best representation of a target audience.

Calling Back Disconnected Numbers. The rate of non-working or disconnected telephone numbers is usually high in most telephone-based studies and a barrier to call center productivity. Predictive dialers or other types of automated calling solutions have helped to identify and remove most of these non-working numbers, but the TCPA regulations now require manual dialing of wireless numbers. Although time consuming, calling non-working numbers again is worthwhile since about 10 percent of these numbers will include persons who re-connected their telephones after paying a past due bill. Calling previously disconnected telephone numbers more than once could be a good investment for improving the low response rates of selected subgroups of respondents, such as the lower income and younger persons.

Interviewing Idiosyncrasies with Multicultural Research Respondents. When discussing differences between multicultural and non-multicultural respondents, it is important to point out that a "difference" between two groups does not necessarily mean that one group exhibits a particular behavior and the other group does not — like a dichotomy. For example, Latinos may show a higher cooperation rate than white respondents in telephone surveys, but this does not mean whites are not cooperative — just less cooperative than Latinos. Table 10 on the following page summarizes some general idiosyncrasies that our interviewing teams have encountered while conducting telephone interviews with multicultural respondents.

Table 10: Interviewing Idiosyncrasies with Multicultural Respondents

Factor	Latino	Black	Asian
Gender	Males are less cooperative & require more persuasion, women usually answer calls, males more suspicious when a male interviewer requests female householder	Males are more difficult to find & require more persuasion; most calls answered by females	Males usually screen calls and limit access to other family members
Calling schedule	Evenings better for immigrants, weekends less productive	Best in daytime and evenings, weekends moderately productive	Evenings better to reach immigrants, no specific days that are better
Multi-generational households	Common, extra screening needed to identify target member	Not common	Common, extra screening needed to identify target member
Language preference	Spanish for immigrants, English for native-born adults and youth, respondents may over or under-estimate language skills due to social desirability	English with some considerations for age-related terminology. May vary by country of origin, i.e., Haitians.	Native language for adults, mostly English for youth
Cooperation rate	Generally high, especially when bilingual interviewers offer language choices	Higher with females and elderly; lower with males and youth	Chinese & Vietnamese very cooperative, Asian Indians & Koreans less cooperative

In my experience, males are generally less cooperative in telephone surveys than females and require more encouragement by interviewers to participate in a survey. Black and Latino males, however, are distinctly less cooperative than Black females and Latinas, and will quickly pass the call to the female head of household if one is present. Our interviewing teams have been trained to provide Black and Latino males added assurance that their opinions are also important to a study — a practice that often results in higher cooperation rates. By contrast, Asian males are often the first household member to answer a telephone call and are particularly careful to screen calls before other household members are allowed to participate in a survey. In terms of the *language of the interview*, we have discovered that foreign-born Latino adults tend to over-estimate their English-speaking skills, while native-born Latinos tend to over-estimate their Spanish-speaking skills — an observation that has been attributed to social desirability.[90] That is, despite choosing a particular language for an interview, Latino adults may still struggle to complete an interview in that language, resulting in invalid or unreliable responses. In such situations, interviewers should suggest to respondents that they switch to another language that they are better able to understand to complete the interview. In terms of the *calling schedule*, evenings have worked better to capture males, especially blue-collar workers, due to their day-time work schedules, while females are generally accessible throughout the week during daytime and evening hours. *Household composition* should also be a point of concern for interviewing schedules. A recent Pew Research study, for example, revealed that multi-generational households were more common among Asian (28%), Hispanic (25%) and Black (25%) households, and less common among white households (15%).[91] This trend has implications for traditional methods that are used to screen household members for inclusion in a study since targeted members may be absent or multiple adults — related and unrelated — may be eligible for inclusion in the study.

Wireless numbers are key to representative studies. Despite their recognized lower response rates, telephone surveys continue to capture representative samples of the U.S. population. However, this observation strongly depends on the manner in which telephone surveys incorporate wireless numbers in their sampling strategy. As summarized by Kohut et al[92] in reviewing the representativeness of public opinion surveys:

> *Despite declining response rates, telephone surveys that include landlines and cell phones and are weighted to match the demographic composition of the population continue to provide accurate data on most political, social and economic measures.*

The most recent information concerning the penetration of wireless and landline households in the U.S. is provided by National Health Interview Survey for the period of January to

June 2019. Table 11 below summarizes the personal telephone status by race-ethnicity. The information reveals that wireless penetration — including wireless only and wireless mostly adults — was high for all race-ethnic groups: Hispanics (87.2%), whites (76.2%), Blacks (76.5%) and Asians (79.1%). Hispanics revealed the highest rate of wireless-only adults (71.2%).

Table 11: Personal Telephone Status of U.S. Adults (Percent)

Telephone Status	Race-Ethnicity				
	Hispanic	Non-Hispanic			
		White	Black	Asian	Other
Wireless only adults	71.2	56.0	54.3	55.5	64.3
Wireless-mostly adults	16.0	20.2	22.2	23.6	17.5
Dual users	5.2	11.0	10.7	12.2	7.3
Landline-mostly adults	2.7	7.1	6.1	3.7	2.8
Landline-only adults	1.9	4.3	4.6	1.8	0.0
Phoneless adults	2.8	1.1	1.7	2.4	3.8
Unknown	0.2	0.3	0.4	0.8	4.3
Total	100.0	100.0	100.0	100.0	100.0

Source: National Health Interview Survey, June 2019

Consequently, it should come as no surprise that Pew Research, coupled with my experience, suggests that it is essential that 75 percent of telephone-based surveys include wireless numbers. Indeed, Pew Research studies have confirmed that telephone surveys completed with an adequate proportion of wireless numbers provide a very close match to the Census demographics of an area's population.[93]

The importance of having a well-executed telephone sampling and data collection strategy was further illustrated in a recent analysis that I conducted of three polls that evaluated community sentiments regarding a proposed $1 billion bond referendum for the Texas Rangers baseball stadium.[94] The ability of each pollster to accurately predict the actual vote on the stadium referendum, however, varied with the quality of their methodological approach. The polls conducted by Survey USA and DHC Data relied primarily on interactive voice response systems that primarily contacted landline telephone households — which systematically excluded wireless numbers that are often used by younger persons and multicultural persons. The telephone poll conducted by Public Opinion Strategies, by contrast, included live interviewers who contacted a larger proportion of wireless numbers for the study. Prior to the completion of the voting for the bond referendum, I had predicted from my analysis of the individual polling methodologies that the methodology used by Public Strategies would more accurately predict the actual voting outcome. Table 12 below summarizes the predicted outcomes by each pollster and the actual voting outcome:

Table 12: Polling Estimates vs. Actual Voting Outcome for Texas Rangers Stadium Referendum (Percent)

Polling Company	Sponsor	Favor	Oppose	Undecided
DHC Data	Save Our Stadium Campaign	38%	46%	16%
Survey USA	WFAA/Ft. Worth Star-Telegram	42%	42%	16%
Public Opinion Strategies	Say Yes Campaign, first poll	54%	40%	6%
	Say Yes Campaign, second poll	56%	37%	7%
Actual Voting Outcome*		60%	40%	-

*Source: Tarrant County Election Results: www.results.enr.clarityelections.com

It is readily obvious from Table 12 above that my initial analysis about the expected accuracy of the polling conducted by Public Opinion Strategies was correct: both of their two polls more accurately predicted the actual voting outcome than the polls conducted by the other two polling companies. As discussed in my blogpost on this topic,[95] research practitioners and sponsors who overlook the importance of including wireless numbers in telephone surveys are out of touch with reality or perhaps stacking the deck in their quest to influence public opinion.

One federal survey underscores the importance of providing language options in surveys of Asian consumers. The Federal Trade Commission conducts periodic telephone surveys of U.S. residents in order to evaluate awareness and victimization related to consumer fraud. In their most recent survey in 2011,[96] an estimated 3,638 U.S. respondents were interviewed by telephone with language support provided in English and Spanish. Although Blacks and Latinos were more likely to be victims of fraud than whites, no data was provided for the victimization rates of Asians. Small sample sizes may have precluded any analysis related to Asian respondents; however, it is likely that the failure to provide Asian-language interviewing support decreased the chances of finding Asians that were victimized. Should one conclude that Asians are not typical victims of consumer fraud? A more recent study of Asian consumers would dispute that theory.

AARP (American Association of Retired Persons) recently sponsored a survey of Asian Americans and Pacific Islanders 50 years or older to explore their experiences with fraud and scams.[97] A key finding was that 39 percent of the survey respondents and their families had been victims of at least one type of fraud, while 71 percent had insufficient knowledge of fraudulent practices. Importantly, the AARP survey was conducted by telephone in six languages (i.e., English, Mandarin, Cantonese, Korean, Tagalog and Vietnamese). Thus, the provision of the appropriate language options enhanced the coverage of Asians and Pacific Islanders, and probably made it easier for victims to disclose their experiences to the telephone interviewers.

In summary, research practitioners are likely to encounter many challenges in conducting telephone surveys with multicultural populations, including the need for multilingual staff, multilingual survey software, and adequate training to ensure that the interviewing team understands the linguistic and cultural nuances that they are likely to encounter. An effective telephone strategy, however, offers the benefit of a two-way conversation with a human being that helps to engage respondents, and the opportunity to probe or clarify responses. Moreover, the telephone mode provides persons with lower literacy levels or visual acuity problems the opportunity to participate in the survey — a barrier that is sometimes overlooked with self-administered paper or online surveys. While telephone data collection may be more costly than other modes, it continues to be an important asset in communities with lower literacy rates and persons who just prefer to talk to a live interviewer. In Chapter 8, more attention is devoted to the key role that telephone surveys play in mixed mode studies that include multicultural populations.

Online Surveys

Despite the many benefits, it took many years for online surveys to gain acceptance in the survey industry as a credible data collection tool. Compared to other modes, online surveys are demonstrably less costly to implement, allow significant control of the interviewing experience, add the capability to evaluate visual and audio stimuli, and generally improve the overall survey experience for the respondent. In the earlier years when internet penetration was under 30 percent, conducting an online survey with a listing of online users, usually accessed via a panel company, was almost universally perceived as "quick-and-dirty" research — a label earned because the sample coverage bias with online panels was usually quite severe and not representative of anyone other than the panel members. For captive audiences — that is, membership lists with email addresses provided for all members — an online survey was the obvious choice for research practitioners who enjoyed the added benefit of selecting a probability sample.

To remove the stigma long associated with online surveys, several panel companies have evolved in recent years to become credible solutions for research practitioners. GfK Knowledge Networks[98] and YouGov,[99] for example, have developed strategies that effectively address the sample bias coverage problem. GfK Knowledge Networks, for example, starts by first selecting a random, addressed-based sample of households, recruiting them into their panel, and providing panel members access to the internet and a computer. Panel members are incentivized to complete online surveys for a defined period of time, then new panel members are recruited. YouGov, on the other hand, explains their sample matching approach as follows:

> *YouGov employs a unique method of sample design to build representative samples of the US population. From a panel of opt-in participants, YouGov draws stratified samples that approximate the characteristics of random samples of the US Population. The YouGov sampling frame has been*

designed to match the population in the American Community Survey conducted by the US Census and has been augmented with voter and consumer databases.[100]

One downside to using these more sophisticated panel vendors is the sticker price, which is higher than most other online panel companies based on quotes that I have reviewed in past years. Nonetheless, the higher price may be worth the investment for the scientific credibility that they provide over lower quality panels.

Despite the recognized elegance of the respective methodologies of these panel companies, it is perhaps safe to say that the typical research practitioner may not have the expertise to develop a panel of survey participants that approximates the technical sophistication of the more sophisticated panel vendors. In addition, the typical research practitioner may not be able to afford to use the services of the more sophisticated panel providers. Recognizing these potential barriers, there are several considerations to keep in mind if you are planning to use an online panel for a study of multicultural populations.

Remain Skeptical. No matter how well a panel company tells you that their members represent a particular segment of the U.S. population, always remain the skeptic and request a demographic profile of panel members for the segment that you plan to survey. This demographic profile can be compared to current Census Bureau data for a specific geographic area, so you can have some idea of how closely the panel members match the general population along key demographic attributes. Be especially skeptical of non-probability online panels which have been shown to produce highly biased estimates of Latino and Black survey responses.[101]

Panel samples are demographically narrow. Panel companies do a much better job of including panel members who are college educated, female, higher income, homeowners, U.S. natives, and English speakers. You can expect difficulties in meeting your sampling targets for African Americans, Latinos and Asians, those without a college degree, and lower-income persons. Interestingly, while internet access is almost universal in the U.S.,[102] it does not always occur to research practitioners that many persons dislike using computers and the internet to communicate their sentiments. In past studies that I have conducted where survey respondents were given a choice of completing the survey by mail, telephone or online, African Americans and Latinos were the least likely to choose the online option, while Asians were the most likely to choose the online option. In a subsequent chapter, we will discuss the wisdom of using mixed-mode methods to accommodate these preferences.

Panel samples have geographic limitations. I have conducted a syndicated telephone-based study of 500-600 Latino consumers in the Dallas/Fort Worth metro area for the past 20 years. In 2016, I explored using an online panel option to conduct the study and contacted two national panel companies to get a quote. The first company quoted me a $50,000 fee for conducting these interviews using their high-end panel solution. The second company did not have a sufficient number of Latino panel members to complete more than 100 online interviews. Neither solution was acceptable, so I decided to conduct the telephone survey with my own interviewing team at a data collection cost of $20,000. The lesson here is that a panel company may be able to support an online survey of multicultural consumers at the *national level*, but the number of panel members available in *local markets* is likely to be too small to complete the desired minimum of 400 interviews. The inability to conduct a local market study using national panel data poses a major barrier to marketers who need to make decisions for local markets.

Effect of using different devices. Online surveys can be readily completed on tablets, cell phones and computers, but the quality of the displays can vary on each of these devices and influence the quality of the responses to surveys. Since Latinos, Asians and Blacks frequently use cell phones and tablets to complete surveys, it is important for the research practitioner to conduct appropriate usability tests to ensure that survey respondents can fully view the questions and response options presented to them. One recent study, however, found that the quality of survey responses was quite similar when compared across laptops, tablets and smartphones.[103] This study, however, included few multicultural respondents. Although the study provides some assurance that device effects may not be substantial when completing online surveys, one should still conduct usability tests to ensure that multicultural respondents do not experience difficulties in completing an online survey on the devices that are likely to be used in the study. Additional tips for designing more mobile-friendly surveys are provided elsewhere.[104]

Online Survey Platforms. The online survey platform used in a multicultural study should meet some minimum standards, including support for multiple languages, provision of accent and diacritical marks that enhance the readability of different languages, attractive presentation screens, support for mixed-mode surveys, various security functions, and excellent technical support. In past years, I have been very pleased with the performance and support of Key Survey, an online survey platform by WorldAPP. Other online survey platforms to consider are Qualtrics and SurveyGizmo.

Despite these caveats, there are circumstances where online panels may be a good option for a multicultural study. For example, I recently had the opportunity to conduct a national study of Latino millennials that evaluated their religious attitudes and behavior. Budget and time constraints suggested that an online panel should be considered, although the desire to target English-speaking, acculturated Latino adults reinforced this option since panel companies are more likely to include this segment of Latinos. The study went well, and the client was pleased with the study outcomes. We were careful, however, not to generalize the study results to Latinos who were not part of the panel sampling frame. Thus, online panels may be a viable option for surveys of multicultural persons, but one must proceed with caution and closely examine the client needs and the fit between the panel demographics and the desired target audience.

Exit Polls and Intercepts

Exit polls, also commonly known as election exit polls, represent a special application of survey methodology used to gain an early understanding of election results since the actual results of many elections may take hours or days to enumerate. Voters are intercepted by interviewers upon leaving the polling locations and asked for whom they voted, the reason for their choice, and their demographic characteristics. In the U.S., the National Election Pool (NEP) — consisting of ABC, AP, CBS, CNN, Fox News, and NBC — pool their resources to conduct a joint election exit poll, which has been conducted by Edison Media Research since 2004.[105] In the U.S., exit polls have come under harsh criticism because they have often been used as a basis for projecting winners before all of the actual voting polls have closed, which can potentially influence election results. Nonetheless, election exit polls continue to have an influential role in our political system.

As a result of their controversial role, it comes as no surprise that the sampling and interviewing strategies used by exit pollsters like Edison Media Research have been the subject of considerable scrutiny, especially as it concerns the potentially inaccurate voter predictions for African American and Latino voters. For example, a recent article by Latino Decisions[106] described the results of the NEP exit polling for the 2008 election as "wildly inconsistent with dozens of pre-election polls demonstrating a larger 3-1 advantage for Secretary Clinton." (p.1). As explained by Latino Decisions, the NEP exit poll estimated Latino support for Donald Trump at 29 percent — a sharp contrast to pre-election poll results by Latino Decisions and four other media-sponsored polls which placed Trump's Latino support at a much lower range of 13 to 19 percent. Aside from these disparate exit polling outcomes, Edison Media Research has been criticized for their lack of transparency regarding the methodology they employ in conducting the NEP exit poll. Nonetheless, Latino Decisions along with expert Nate Silver, separately offered three key reasons that exit poll results tend to be flawed:

The exit poll sampling methodology was not designed to accurately capture sub-groups of the voting population. The cluster sampling methodology focuses on a handful of thousands of possible precincts, which creates a margin of error that is between 50 to 90 percent higher than comparable telephone surveys. Few high-density Latino or African American precincts are included in exit polls, while African Americans and Latinos with higher income and education are over-represented.

Few Latino voters are interviewed in Spanish in exit polls. Despite the fact that an estimated 30 percent of Latino voters are foreign-born and primarily Spanish speaking, only 6 to 7 percent of Latino voters in past exit polls have been interviewed in Spanish. Since Spanish-dominant Latinos are more likely to identify as Democrats, exit poll results are thus likely to under-estimate support for Democratic candidates.

The failure to adjust exit poll results by including the outcomes of early and late voters also generates inaccuracies. In some precincts, absentee or early voting can be significant, while late voters sometimes arrive at the polling place after the exit pollsters have left. The exclusion of these two groups, which may include many blue-collar workers, further renders exit polls less accurate.

Unless working for a political campaign, a research practitioner may have little interest in the problems associated with exit polls. However, the types of problems associated with exit polls are relevant to a more common method of collecting data in the marketing research industry known as intercept interviews — a quick turnaround method that is used to collect consumer opinions at a variety of locations, such as retail stores, airports, bus stations, movie theaters, and shopping malls. While intercept interview studies attempt to employ random selection techniques to achieve a probability sample (i.e., nth sampling), in actual practice it is difficult to achieve due to the uncontrolled nature of public places. I have conducted numerous intercept studies in past years with multicultural consumers and have learned that the results of such studies are generally well accepted if they are planned and executed appropriately. Following are some lessons learned from my own experience with studies using intercept interviews:

Unplanned interruptions. Your best plans to execute an intercept study will sometimes be subject to events that you cannot control. In one of our past studies, our interviewing team intercepted passengers at a Greyhound bus station as they arrived in order to complete a 30-minute evaluation of a video advertisement. Things were going well until a team of immigration officers arrived on the scene and segregated the passengers, mostly Mexican immigrants, into a separate room to screen their immigration status. The interruption delayed the study progress, which continued in the following days.

Indifference to Language Options. A research supplier for McDonald's once contacted us to conduct intercept interviews of their customers at locations in the Dallas-area with heavy Latino traffic. When asked if a Spanish and English version of the survey instrument was being provided for this assignment, the research supplier responded that an English-language instrument was the only one being provided. I challenged this decision and pointed out that 6 in 10 Latinos in Dallas prefer a Spanish-language interview, and that their opinions are equally important. To my surprise, the research supplier instructed us to "not worry about it" and focus only on English-speaking customers. Feeling very disappointed with his response, I decided to turn down the assignment which I believed would create ill will among Spanish-speaking Latino customers. The extra time and cost that would be required to provide Spanish-language interviewing support was not substantial and would have been balanced by a higher response rate in the study.

Are Mall Venues a Good Choice for Intercept Interviews? Shopping malls have been popular locations for conducting intercept studies due to the constant flow of shoppers. Many malls, however, already have a research shop with an exclusive right to any research that is conducted in that mall; consequently, you will likely need to contract such shops to implement your intercept study. Whether or not a research shop currently offices in the mall, you will need to study the mall's shopper demographics carefully before choosing it for a multicultural intercept study. Why? Because unless the mall is located in a major urban center, the number of African American, Latino and Asian visitors may be insufficient to complete your study. Moreover, their socioeconomic profile may not match your client's target audience. Ideally, you want a mall that attracts a mix of multicultural visitors that represent different socioeconomic levels. If the mall does not provide you a demographic profile of their visitors, you should take the time to visit a few malls to make your own observations about the mall's visitor diversity. If your intercept study is focused on only one of the multicultural segments, it may be more productive to select a supermarket located in the appropriate neighborhood and strike an agreement with the supermarket store or chain to provide your research team access to their store.

Creative Use of Malls in Legal Studies. In recent years, malls have been used by legal consultants to address issues related to brand confusion or other trademark issues in the marketplace. In brand confusion cases, a company that owns a well-established "senior" brand is typically suing a "junior" brand owned by another company that is trying to capitalize on the success achieved by the senior brand and is required to establish in court that consumers in the marketplace are indeed confusing the two brands. To prepare for litigation, attorneys representing clients in such cases usually engage a legal consultant or expert to conduct research that will address important issues to be argued in court. Malls have become a common venue for such studies due to their proximity to potential shoppers. However, rather than rely on the shoppers that a mall attracts on a daily basis, such studies instead engage research shops in targeted communities across the U.S. to select random samples of households surrounding a mall and screen persons to participate in a study scheduled to take place at the mall. Once recruited, the local research shop conducts the brand confusion experiment for the legal consultant, pays the participant an incentive, and submits the study data to the consultant. This process is repeated in the malls that have been previously selected in the approved sampling plan. These studies are very costly to the plaintiffs and defendants engaged in litigation and subjected to considerable scrutiny by the courts. Although the courts require that such brand confusion studies include only study participants who represent the current or potential buyers of a particular product or service, they fall short in one important respect: all of the study participants are English-speaking consumers, while no accommodation is made to include participants who are not English speakers. This is a serious shortcoming for two reasons. First, persons with low proficiency in English are frequently a significant part of the consumers who buy the product or service under litigation. Secondly, the level of brand confusion could be higher among persons with lower English proficiency, thereby leading to an incorrect conclusion that the level of brand confusion is insufficient — a costly and incorrect conclusion for the plaintiff that owns the senior brand. Such brand confusion studies, in my opinion, should expand the sample of respondents to include shoppers with lower English-language proficiency, and provide a bilingual interviewing team to ensure that these participants can complete the experiment in the language of their choice. When it comes to such high-stakes litigation, it appears that the courts have lowered the standard to the detriment of plaintiffs by removing limited English speakers from brand confusion studies.

Managing the Intercept Interview. Since mall or retail shoppers are typically pressed for time and often accompanied by family members, you will need to make the best use of time once a shopper is intercepted. The intercept interviewing team should include persons who have the language skills needed to communicate effectively with the target audience, while a balance by race-ethnicity is usually a plus in personal interviews to establish rapport initially. A relevant incentive is essential, whether it is cash or a gift, to facilitate cooperation. The interview should be kept short — about 5 to 10 minutes — during which time you will be able to conduct a variety of tasks, such as a taste test, evaluate exhibits, or obtain reactions to other physical or visual stimuli. A longer interview should be accompanied by a more valuable incentive. You can expect family members, especially children, to be a distraction in the interview unless you provide some options — like a play area with toys — to entertain them.

In summary, exit polls and intercept interviews are effective data collection tools for rapidly capturing important information from large audiences in targeted locations. A major downside, however, is the difficulty in implementing a random sampling strategy that meets the standards of scientific credibility. The appropriateness for studies of multicultural populations will require staffing and other resources to permit an efficient data collection experience. Nonetheless, the ability to conduct face-to-face interviews, present exhibits, and conduct other product testing in the language and context that is most familiar to the study respondents has considerable merit.

Use of Incentives

Given the declining response rates associated with all types of surveys, you would be overlooking an important opportunity if you did not explore the use of an incentive to improve the response rate in your study. There are many potential incentives at your disposal, and there is a substantial amount of research that discusses the benefits provided by incentives in survey research. Unfortunately, much of this research does not provide guidance on the effectiveness of different types of incentives in studies of multicultural populations. Nonetheless, I will discuss some general findings about the use of incentives in surveys and supplement this discussion with some of my own insights and past experiences.

Among the various strategies available to maximize response rates, the payment of incentives has been shown to most consistently increase response rates. Although considerable research has been done on the different types and levels of incentives used in experiments and surveys, much has yet to be learned about the potential impact of incentives. The decline of response rates in federal surveys, which often are more complex in scope, has generated attention on the impact of incentives on survey response rates. Following are some observations from a recent review of federal surveys:[107]

- "Incentives increase response rates to surveys in all modes, including the Web, and in cross-sectional and panel studies;
- Monetary incentives increase response rates more than

gifts, and prepaid incentives increase them more than promised incentives or lotteries, though they are difficult to implement in Web surveys;
- There is no good evidence for how large an incentive should be. In general, though response rates increase as the size of the incentive increases, they do so at a declining rate.
- Relatively few studies have evaluated the effect of incentives on the quality of response. Most studies that have done so have found no effects, though the variables used to assess quality have generally been limited to item nonresponse and length of responses to open-ended questions. Research is needed on what effect, if any, incentives have on reliability and validity.
- Relatively few studies have examined the effect of incentives on sample composition and response distributions, and most studies that have done so have found no significant effects." (p. 34)

Interestingly, the study authors explain, incentives have a clear potential for *both* increasing and reducing nonresponse bias. On the one hand, if they can be targeted to sample members who would otherwise fail to respond, they may reduce nonresponse bias. However, if they affect all sample members in the same manner, they are *unlikely* to affect nonresponse bias. Lastly, if they bring into the sample more of those who are already overrepresented, they may increase whatever nonresponse bias exists.

Based on their experiments related to the use of incentives in mail surveys, Dillman et al.[108] also confirm that response rates to mail surveys are higher when using pre-paid token cash incentives rather than promised incentives, and that lotteries or prize drawings have minimal effects.

Thus, before investing too much time and money into any single incentive strategy, I strongly recommend you conduct a pilot survey of a random sample of the survey audience that reflects a mix of multicultural respondents. In this pilot survey, randomly assign households to receive one of three types of incentives; conduct about 100 surveys, then check the responses to determine which incentive strategy produced the best outcomes for multicultural respondents, including response rates, response quality and demographic composition of the respondents. This pilot study might require a little more time to implement and some extra budget, but the benefits to the overall project will become obvious to you and your client.

In past experiences, I have had very few opportunities to include incentives in studies of multicultural populations since many of these past studies were telephone-based and typically did not provide incentives. One noteworthy experience involved a national study of African Americans, Latinos and Asians that utilized a mixed-mode method approach coupled with a sweepstakes program that rewarded early completions of surveys at different monetary levels. The sweepstakes was especially effective with Asian respondents who easily surpassed the sampling targets for the study. This outcome was not surprising since prior research confirms that Asians[109] and Latinos[110] were particularly attracted to games of chance, such as gambling. Indeed, Las Vegas casinos have observed this behavior for some time. Consequently, it makes sense for survey practitioners to explore the use of sweepstakes and other games of chance to further engage multicultural survey respondents.

Chapter Summary

This chapter covered several topics related to decisions about data collection strategies in multicultural communities, pointing to the limitations of mail, telephone, and online surveys; exit polls and intercept interviews; and the use of incentives. Although various factors enter the decision-making process regarding which data collection strategy is best for a study of multicultural populations, the best strategy will ultimately rest on the following considerations:

- How well do you know your target audience? Current Census data and past research about the target audience is essential, including race-ethnicity, gender, age, nativity, household income, and English language proficiency.

- Which languages will need to be supported by the study? A substantial presence of immigrants and knowledge about limited English-language proficiency should be early indicators of the need for languages other than English, while knowledge about specific ethnicity or country of birth can define the specific languages requiring support in the targeted community.

- Which data collection strategy makes the most sense for a specific study? Although the available budget is always a consideration, it should not be the most important one in a study of multicultural populations. Other important considerations should include (a) coverage bias of the sampling frame, (b) language support by staff, (c) timeline, (d) need for a probability sample, (e) inclusion of visual exhibits in the survey, (f) respondent limitations in terms of reading ability, physical disabilities related to speaking, hearing and writing, and (g) access to technology like the internet, smartphones, and computers.

- Are incentives needed to motivate multicultural respondents? If so, what types of incentives should be used? The general conclusions from past research suggest that incentives are effective in engaging research participants and improving survey response rates. However, the types of incentives vary considerably by the type of study and survey respondent included. Relatively few studies have documented the types of incentives that are more effective with multicultural populations, although there is some evidence that sweepstakes or similar games of chance show promise in engaging Asian and Latino persons. Given the current state of knowledge on incentives, it seems best to conduct your own pilot study with two or three different types of incentives and analyze the outcome by the demographic characteristics of the respondents. Such a pilot study would provide the market intelligence needed to plan the best use of incentives in a multicultural study.

In 2019, the Census Bureau released the results of a comprehensive predictive analytic study that was designed to encourage households to self-respond to the 2020 Census without follow-up from the Census Bureau enumerators.[111] Coupled with their communications contractor, Team Y&R, the research helped to identify and deliver messages to the public in the manner and at times and locations that were most effective for the 2020 census communications campaign. The reader is encouraged to read this innovative study which illustrates how segmentation research can be used to estimate response rates by mode across a wide spectrum of demographic and attitudinal characteristics.

In the following chapter, I discuss some solutions for common data analytic problems that a research practitioner is likely to encounter in conducting a multicultural study, including missing

Limitations of Traditional Data Collection Methods

data on key variables, language support, response sets, margin of error, using outdated Census data, and weighting of survey data.

Chapter 7: Solutions for Common Data Analytic Problems

Despite all the planning and precautions a research team may have considered prior to the data collection phase, there will always be a few bases that were not covered or considered thoroughly. In addition, if no one was monitoring the data collection process while it was taking place to check for unusual response patterns, then it is likely you will encounter several problems commonly associated with studies of multicultural populations. While some of these problems may be encountered in surveys of the general population, they are more likely to occur in multicultural studies since they tend to be more complex and are often conducted by survey practitioners with more limited resources. These problems are likely to influence the statistical analyses of the survey and the conclusions based on these analyses. Following are some of the most common problems I have encountered as well as some suggested solutions.

Missing Data on Key Study Variables

It is often the case that some respondents will refuse to respond to questions related to race, ethnicity, and household income — questions which are very important in monitoring progress toward sampling targets and subsequent statistical analyses. Once the data collection activity is completed, however, there are only a few limited options for correcting this problem. First, an experienced interviewer with the right "charm" should be assigned to re-contact respondents with the missing data and emphasize that the data is important to ensure that a representative picture of their community is obtained. Secondly, missing race or ethnicity data can be imputed from other survey data, such as country of birth or parental ancestry, if it was collected. Thirdly, one could complete a few additional surveys over the planned sampling targets as replacements for surveys that cannot be corrected through other methods. And fourthly, statistical programs allow for substitution of the mean for selected variables although this should be used as a last resort by the analyst.

Too Many Interviews Conducted in English

A comparison of the proportion of foreign-born adults in a community with the proportion of survey interviews completed in English will usually reveal important information about the quality of native language support provided by the research vendor. Our past industry experience confirms that, when provided a choice, about 60 percent of Latino adults and 80 percent of Asian adults will choose a native-language interview. Survey data that reveals that 60 percent or more of the interviews were completed in English points to the possibility that the research vendor provided minimal or no support to native-language respondents, who are usually immigrants. The research data would thus be biased by placing more weight on the opinions and behavior of English-speaking native-born respondents.

Evidence of Response Sets

Survey responses by Latinos, and to some extent Asians, will likely show evidence of response sets that result from the need for social desirability, the tendency to be agreeable, providing extreme responses on scales, and a reluctance to self-disclose on sensitive questions. Although some investigators believe that such response sets may be a result of cultural values,[112] others have argued that they represent errors in measurement that should be adjusted or minimized through statistical formulas — an issue that is discussed in more detail in Chapter 8. My own perspective is that cultural values may play a role in such response sets; however, inexperienced or improperly trained telephone interviewers also contribute to the problem of response sets when they fail to correct the problem once they observe a response set pattern. A survey respondent, for example, may not understand the directions for choosing scalar responses and not realize that it is acceptable to select a range of responses instead of just extreme values. In observing the pattern, an interviewer can repeat or clarify the question instructions and thus ensure more valid responses. Assuming the interviewing team was conducting the survey interview appropriately, I would not recommend a statistical adjustment of the response patterns since they are likely the result of cultural values, not measurement errors. In my experience, Latinos and Asians make concerted efforts to please and agree with others and refuse to answer questions that are deemed too sensitive. It seems illogical to distort reality by statistically adjusting these values to conform to some other standard of behavior. SurveyGizmo is one online survey platform that includes a feature that checks completed surveys for the presence of response sets, like straight-lining, and flags the survey as potentially unusable.

In the Marín and Marín publication,[113] the authors provided a useful discussion about response sets and how they can influence the quality of survey responses by Latinos. They define a response set as the tendency for individuals to provide inaccurate data, socially desirable responses, and other undesirable behaviors. In general, their research tells us that Latinos are:

- More likely to provide socially desirable responses, stemming from a tendency to give correct responses, please others, or being polite
- More likely to acquiesce or be agreeable, which stems from a need to be accepted by others, feelings of submissiveness, or presenting a good face
- More likely to choose extreme responses on a rating scale that may be a function of being more sincere, whereas mid-scale responses are considered to show less commitment
- Less likely to self-disclose on topics that create discomfort, such as sexual practices, deviant behavior, and similar behaviors
- More likely to leave questions unanswered

A reluctance to guess also contributes to the problem of unanswered questions and an unwillingness to self-disclose. Hispanics, for example, are less likely to guess or estimate their household income, leading to higher refusal rates unless an interviewer encourages the respondent to just provide their best guess. The reluctance to guess is also evident in tests of ability where test takers show a tendency to leave a test question unanswered rather than provide a "good guess" that could actually benefit their total test score. In my survey practice, reassuring respondents that the income information is needed simply to ensure that the study captures a cross-section of the community at all income levels has worked well in obtaining responses to income questions.

One study conducted in the Netherlands demonstrated how response strategies and styles by culturally diverse groups can influence responses to Likert-style attitudinal statements.[114] The study compared one group of residents who were more accustomed to the Dutch language, heritage and culture (Surinamese and Antilleans) with a minority group (Turkish and Moroccans) who were less familiar. Analysis of cognitive interviews revealed that respondents used three types of response strategies to overcome difficulties of responding to attitudinal statements in a cross-cultural survey. Cross-cultural differences resulted, for example, if respondents based their responses primarily on (a) the host country, (b) their own cultural background, or (c) their personal experiences. Extreme responses to attitudinal statements were more likely the closer the topic was associated to the respondent's culture. According to the investigators, the problem of measurement non-equivalence can be reduced by including a short introduction that clarifies the domain of interest — the host country, cultural background or personal experiences. This clarification will help the respondent understand the information that the researcher wishes to know, and more validly reflect the construct that is being measured.

Response sets can have serious implications for the quality of survey data and underscores the need for research practitioners to closely monitor survey responses on a regular basis and remove or modify question formats that encourage undesirable response sets.

Descriptive vs. Multivariate Analyses

Once the survey is completed, the typical analyst will conduct a variety of descriptive analyses to evaluate data distributions, create new variables, and conduct the statistical analyses to address the research questions or hypotheses defined in the planning stages of the study. However, it is a mistake to wait until a survey is completed or near completion to check for common data problems related to outliers, errors of omission and commission, achievement of sampling targets, missing data on key study variables, programming errors, and interviewer behavior. The survey data should be monitored on an on-going basis by the research practitioner so that solutions can be implemented before the expected survey completion date.

A common problem in the data analytic stage is the lack of an analytic strategy. For example, one national study of multicultural consumers involved a rather lengthy questionnaire with numerous variables. Several boxes of crosstabs were requested by the client, which did not have a clear analytic focus. Moreover, the numerous crosstabs that were produced resulted in a multitude of statistically significant relationships just from the sheer number of comparisons that were made. Like many similar studies, the presentation of the data focused primarily on univariate and bivariate relationships in the data and overlooked a higher-level analysis that could have been more meaningful.

Too many multicultural research studies, in my opinion, rely on simplistic descriptive analysis of the data and avoid the use of multivariate procedures that could yield more meaningful insights, such as discriminant analysis, cluster analysis, regression analysis, logit analysis, and conjoint analysis. This trend may reflect a tendency for multicultural investigators to focus on questions that are less complex or easier to analyze, or perhaps a tendency to "keep it simple" for the benefit of executives or other audiences. Regardless of the motivation, there is a need for more expanded complexity in the design and analysis of multicultural studies.

One common example evident in multicultural studies will hopefully illustrate the point here. It is a common practice to segment multicultural consumers by their level of acculturation, an index that is usually derived by combining such attributes as nativity, language usage and media behavior, and produces distinct groups with low, medium and high acculturation levels. While many studies have confirmed relationships with acculturation levels and various consumer behaviors, the scale is limited in its usefulness because it overlooks the respondent's relationship or experience with the service or product in question, which may be more important than the demographic or media attributes that are incorporated into acculturation scales. Knowing that a low-acculturation person differs from high-acculturation persons on a specific behavior assumes that persons within each of these two groups are psychologically similar, which may or may not be accurate. As a case in point, we recently conducted a national study of DIY (Do-it-yourself) behaviors among Hispanic homeowners in major U.S. metropolitan areas with a specific focus on paint products. Although the study could have been simplified by analyzing acculturation levels and DIY behaviors, I recommended the development of an attitude scale that measured specific DIY attitudes that were related to the use of paint products, then conducted a multivariate cluster analysis that produced three meaningful segments of respondents based on their similarities and differences on the DIY attitudes. Within each of the three clusters, there were a mix of respondents who differed demographically — that is, men and women, English and Spanish speakers — but that nonetheless shared similar DIY attitudes. The client was thus in a much better position to target each of these three clusters or segments with a distinct message in their advertisements and understand the types of consumers who are geographically concentrated near their retail outlets.

Confusion Regarding Margin of Error

In reviewing a recent report about an online survey of 40,000 transit agency customers, I observed that the study investigator reported a margin of error of 0.5 percent at a confidence interval of 95 percent. This level of "precision" apparently gave the study sponsors a great deal of confidence about the accuracy of the survey results. The reported margin of error, however, provided a false sense of accuracy for one main reason: the respondents were not selected at random, but rather were self-selected in response to the client's promotional campaign for survey participation. An article by the Pew Research Center on the topic of sampling error puts it this way:[115]

> *Non-probability sampling does not permit the computation of a margin of sampling error in the same way that probability sampling does. As a result, there is much greater uncertainty about the accuracy of results from such samples.* (p.1)

Although this study did not focus exclusively on multicultural respondents, nearly half of the population in the targeted geographic area included multicultural residents. Thus, it seems apparent that the study sponsors accepted this incorrect estimate of the survey's accuracy and may have inappropriately acted on service or program changes based on the undeserved confidence in the survey's accuracy. Indeed, history tells us that a large sample offers no guarantee about a sample's accuracy. The presidential poll conducted by the Literary Digest in 1936 incorrectly predicted the actual voting outcome by a large margin despite the inclusion of 2.5 million respondents. It was determined that non-response bias was the problem since the sampling frame was over-represented by wealthier members in the listings utilized.[116]

Solutions for Common Data Analytic Problems

Problematic Weighting Practices

The computation and application of weights in surveys is especially important in studies of multicultural populations since special efforts are often required to ensure their adequate representation. For example, a simple random sample of households in a specific community may produce fewer households of Latinos, Asians or African Americans than is desired. Over-sampling of these under-represented households would thus be necessary, and a *design weight* would be required in the statistical analyses to compensate for the over-sampling of such households. On the other hand, it is often the case that females are over-represented in a survey, an outcome of lower cooperation rates among males or an interviewing team that finds it easier to complete surveys with females. In either case, a *post-stratification* weight would be needed to adjust the proportion of males and females to the proportions from an objective source that provides the correct proportion of males and females in that geographic area. The American Community Survey (ACS) is often the most current and objective source to use for post-stratification weighting since it includes various demographic characteristics of the U.S. population that are collected annually by the U.S. Census Bureau. Despite its obvious need for ensuring accurate survey estimates, I have observed four specific problems with the application of weights in studies of multicultural populations. For example:

A. **Using Outdated Census Data.** Research practitioners do not always use the most current Census data available for weighting survey data. I have frequently seen research reports using older Census data as weights for surveys despite the availability of more current information. This practice, of course, is likely to misrepresent the survey findings for that study sample unless the demographic indicators used for weighting purposes have not changed much between the Census and survey period.

B. **Using Flawed Data as Weights.** In its television ratings, The Nielsen Company has used the results of language dominance questions collected by their own telephone surveys of U.S. Latino communities to weight or adjust the results of television audience ratings. I have critiqued this practice because, in my view, the self-reported language data collected in the Nielsen telephone surveys over-sampled foreign-born Latinos, which produced an adjusted television rating that unfairly favored Spanish-language television programs.[117] A more objective and reliable weighting approach would have been to use the most current Census data that presents the correct proportions of native and foreign-born Latinos to adjust the television ratings — a practice that might have prevented the cancellation of promising television programs in English with multicultural content.

C. **Using Weights to Compensate for Poor Interviewing Practices.** Research practitioners, especially those with fewer multicultural capabilities, will often fall short of achieving their interviewing targets for African American, Latino or Asian respondents. Moreover, the lack of multilingual interviewers often results in the systematic exclusion of native-language respondents from surveys since it becomes more convenient to complete English-only interviews. Rather than improve their interviewing practices, however, some survey practitioners find it more convenient to apply post-stratification weights to "fix" the imbalances in the survey results that resulted from poor interviewing practices. Moreover, the application of large weights introduces more instability into the survey data by increasing standard errors. To check for this practice, it is a good idea to require the presentation of un-weighted and weighted tables in the methodology section of the report. Another check is to review the proportion of interviews completed by language — in many cases, you can suspect the presence of an interviewing bias if over half of the interviews with Latino or Asian adults were completed in English. You should also make it a practice to check the most current or relevant Census data to determine the proportion of native and foreign-born adults in the targeted community since language choices correlate highly with nativity in our experience. Although survey software programs or online platforms provide features that allow the calculation of weights for simple sampling plans, it is a good practice to engage a sampling statistician for the calculation of weights for complex sampling plans.

Chapter Summary

This chapter underscored the importance of on-going data audits as a tool for identifying common analytic problems associated with multicultural research studies, such as missing data on key study variables and a disproportionate number of English-language interviews among Latino and Asian immigrants. Potential solutions to these analytic problems were discussed, while the practice of statistically adjusting responses that are considered extreme or departing from some standard was considered inappropriate since cultural values could be a factor in explaining behaviors that are identified as response sets. The relative absence of multivariate analyses in studies of multicultural populations was considered a limitation in the understanding of the breadth and complexity of this population segment. The confusion related to the calculation of sample accuracy was considered a factor that contributed to a false sense of survey accuracy that can potentially mislead decisions about programs and policies.

Concern was also raised about the problems associated with the weighting of survey data. These decisions are best made by a trained sampling statistician; however, one may not always be available or affordable for a specific study. Weighting data is very important in studies that have utilized different selection strategies for subgroups of respondents. Weighting is also important in studies that end up with sample imbalances along key demographic characteristics, such as race-ethnicity and gender — called post-stratification weights. Without the appropriate weights, survey findings can misrepresent the sentiments or behavior of a community. In some situations, the sample selected is self-weighting and may not require post-stratification weight adjustments unless non-response differences need to be corrected. However, because simple random sampling does not always produce a proportionate representation of persons or households by key demographic characteristics, more complex sample designs with weighting adjustments are often required in survey research.

In the following chapter, I review mixed mode studies, the different approaches utilized, and the potential benefits for the study of multicultural populations. Examples of past mixed mode studies of multicultural populations are also discussed.

Chapter 8: Mixed Mode Methods — An Intuitive Solution

Frustrated with the shortcomings of traditional data collection approaches, research practitioners began to experiment a few decades ago with the idea of using more than one mode of data collection to improve their survey outcomes. Aside from the problems related to declining response rates, sample coverage bias, and technological changes, the concept of mixed mode methods has always made intuitive sense to me for another important reason: Why require survey respondents to share their sentiments using *only one mode of data collection*? Moreover, why are respondents often provided *only one language option*? After all, many persons in the U.S. cannot read or see well, have trouble hearing, or struggle with the English language. The information presented in Table 13 below illustrates this point:

Table 13: Percentage of U.S. Adults with Reading, Vision and Hearing Limitations, by Race-Ethnicity

	White	Black	Hispanic	Asian
Percent of U.S. Adults who read below basic English prose literacy	7%	24%	44%	14%
Percent of U.S. adults with a vision limitation	8.4%	9.3%	9.4%	5.7%
Percent of U.S. adults with hearing trouble	16.2%	10.0%	11.2%	9.7%
Percent of persons 5 years or older who are limited English speakers	-	-	30.9%	33.8%

Sources: U.S. Department of Education 2003,[118] Vital and Health Statistics,[119] 2014, ACS 1 Year Estimate 2016[120]

With such limitations in vision, hearing, reading or speaking English, how does one justify excluding the opinions of these individuals from research studies? Indeed, are they not also residents who pay taxes and consume products and services? While some industry experts have demonstrated the benefits of well-designed panels that can accurately capture the sentiments of the U.S. population using only online surveys, the vast majority of research practitioners will not likely have the financial resources or technical knowledge to develop these high-end panels and will continue to use traditional data collection approaches. Thus, mixed mode studies make sense as a more practical tool to expand access to persons with physical, linguistic and literacy limitations — many that are likely to include multicultural persons. Thus, people with poor hearing need a survey that is self-administered; those with low reading literacy will need an oral survey administered; and those with limited English-language proficiency will need a native-language option.

The Logic of Mixed Mode Methods

Mixed mode methods are not new to the research industry. Indeed, mixed mode methods have been employed in past years in various federal surveys of the population.[121] Table 14 on the following page summarizes several of these federal surveys, the modes utilized to collect the data, and the language support provided. It is evident in reviewing this table that federal surveys utilize multiple modes of data collection to capture primarily factual information about U.S. residents, a sharp contrast to a previous point in time in 1981 when 80 percent of all federal surveys used a single mode of data collection.[122] During the earlier years, conducting surveys in multiple modes was complicated by the lack of technology and knowledge: indeed, mixed mode surveys require more sophisticated survey platforms, interviewing software that accommodates different modes, and staff who can manage the added complexities. Declining telephone survey response rates, however, provided the needed stimulus for research practitioners to explore other approaches for improving survey response rates, response quality, reduce costs, and expanding coverage.

Table 14: Federal Surveys Using Mixed Modes

Federal Survey	Sample	Mode of Data Collection	Language Support
Census 2020	Total Population in U.S. and Puerto Rico	Internet, mail, telephone, personal interviews; several reminder letters or postcards	Online will support Spanish, Chinese, Vietnamese, Korean, Russian, Arabic, Tagalog, Polish, French, Haitian Creole, Portuguese, Japanese / Mail survey will support Spanish / field enumerator supports Spanish
American Community Survey	Annual samples of the population, provides 1-year, 3-year, and 5-year estimates	Internet, mail, telephone, and personal visit; repeated mailings	Cover letter in English and Spanish; Spanish mail survey package can be requested in Spanish; toll-free telephone assistance in English, Spanish, Russian, Chinese, Korean and Vietnamese upon request
Current Population Survey	Sample of U.S. households	Telephone and personal interviews	Concerted efforts made to support Spanish-language telephone interviews
Consumer Expenditure Survey	Sample of U.S. households	Pre-notice by mail, personal interviews, some telephone interviews.	No information provided on support for non-English languages
Survey of Income and Program Participation	Sample of U.S. households	Personal interview, telephone interviews	No information provided on support for non-English languages
Hospital Consumer Assessment of Healthcare Providers and Systems	Patients in U.S. hospitals	Mail, telephone, mail with telephone follow-up, or interactive voice recognition	English, Spanish, Chinese, Russian, Vietnamese and Portuguese
Pregnancy Risk Assessment Monitoring System	Surveillance of pregnant women in participating states	Mail, online and telephone	English and Spanish, some states provide Mandarin support

Table 14: Federal Surveys Using Mixed Modes (continued)

Federal Survey	Sample	Mode of Data Collection	Language Support
Consumer Fraud in the United States, 2013	Sample of telephone households in U.S.	Telephone	English and Spanish
Behavioral Risk Factor Surveillance System (BRFSS)	Adult population in 50 states in the U.S.	Telephone (landline and wireless)	If a significant portion of any state's population does not speak English, states have the option of translating the questionnaire into other languages.

Note: Information was accessed from the web sites for each federal survey.

The U.S. Census Bureau was among the early pioneers to explore the use of mixed mode methods in the execution of its decennial census and annual American Community Survey by including a mix of such modes as mail surveys, online surveys, telephone follow-up and household interviews. Indeed, the 2020 Census begins its data collection process by sending a letter that invites respondents to complete an online version of the Census questionnaire with the hope of reducing costs. While federal agencies have shown a willingness to incorporate mixed mode methods into their data collection practices, my observation of practices in the private sector suggests that the use of mixed mode methods has progressed at a much slower pace, no doubt due to the added complexities and financial investment required by such studies, and the relative lack of attention to the mixed mode methodology in traditional survey research methods courses.

In one of the most comprehensive literature reviews regarding mixed mode methods, de Leeuw traces its evolution, major benefits and shortcomings. As she explains in this review:[123]

When designing a survey, the goal is to optimize data collection procedures and reduce total survey error within the available time and budget. (p. 235)

As de Leeuw explains it, the limited coverage and declining response rates associated with traditional telephone and web surveys provided the impetus for the evolution of mixed mode surveys, which provided the motivation to explore other alternatives for engaging the survey respondent. Declining response rates focused more concern on the consequences of non-response bias as the studies documented distinct demographic differences between survey respondents and non-respondents who were excluded due to limited sampling or lack of access to telephone or the internet. To achieve higher response rates while keeping overall costs low, the thinking among earlier pioneers was that mixed mode strategies should start with the less costly method first and follow up with the more costly methods. As shown in the previous Table 14, the American Community Survey continues to use a mixed mode strategy that includes several steps: a web-based survey, a mail survey, telephone follow-up calls to non-respondents, and a final face-to-face interview to households that did not respond to previous efforts.[124] As de Leeuw observes, telephone follow-ups have been effective in increasing response rates and reducing non-response bias in mail surveys,[125] while other investigators have observed that mail surveys can be a valuable tool in improving survey response rates.[126, 127]

Mixed mode surveys generally fall into two categories: uni-mode and multi-mode.[128] A uni-mode survey utilizes only *one mode to collect respondent information*, and may include pre-notifications and follow-up reminders using mail, internet or telephone. A multi-mode survey, however, offers respondents *more than one mode to collect their information* — mail, online, telephone, face-to-face interview, IVR (interactive voice response) — and may also include pre-notification reminders and follow-up reminders using different methods.

Figure 13 below presents an example of the process for a uni-mode design. Note that only one mode is utilized (mail survey) to collect the data while including multiple contacts.

Figure 13: Uni-mode Design: Single Mode Used to Collect Data

Figure 14 on the following page illustrates the process for a multi-mode design, which includes two different modes (mail and telephone) used to collect the data as well as multiple contacts. Importantly, the telephone follow-up in the multi-mode design would allow completion of the interview by telephone.

**Figure 14: Sequential Multi-Mode Design:
Two Modes Used to Collect Data**

The key advantage of the uni-mode method is that it minimizes measurement error since the survey questions are presented consistently in only one mode to all the respondents. That is, uni-mode questions work well across all modes.[129] A key advantage of the multi-mode design, however, is that it can improve response rates and reduce non-response bias by giving respondents more than one mode choice to complete the survey; however, it can introduce more measurement error since questions can appear differently for each mode and lead to mode-related variations in responses to a question. The measurement error for a demographic question like gender, however, would be similar regardless of mode.

Reviews of the mixed mode survey literature by de Leuww[130] and Dillman et al.[131] have documented a variety of uni-mode and multi-mode study designs, and the outcome resulting from these studies regarding survey response rates, non-response bias, and data quality. The reader is encouraged to study these publications to obtain a broad understanding of the creative designs that are being employed in the survey research industry. Although not an exhaustive list, following are some of the lessons learned from these two literature reviews of mixed mode surveys:

- Self-administered surveys, when completed privately using a computer or paper survey, lead to more accurate reporting of socially undesirable attributes, i.e., drug abuse, marital infidelity.

- Topics that are common in government surveys — education, work, expenditures — are relatively immune to changes in the data collection mode.

- Questions that utilize scales sometimes produce more positive ratings when there is no visual display of the scale, i.e. telephone interviews. The desire to please the interviewer, or social desirability, is considered one of the reasons for this finding.

- A mail survey accompanied by a telephone follow-up interview has been shown to improve response rates and lower non-response in mail surveys.
- Rotation of response categories is not recommended when conducting multi-mode surveys since it may not be implemented consistently across the different modes.
- Pre-notification letters or post cards make it easier to establish legitimacy and trust among survey respondents.
- Questions in mixed mode surveys should be asked in the "lowest common collection denominator."[132]

In June of 2007, the U.S. Census Bureau produced a comprehensive checklist to guide survey practitioners in the design of mixed mode surveys.[133] As explained in this publication, the underlying principle for these guidelines is Universal Presentation: all respondents should be presented with the same question and response categories, regardless of mode. The guidelines apply the principle of Universal Presentation to nine major aspects of instrument design — question wording and instructions, examples, response categories, formatting of answer spaces, visual design elements, question order and grouping, flashcards, prompts and help — a principle that was intended to minimize mode effects. I strongly recommend that you add a copy of this publication to your mixed mode methods library.

Concerns About Mode Effects

There is no consensus in the survey research industry about the presence or significance of mode effects. But consensus may not be possible because mode effects depend on various factors, including the construct being measured (factual vs. attitudinal), the question asked, the mode, and the population. Mode effects are more likely to influence the more subjective or opinion-related questions, and less likely to influence responses to factual questions, such as demographic characteristics. Several investigators, however, have concluded that there are few observable differences by mode;[134, 135] that minimal differences are observed by demographic attributes, but that differences are more likely when measuring attitudes.[136] Another survey expert explained the trade-off in survey error in this manner:

> *In survey design, we are always trying to balance and minimize several types of error. We are not saying that mode effects don't exist. The point is that using several modes might greatly reduce coverage error and non-response error (especially culturally-based non-response error) and these gains may greatly outweigh a possible increase in measurement error on a few questions.*[137]

It is noteworthy that many mixed mode studies have generally included racially homogenous samples of respondents with few African Americans, Latinos or Asians — a trend that appears characteristic of the many books and published articles I have reviewed related to mixed mode methods. In a subsequent section, we will discuss the experience of multicultural persons in selected mixed mode studies and the influence of language preferences.

Adjustment for Mode Effects

As previously discussed, attention is often focused on the survey error introduced by mixed mode studies that utilize different modes for collecting data. The concern arises from the fact that a question format will likely appear differently from one mode to another and perhaps lead to unwanted variation in the responses to a question. In a recent review of mixed mode studies and adjustments typically made for mode effects, Hox et al.[138] explain:

> *...the strength of mixed mode surveys is "their potential to reduce coverage and non-response problems, while at the same time attract as many respondents as possible for an affordable budget....the differences in coverage and nonresponse may arise because different modes attract different respondents. These differences are not problematic; in fact if different modes attract different segments of the targeted sample, the coverage of the target population is likely to improve, which is an intended effect and one of the reasons to use a mixed mode approach (e.g. web-mail).*

Given that there are two components included in any mode differences, de Leeuw advises that "You should NOT adjust for mode selection effects, only for mode measurement effects."[139] Hox et al. discuss an example of the confounding that occurs between mode selection and measurement selection effects. A study of drinking behavior used a web survey to attract younger respondents than traditional interviews. Web surveys are known to elicit less socially desirable responses. Since the web mode is confounded with age, if the web respondents reported more extreme drinking behavior, we would not know whether it points to a real relationship of extreme drinking with age or is just the result of lesser social desirability in the web mode. This confounding makes adjustment for mode effects difficult.

To remove or reduce such "mode effects," some investigators have devised formulas for adjusting survey results — a practice that has generated some controversy in the survey industry. The design and implementation of the HCAHPS — Hospital Consumer Assessment of Healthcare Providers and Systems — provides an excellent case analysis of the rationale and issues involved in mode adjustments. First, let's review some background information about the HCAHPS.

As described on their website,[140] the HCAHPS is "a 32-item survey instrument and data collection methodology for measuring patients' perceptions of their hospital experience...HCAHPS has allowed valid comparisons to be made across hospitals, locally regionally and nationally." The literature further explains that the HCAHPS has been extensively researched and accredited by the National Quality Forum, a national organization that represents the consensus of many healthcare providers, consumer groups, professional associations, purchasers, federal agencies and research organization. Importantly, HCAHPS performance has been tied to incentive payments to U.S. hospitals — so the results of this survey have cost implications for hospitals. HCAHPS is usually administered to a random sample of adult inpatients between 48 hours and six weeks after discharge. Hospitals have four mode options for administering the survey: mail, telephone, mail with telephone follow-up, or active interactive voice recognition (IVR), each of which requires multiple attempts to contact patients. The HCAHPS is available in English, Spanish, Chinese, Russian and Vietnamese versions. More detail about the sampling, data collection, coding and submission of the survey can be found in the HCAHPS Quality Assurance Guidelines manual on the official HCAHPS website, www.hcahpsonline.org.

To ensure that publicly reported HCAHPS scores are fair and allow accurate comparisons across hospitals, the survey sponsors adjust for factors that are not directly related to hospital performance but which affect how patients answer survey items — such as mode effects and patient-mix characteristics like age, language, education, and others.

Adjustments are applied to remove any advantage or disadvantage in scores that may result from the survey mode used or from characteristics of patients that are beyond a hospital's control. The statistical computations to achieve these adjustments are complex. In general, however, the mail survey mode is used as a "reference" category against which survey responses in the other modes are compared against. For example, it is generally known that telephone interviews result in more positive evaluations than other modes that are self-administered like mail and online surveys. The effect of the adjustment formula is to reduce the positive evaluations from surveys completed by telephone by certain percentage points. More specifically, if one hospital has a higher number of survey respondents who complete the HCAHPS by telephone, then its satisfaction ratings would be lowered due to the calculated mode effect. Similarly, if a hospital has a patient base that is predominantly Latino who are known to provide more positive evaluations than non-Latinos, then the patient-mix adjustment would lower the positive evaluations by Latino respondents.

Although extensive scientific research was dedicated to the development of the HCAHPS survey instrument and adjustment procedures for the purpose of allowing a fair comparison across different hospitals, there is a sense from some industry experts that the process is not well conceived. For example, Bill Mockovak with the Bureau of Labor Statistics Office of Survey Research Methods shared some reservations regarding the practice of mode adjustments:[141]

> *From a research perspective, the impact of multiple modes on measurement error is also difficult to determine because choice of mode is often determined by the respondent either explicitly or implicitly (for example, by failing to respond via the desired mode). Therefore, self-selection can lead to differences that are confounded with the data collection mode.*

In addition, Robert Santos reviewed the HCAHPS mode adjustment methodology and shared some concerns as well. He is Chief Methodologist and Director of the Statistical Methods Group at The Urban Institute, and President-elect of the American Statistical Association (ASA). The following comments were communicated to me by Mr. Santos via email:[142]

> *The stated goal of their PMA Model is: 'The goal of adjusting for patient-mix is to estimate how different hospitals would*

be rated if they all provided care to comparable groups of patients.' I see that as DOA... a fundamental flaw. Hospitals are what they are and have specific clientele reflecting specific demographic profiles. It makes no sense to me to create a score for a hypothetical population for a hospital that might never exist. If a hospital historically serves mostly elderly and a few young adults, and the young adults hate it, but the vast majority of elders love it, then the hospital should get a good rating based on the majority of its clientele that like it. Weighting down the score to increase the representation of young adults just makes no realistic, substantive sense to me. It's like weighting down the "good score" of clientele of gourmet restaurants because the folks who don't patronize them (and never will) prefer the taste of McDonalds.

Dr. Edith D. De Leeuw, Professor of Methodology & Statistics at Utrecht University, has written extensively on mixed mode studies and approaches for adjustments of mode-related differences. In reference to the adjustments made to the HCAHPS survey, she concluded:

> ...the respondents that answer by phone could be different (i.e., older or less educated). You want these people. They could also have a different evaluation, not because of mode effect, but because they are older...I have the feeling that there is an over-correction due to correcting falsely for the mode selection effects....modern techniques can do it correctly.[143]

I agree with these experts. Based on my experience in conducting research studies for various hospitals, I believe that the well-intentioned effort by the HCAPHPS developers to create a fair accountability system on hospital performance has achieved the opposite result. For example, a hospital that treats a large number of indigent Latino patients may achieve positive ratings on the HCAHPS but may have these ratings routinely lowered for two reasons: Latinos are known to provide more positive ratings than non-Latinos (a patient mix adjustment), or Latinos are more likely to complete surveys using the telephone mode which also produces more positive ratings (a mode adjustment). Ironically, the great job that this hospital is doing is hidden by the HCAHPS patient mix and mode adjustment formulas — a distortion of reality. Hospitals located in major metropolitan areas are treating increasing numbers of multicultural patients and may actually work harder to earn their praise on such surveys. Such hospitals should be rewarded, not penalized, for their exceptional performance when it is recorded as such by their patients.

Race and Language Factors Overlooked in Mixed Mode Research

It is indeed a major shortcoming that mixed mode investigators have not focused much attention on the differential outcomes of mixed mode methods for U.S. respondents who are linguistically and culturally diverse, especially since there are some mixed mode studies that reveal some interesting patterns related to race-ethnicity and language preferences. Perhaps one of the earliest exceptions to this trend is a study that was discussed by de Leeuw in her extensive review of mixed mode studies[144] wherein the study investigators incorporated a mixed mode design to improve the response rates of Medicaid patients that were ethnically diverse. To raise response rates, the study implemented three techniques: (a) adding a statement in multiple languages to the English-language mail survey cover sheet to encourage respondents interested in completing a telephone survey to contact the survey center where bilingual interviewers were available to complete an interview, (b) incorporating a pre-paid, unconditional incentive of $2.00 for a random subset of the sample, and (c) adding mail and telephone follow-up calls to non-respondents. The study found that response rates improved considerably with the inclusion of a telephone follow-up, especially among the ethnic groups in the study (e.g. African Americans, Latinos, Somalis, Hmong, and American Indians). The small incentive ($2.00) also added to a smaller improvement in response rates beyond the telephone follow-up. The study investigators concluded:

> *Although decisions on whether or not to use a mixed-mode mail and telephone methodology or incentives must be based on the specific goals of the study, the results suggest that the coupling of such a data collection protocol with a small prepaid cash incentive provides an affordable means of increasing participation among a sample of low-income and minority individuals.* (p. 414)

This study is noteworthy because it underscores the potential benefits of including race-ethnicity and language factors in mixed mode studies and their relationship to survey response rates and perhaps quality of the data. The importance of language and cultural factors in the survey industry is certainly not lost, as Dillman et al. affirmed in their recent book *Internet, Mail and Mixed-Mode Surveys: The Tailored Design Method*.[145]

> *Multiple language surveys, once rare, are increasingly becoming the norm for very important national surveys, a trend that coincides with larger cultural changes. (p. 454)*

To reinforce their observation, Dillman et al. discuss three ways in which survey practitioners have been adapting to these cultural changes: (a) providing English and Spanish-language options in telephone surveys, (b) responding to an increasing demand for bilingual interviewers to avoid transferring respondents to another interviewer or calling back to offer a language other than English, and (c) printing separate language questionnaires or formatting questionnaires with English and Spanish-language columns on the same page. The authors further emphasized that translation is perhaps the most important challenge in multiple language surveys because translators are often focused on *literal* translations when the focus should be on *conceptual* equivalence of translated surveys. The authors discussed one example of a simplified solution to the challenge of conducting mixed mode surveys in the global arena. The Gallup World Poll, for example, opted to use dichotomous yes/no questions in 130 different countries in order to limit the use of scalar questions that are more difficult to translate across languages and culture. The Gallup World Poll was further challenged by the country-specific variance in the availability of different technologies and uses different modes to overcome this barrier. Interestingly, the book chapter in Dillman et al. that focused on mixed-mode studies did not include any studies that focused on the influence of linguistic and cultural factors — a troubling omission that limits our collective knowledge about the differential benefits and problems related to the use of mixed modes in survey research.

Despite the noted efforts in the survey industry to adapt their practices to meet the growing demand for linguistically diverse populations, I am less optimistic than Dillman et al. about the progress being made by survey practitioners for several reasons:

- While national surveys are increasingly incorporating multiple language surveys, the vast majority of mid-size to smaller survey firms in the U.S. continue to offer only one language option — English — based on my own observations and review of the methodology section of numerous industry survey reports.

- When language options are offered by survey firms, the implementation is often less than optimal. A non-English speaking respondent is usually required to request a native-language mail questionnaire or told in a telephone survey that a native speaker will call them at a later time — both tactics that lead to increased non-response rates. Indeed, it is not difficult to determine when a survey firm has done a poor job of making a language option available since the percentage of Latinos or Asians that complete a survey in their native language is often very low. When language options are properly presented, my own survey experience has consistently shown that 50 to 60 percent of Latino adults will usually select a Spanish-language option, while 80 percent or more of Asian adults will select a native-language option. The choice of native-language options is strongly correlated with the proportion of foreign-born adults — that is, most foreign-born adults will select a native-language interview when provided the choice.

- In the absence of bilingual interviewers, survey firms will often out-source native-language interviews to survey shops or call centers in foreign countries. Interviewers in foreign countries may offer the desired language support, but U.S. Latino or Asian consumers may not readily understand the different dialects used by foreign interviewers. Moreover, interviewers in foreign countries may be unfamiliar with the correct pronunciation of U.S. brands and institutions, which further complicates the communicative process. If you have no other option other than out-sourcing to a foreign country, be prepared to closely monitor the interviewing process on a periodic basis to check for potential problems, especially with first-time vendors.

- I fully agree that translation is one of the most important challenges in multiple language surveys, and that survey practitioners should incorporate the recommended team or committee approach for the translation of survey instruments. Organizations that lack the resources or time to employ a team translation approach should at least conduct cognitive interviews or pilot studies with the

- The tendency for translators to use literal instead of conceptual equivalence in translating survey instruments continues to be problematic. In their book on Hispanic marketing, Korzenny and Korzenny underscored the same concern about placing more emphasis on conceptual translations.[146] However, possibly more problematic is the practice by survey practitioners of accepting "professionally" translated questionnaires and not adequately pilot testing them with the intended audience — which can frequently expose unexpected problems.[147] Thus, the last word on the adequacy of a translated survey questionnaire should be the results of a pilot, usability or cognitive interviewing study with members of the intended audience — not just the formally trained translator(s) who may or may not be in touch with the linguistic nuances of the target audience.

Two interesting studies provide further evidence that survey practitioners have much more to learn about multicultural persons beyond the translation of a survey instrument. The importance of conducting a usability study with limited English speakers was underscored by two recent studies of Asians and Latinos. The first study evaluated the "cultural fitness" and usability of a Chinese translated version of the 2020 Census. The study discovered several problems with the translated version: the incorrect application of English sentence structure to Chinese sentence structure; incorrect grammar; the lack of context when needed; incorrect order of first and last name; and problems with validation rules.[148] The second study focused on Spanish-dominant Hispanics and their ability to use mobile devices to complete a web survey.[149] The study investigators found that despite having access to computers, smartphones, and tablets, Spanish-dominant Hispanics lacked familiarity with these devices — that is, they experienced problems with entering URL addresses, scrolling, recognizing hyperlinks, used a very limited number of internet applications other than social media, and had limited data plans that limited their access to the internet. Indeed, while the survey industry has made progress in expanding the language options in studies of multicultural populations, there are other potential problems that go beyond the provision of a language option.

Review of Multi-Modal Studies with Multicultural Populations

As pointed out in previous sections, much of the published studies utilizing mixed mode methods have provided limited information on the demographic characteristics of the survey respondents by the mode of data collection. This is especially true as it concerns the role of cultural and linguistic factors in mixed mode studies. This shortcoming is a significant omission since it limits our collective understanding of factors that could be used to improve response rates and response quality. To address this information void, I would like to review recent findings regarding the demographic characteristics by mode of respondents to the American Community Survey 2010 to 2017. This discussion will be followed by a discussion of general findings of five unpublished studies that I have conducted in recent years that utilized our version of the mixed mode methodology that I call SERENITY® — a multi-modal, multilingual data collection strategy.

American Community Survey. On October 11, 2018 the Census Bureau posted a website entitled "What People and Households Are Represented in Each American Community Survey Data Collection Mode?" Following is a verbatim description of the goal of this tool:

> *This visualization allows you to explore multiple housing and people variables. It provides the overall distributions, as well as the information on response metrics for the four ACS response modes that include Internet, mail, telephone interviews and personal interviews. You are also able to switch the year of data collection to see a specific year, or toggle through the years to observe changes, such as the addition of the Internet response mode in 2013.*[150]

The publication of this website is an important milestone in the mixed mode research industry because it provides the first clear snapshot of the modes that different demographic subgroups are more likely to utilize given multiple alternatives. The American Community Survey is a sequential multi-modal survey that provides two self-response modes initially — that is, the internet and mail modes — but also includes non-response modes such as a telephone interview and personal interview. The telephone interview, however, was discontinued in October 2017. Figure 15 on the following page includes a summary of selected demographic characteristics by mode of response I generated using this ACS website including race, Hispanic origin, citizenship, language spoken at home, age and educational attainment.

The mode profiles reveal distinct patterns:

- **Online Mode.** More likely to be utilized by whites and Asians, non-Hispanics, U.S. citizens, persons speaking English very well, younger persons and the college educated.

- **Personal Interview Mode.** More likely to be utilized by Blacks, Hispanics, some non-whites, not U.S. citizens, Spanish speakers who do not speak English very well, younger persons and persons with less than a college education.

- **Mail Mode.** Generally utilized about 18-20% of the time across demographic subgroups but more frequently used by persons 65 years or older.

Survey practitioners should glean two important lessons from these results: (a) Online surveys are very limited in their ability to capture a cross-section of multicultural persons, and (b) the personal interview, while more costly, is a valuable tool for capturing responses from multicultural persons. Since the ACS discontinued the use of the telephone interview in 2017, its value cannot be judged by these tables but require some attention to the years from 2010 to 2016 when telephone interviewers were being conducted. Interestingly, a review of the percentage of ACS surveys completed by telephone interview during the 2010-2016 period revealed a declining pattern for each race-ethnic group: Hispanics (11.0% to 3.2%); whites (9.5% to 3.7%); Blacks (10.4% to 4.9%); and Asians (7.8% to 2.3%). Research practitioners are not likely to employ the more costly personal interviews in local studies and will likely depend more on the mail and telephone interview modes. So, what results can one expect for smaller scale studies using mixed modes with online, mail and telephone options? The next section will provide several case studies to address this question.

THE CULTURE OF RESEARCH

Figure 15: Demographic Profile of ACS Respondents by Mode of Response, 2017

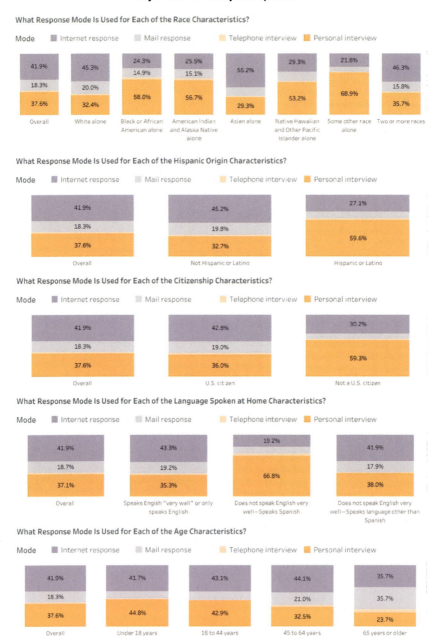

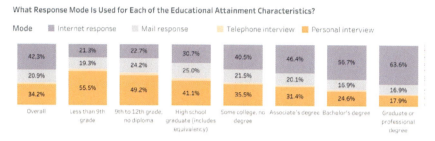

Figure 15: Demographic Profile of ACS Respondents by Mode of Response, 2017 (Continued)

Mixed Mode Case Studies

In this section, I discuss five studies that describe the mode of data collection chosen by specific race-ethnic groups, the language preference by mode for Latino and Asian respondents, and a description of the "mode profile" — that is, the general characteristics of the respondents that completed a survey for each mode. Perhaps it would be helpful to first explain the general steps that are followed in our SERENITY® multi-modal, multilingual model. Following are some of its key features:

- **Sample Selection.** An addressed-based sampling (ABS) is used as the starting point to ensure a nearly 100 percent penetration of targeted households, thereby greatly reducing coverage bias and providing a solid foundation for probability sampling. As mentioned by one survey expert, "ABS is high on penetration but low on participation…trades off one source of error for another one."[151] Nonetheless, the expectation is that the lower participation will be offset to some extent by using multiple modes and languages, and optionally a pre-paid incentive.

- **Telephone Matching.** We match the available landline and cell phones with the sample of household addresses in order to conduct telephone follow-up surveys with an expected match rate of 30 to 40 percent. ABS listings that include proportionally more renters than homeowners typically provide lower match rates.

- **Instrument Design.** The questionnaire is designed in English and the native language(s) relevant for the target audiences following the universal principles of the same question format for each mode. A pilot test is strongly recommended for each language version of the questionnaire in order to identify comprehension and navigational issues.

- **Data Collection.** We generally provide two self-response modes of data collection — an initial mail survey with an online option included in the cover letter — and a non-response mode that includes a telephone follow-up interview of non-respondents with a telephone available — all of which are provided in multiple languages; that is, the mail and online surveys include both an English and a native language questionnaire, and the telephone interview follow-up of non-respondents utilizes interviewers that are bilingual in the relevant languages. A password security system is part of our web-based survey system that ensures respondent integrity and prevents duplicate responses when using multiple modes.

- **Incentives.** Pre-paid incentives, included in the initial mail survey package, are recommended when the budget allows and there is justification for including additional motivation to increase response rates. A $2.00 bill is commonly used in many mail surveys although a pilot study should provide further guidance on whether a different incentive would be more effective with multicultural respondents.

Following is a brief description of each of the five studies which were conducted between 2008 and 2015.

Case Study 1

The first study included a national addressed-based sample (ABS) of African Americans, Latinos and Asians. The study included a sweepstakes that rewarded respondents for submitting early responses via mail or online methods. The estimated yield rate was 12.0 percent while a precise response rate could not be calculated because we were unable to retrieve the mail that was undeliverable using bulk mail postage rates.

Case Study 2

The second study was conducted with a statewide random sample of 1,200 Texas residents who were homeowners and racially diverse. The estimated response rate was 10.3 percent.

Case Study 3

The third study was conducted with a random sample of 1,200 Dallas County low-income female patients — mostly Latinas — for a hospital serving indigent community residents. The estimated response rate was 25.4 percent.

Case Study 4

The fourth study was conducted with a random sample of 2,981 Texas Medicaid program participants, which required an adequate representation by race and ethnicity. The estimated response rate was 25.3 percent.

Case Study 5

The fifth study was conducted with a random sample of 1,200 Dallas County residents that was racially diverse and representative of all income levels. The "White-Other" group primarily included self-identified white respondents and a small number of "other race" respondents. The estimated response rate was 19.0 percent.

The questions we attempted to address in the analysis of the five case studies were:

- Which mode choices are made by multicultural survey respondents when they are presented with two distinct modes for completing a survey — mail or online? How effective is a telephone follow-up call as a third mode?

- What language choices are made by Latino and Asian survey respondents for the survey mode that they selected?

- What is the mode profile, or characteristics, of multicultural survey respondents who utilized a particular mode?

Mode Choices by Race-Ethnicity

Figure 16 on the following page presents the mode choices by race-ethnicity for the five case studies. To clarify the term "mode choices," the respondents typically made a choice between an online or mail mode, while the telephone option did not represent an actual choice but rather the default follow-up mode to persons who did not respond using the online or mail modes and had a matching telephone number available. Given this clarification, it is clear to see that the selected modes varied considerably across the five studies as well as by race-ethnicity. For example, Case Study 1 revealed that the mail mode was utilized more frequently by all three race-ethnic groups, while the online mode was a distant second choice although more popular among Asians; the telephone mode was equally popular for Latinos and African Americans. The sweepstakes utilized in this study was an important factor in driving responses by mail.

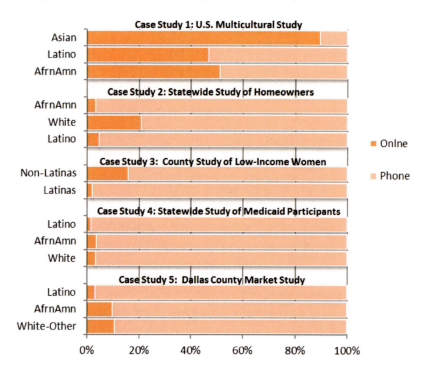

Figure 16: Mode Preference by Race-Ethnicity for 5 Case Studies

Case study 2 also showed a strong reliance on the mail mode by African Americans and whites, and relatively more utilization of the telephone mode by Latinos. Minimal usage was made of the online mode by all race-ethnic groups. Case studies 3 and 4 both focused on lower-income respondents, which revealed considerably higher usage of the telephone mode. Case study 5, which targeted a cross-section of respondents by race-ethnicity and income levels, also revealed a high utilization of the telephone mode, modest use of the mail mode, and minimal use of the online mode.

One additional observation concerns Case Studies 3 and 4

which yielded the highest response rates of 25.4 percent and 25.3 percent, respectively. It is clear these higher response rates were associated with higher completions using the telephone mode — reinforcing the important role that the telephone mode plays in mixed mode studies. By contrast, Case Studies 1 and 2 showed the lowest response rates but relied primarily on the mail mode.

Language Choices by Mode

For each of the five case studies, the respondents were provided the choice of an interviewing language in all modes. Figure 17 below presents the language choices made by Latino respondents for each mode employed across the five case studies. The most obvious pattern that emerges is that studies that included a cross-section of Latinos — such as case studies 1, 2 and 5 — were more likely to complete a survey in English. By contrast, studies that focused on lower-income Latinos — such as case Studies 3 and 4 — were more likely to complete a survey in Spanish. In general, surveys that were completed online by Latinos were usually completed in English.

Figure 17: Mode Preference by Language for Latinos, 5 Case Studies

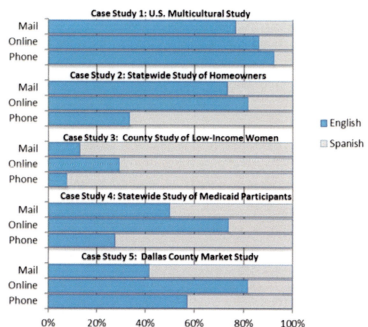

The language choices made by Asians were captured only for Case Study 1. As shown by Figure 18 below, surveys were more likely to be completed in English when using the online mode and to a lesser extent by the mail mode. The mail mode captured a broader diversity of Vietnamese, Chinese and Korean languages, while the telephone mode was especially popular among Vietnamese respondents.

Figure 18: Mode Used by Language for Asian Respondents, Case Study 1

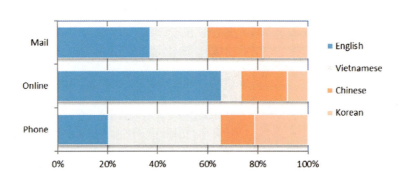

Mode Profiles

Thus far, we have determined from an examination of these five case studies that mixed modes are able to capture a broad diversity of survey respondents in terms of race-ethnicity and language preference. But are these respondents essentially similar, regardless of the mode chosen, or do they differ in other important ways? In reviewing the demographic and socioeconomic characteristics of the survey respondents across the five case studies, the following four mode profiles emerged.

African American Mode Profile. Respondents who completed a mail survey tended to be lower income, less educated and older. Online respondents were typically higher income, more educated, and balanced by age. Telephone respondents were generally lower income and balanced by education and age.

Latino Mode Profile. Respondents who completed a mail survey were balanced by language dominance and education, lower income, older, and more likely to be foreign-born males. Online respondents were typically English dominant, higher income and education, balanced by age, and more likely to be native-born females. By contrast, telephone respondents were typically Spanish dominant, lower income, less educated, and older.

White Mode Profile. Respondents who completed a mail survey were balanced by education and age, and less educated. Online respondents, on the other hand, had higher incomes, more educated, and included more middle-aged males. Telephone respondents were balanced by age and income, less educated, and included more females than males.

Asian Mode Profile. Respondents who completed the mail survey were more likely to be native-language dominant, older and balanced by income. The mail option captured a broader diversity of Asians by language dominance, including Chinese, Korean and Vietnamese. By contrast, online respondents were generally higher income, younger, native-born and more likely to complete a survey in English. Telephone respondents were balanced by income and age and captured a broad diversity of languages. The telephone mode was especially effective in capturing responses in Vietnamese.

These five case studies provide convincing support that mixed mode studies, when coupled with language options, are effective in capturing demographically distinct segments of multicultural populations. With few exceptions, the choice of an online survey was minimal — a troublesome outcome given our industry's obsession with advocating for the expansion of online surveys — but nonetheless consistent with outcomes related to the American Community Survey. Perhaps the process for completing an online survey is too burdensome and needs to be further simplified to expand its usage. Moreover, it seems clear that reliance on only one survey mode would have resulted in survey outcomes that may have been less representative of the target communities.

How Do Multi-Modal, Multilingual Study Respondents Compare to Respondents in the American Community Survey?

Aside from the ability of multi-modal, multilingual studies to expand the demographic diversity of their study respondents, it is equally important to evaluate the extent to which mixed mode studies represent the population of interest. To address this issue, we compared the demographic characteristics of respondents in Case Study 5 with similar characteristics in the American Community Survey 2014. Case Study 5 was chosen for this discussion because the study targeted a cross-section of all households in Dallas County, and its timing coincided closely with the ACS 2014. Each of the five studies used our multi-modal, multilingual methodology but targeted distinctly different populations; consequently, the following discussion regarding Case Study 5 is unique to Dallas County and the reader should not generalize this analysis to other markets. Table 15 below presents this comparison. Importantly, Case Study 5 percentages were *un-weighted* in order to compare the actual results from the multi-modal, multilingual methodology with the American Community Survey population characteristics for 2014.

Table 15: Comparison of Demographic Characteristics, Case Study 5 with American Community Survey 2014 One-Year Estimates

Characteristics	Survey Mode Choices -Unwtd. Percents				ACS 2014	ACS-Survey Difference
	Mail	Online	Telephone	Total		
Gender						
Male	42.5	67.6	49.3	48.9	48.8	-0.1
Female	57.5	32.4	50.7	51.1	51.2	0.1
Total	100.0	100.0	100.0	100.0	100.0	
Race-Ethnicity						
White/Other	53.1	56.2	39.8	43.8	43.7	-0.1
African American	20.5	28.8	22.1	22.1	21.9	-0.2
Hispanic	26.4	15.1	38.1	34.1	34.4	0.3
Total	100.0	100.0	100.0	100.0	100.0	
Age						
Less than 30 years	2.9	5.4	14.2	11.1	24.5	13.4
30-59 years	47.4	58.1	50.9	50.6	55.7	5.1
60 years and over	47.4	35.1	33.7	36.9	19.8	-17.1
No answer	2.2	1.4	1.2	1.4	0.0	-1.4
Total	100.0	100.0	100.0	100.0	100.0	
Education						
HSG or less	32.4	23.0	38.9	36.4	37.3	0.9
Some college, tech schl., Assoc.	31.2	20.3	29.7	29.5	30.3	0.8
Bachelor degree or more	34.6	55.4	28.8	31.8	32.4	0.6
No answer	1.8	1.4	2.6	2.3	0.0	-2.3
Total	100.0	100.0	100.0	100.0	100.0	
Household Income						
Less than $40K	47.4	23.3	36.6	38.2	40.9	2.7
$40K plus	42.2	69.9	45.5	46.3	59.1	12.8
No answer	10.4	6.8	17.9	15.5	0.0	-15.5
Total	100.0	100.0	100.0	100.0	100	
Tenure						
Own home	61.8	72.6	59.0	60.5	50.2	-10.3
Renting	29.4	23.3	29.3	28.9	49.8	20.9
Other living arrangement	5.5	2.7	10.0	8.5	0.0	-8.5
No answer	3.3	1.4	1.8	2.1	0.0	-2.1
Total	100.0	100.0	100.0	100.0	100	
Language of Interview						
English	84.2	97.3	83.6	84.6		
Spanish	15.8	2.7	16.4	15.4		
Total	100.0	100.0	100.0	100.0		

With some exceptions, it is readily apparent from the percentages shown in the "Total" column for Case Study 5 that the demographic representation of respondents in this survey closely mirrored the percentages shown for the ACS 2014. Race-ethnicity, gender and education were well represented by this survey, although it is apparent that older respondents were over-represented while younger respondents were under-represented. In terms of household income, the lower-income respondents were adequately represented by the survey, but the higher-income segment appears under-represented — a possible consequence of the higher number of "no answer" responses in the telephone mode. Renters, who tend to be younger, were also under-represented in the survey. Younger respondents may have been less engaged in the study topic due to its focus on healthcare.

It is also worth noting that each mode in Table 15 above captured a different distribution of multicultural respondents. Table 16 below summarizes the relevant percentages from Table 15. In comparison to the race-ethnicity percentages from the ACS 2014, it seems clear that both the mail and online modes over-represented White-Others and under-represented Hispanics; however, the telephone mode more closely matched the ACS 2014 distribution. Importantly, the best match to the ACS 2014 is evident when compared against All Modes.

Table 16: Distribution of Race-Ethnicity by Mode

Race-Ethnicity	Mail	Online	Telephone	All Modes	ACS 2014
White-Other	53.1	56.2	39.8	43.8	43.7
African American	20.5	28.8	22.1	22.1	21.9
Hispanic	26.4	15.1	38.1	34.1	34.4
Total	100.0	100.0	100.0	100.0	100.0

Overall, the demographic representation resulting from this multi-modal, multilingual study compared favorably to an industry gold standard like the American Community Survey. While the study adds evidence to our current knowledge about mixed mode research with multicultural populations, it is not conclusive and underscores the need for further research. The multi-modal, multilingual methodology is not a one-size fits all solution, but it is highly adaptable.

Promising Research on Data Quality

Although none of the five case studies previously discussed focused on how survey mode choices influence indicators of data quality, its importance is not lost here. Indeed, it seems obvious that more valid responses to a question will be obtained if a respondent (a) is provided a language that he/she understands, (b) can read or hear clearly, (c) understands the construct being measured, and (d) is able to write or record their responses. There is one study conducted in Sweden that provides strong evidence that poorer response quality can be expected the further removed a person is linguistically and culturally from the mainstream culture.[152] The study investigators analyzed the quality of responses from two national multilingual telephone interviews in Sweden that included native-born and immigrant adults. A key aspect of their data analysis focused on several response quality measures such as:

- **Don't knows.** The proportion of don't know responses, for individuals across all questions asked;
- **Extreme coding.** Number of responses at the extreme beginning or end points of a scale;
- **Mid-5 responding.** Proportion of responses at the center point of an 11-point scale;
- **Recency effects.** Proportion of responses that selected the last-mentioned item from a list of four or more items for all applicable questions; and
- **Straight-lining.** Proportion of blocks where responses were identical (i.e., same selected response category) across blocks of questions with the same stem and response format.

After adjusting for socioeconomic factors, the results revealed consistently reduced response quality across the different measures for immigrants when compared to the resident group, which included significantly higher levels of don't knows, recency effects, extreme responses, mid-5 responses, and straight-lining. Some of the question elements recognized as contributing to poorer response quality included increased complexity, use of infrequent words, memory demands, increased subjectivity, and longer formats — all of which created more cognitive demands among lower-educated people, the elderly, and those with limited language proficiency. The results of this study should encourage survey practitioners, especially those involved in mixed mode studies, to expand their interest in mode effects by also evaluating the influence of mixed modes on data quality for culturally diverse groups.

Aside from evaluating response quality, however, some experts have argued that cultural relevance may be more important than the response process.[153] Indeed, if the respondent cannot even understand what is being asked, then why should anyone be concerned about the response quality? Health-related studies, for example, have shown that certain measures of mental health in Western medicine are not easily measured in other cultures. Conversely, there are mental health illnesses recognized in some cultures that do not have a parallel illness in Western medicine.[154] Thus, the analysis of response quality in multicultural studies should always be accompanied by considerations for the cultural relevance of the construct being measured.

Budget Planning for Multi-Modal, Multilingual Studies

Studies using our recommended multi-modal, multilingual methodology (MMML) offer considerable promise in reducing coverage bias and expanding the demographic composition of survey respondents. However, the research practitioner will be challenged in developing an adequate budget for studies using the MMML approach since consideration needs to be devoted to both fixed and variable costs that will vary based on the uniqueness of each geographic market. Having conducted several multi-modal, multilingual studies over the past 13 years, I have developed an understanding of the relevant costs I would like to share with practitioners who are planning to use the MMML methodology for a multicultural study or perhaps another mixed mode design. While not exhaustive, the discussion should help practitioners in planning a budget that includes the most essential cost factors.

A hypothetical example should help to illustrate the relevant cost factors to consider in the budget planning process. As is often the case, let's assume that the survey sponsor is motivated by a strong desire to reduce coverage bias of key demographic segments in their communities of interest, and would like to complete 800 to 1,000 surveys in a hypothetical U.S. county that is racially and linguistically diverse. To achieve this objective, past experience suggests that you will likely need to send 20,000 mail surveys to an addressed-based sample of households — which is likely to provide an overall yield rate of 5 percent and a response rate that ranges from 15 to 25 percent. Let's further assume the mail survey package includes (a) an 8-page English-language questionnaire in booklet format (including a cover letter), (b) a native-language questionnaire for Latino and Asian households and (c) a business reply envelope. The cover letter will also include a link to an online survey in the relevant languages, and follow-up telephone calls will be made to non-respondents with a previously matched telephone number. Importantly, the total weight of the survey package is kept under 3 ounces in order to get the best first-class mail postage rate since higher rates will apply above 3 ounces. Unless you conduct a well-designed pilot study to estimate the likely response rates and completions by the mail and online modes, you will not know the number of telephone surveys that will be needed to achieve the sampling targets for the study — a difficult situation because telephone surveys are more costly, require more staff resources, are limited by the availability of matched telephone numbers, and often blocked by call protect features. Thus, you will need a game plan that will help you manage your budget and the resources to meet the study objectives. Let's work through a possible budget scenario for this hypothetical study by reviewing Table 17 on the following page.

The calculations shown in the Rate column reflect actual rates from recent similar studies I have conducted using the MMML methodology. Fixed Costs represent the estimated costs required to launch a mail survey to 20,000 households. The Variable Costs, however, will vary with each market since one cannot determine, without the benefit of a pilot study, the mode choices that will be made by the survey respondents in a specific geographic area. In some of our past MMML studies, the survey respondents completed surveys primarily by mail and relatively fewer by online or telephone modes. However, in other MMML studies we have completed, respondents utilized the mail and online modes less frequently and required us to dedicate more telephone interviewing effort in order to achieve the survey completion targets. Trying to estimate the cost of telephone interviews using incidence indicators is difficult and likely to under-estimate the needed budget, especially if a pilot study was not conducted. Instead of relying on questionable incidence indicators, it may be wiser to quote an hourly rate for telephone interviewing and bill the survey sponsor for the number of hours required to achieve a targeted number of telephone interviews. One should also keep in mind that the total number of telephone surveys that can be completed will depend on the number of telephone numbers that are produced from the matching process with selected households — which typically provides a 30 to 40 percent match rate in my experience.

Table 17: Hypothetical Budget for Multi-Modal, Multilingual Survey

Task	Rate	Cost
Fixed Costs		
Household random sample	20,000 x .05	$1,000
Printing & fulfillment	20,000 surveys x $1.50	$30,000
Outbound Postage 1st class	20,000 surveys x $0.42	$8,400
Programming for online surveys, monitoring	40 hrs. x $75/hr.	$3,000
Project Management	100 hrs. x $100/hr.	$10,000
Translation of surveys	3 languages x $750	$2,250
Matching landline and wireless numbers to households	8,000 matches x $0.12	$960
Subtotal Fixed Costs		$55,610
Variable Costs		
Telephone interviewing hours	100 to 400 hrs. x $40/hr.	$4,000 to $16,000
Postage for in-bound mail surveys	300 to 500 x $1.38	$414 to $690
Subtotal Variable Costs		$4,414 to $16,690
Optional Costs		
Pre-paid incentives	20,000 x $2.00	$40,000
Reminder postcard: printing, fulfillment and postage	20,000 x $0.80	$16,000
Pilot study		$1,000 to $2,000

The Optional Costs include features I have typically not utilized in past similar studies, but which could enhance survey response rates, such as pre-paid or post-incentives and reminder postcards. Additional contacts designed to enhance survey response rates and reduce coverage bias — such as pre-notification letters, a second survey package or other postcard reminders — would clearly raise the budget for this hypothetical study. However, the additional contacts may be necessary if completions by mail or online modes are unexpectedly low, or if the number of matched telephone numbers available to support the telephone operation is insufficient to meet the completion targets. Regarding the Hispanic-targeted studies, it might be a good idea to anticipate lower response rates due to the chilling effect generated by the current political environment, that is, by planning for a larger sample and using incentives.

In summary, the survey budget and project timeline will often dictate the scope and quality of a survey that utilizes a multi-modal, multilingual methodology. The survey practitioner should ensure that the proposed study budget is adequate to implement the key elements of the study and that additional funds are available if key changes are made to the methodology. Since relatively few mixed mode studies of multicultural respondents may be available to guide your survey planning effort, you are strongly encouraged to include pilot studies with experimental designs to evaluate the effectiveness of different survey modes and incentive offers on response rates and response quality.

Chapter Summary

Mixed mode methods are intuitively appealing because they provide research respondents more choices for sharing their opinions and have the added benefits of reducing non-response bias, expanding the demographic diversity of the study sample, and potentially improving response rates and response quality. The potential benefits of mixed mode methods, however, have been limited due to the use of demographically homogenous survey participants and an industry that has focused little attention on factors related to race-ethnicity and language behavior. Although the resources required to conduct mixed mode studies of multicultural populations involve more complexity and financial investment, the potential benefits seem worthwhile. Following are some insights to keep in mind from this chapter in the design and execution of a multicultural study:

Focus on respondent needs. Remember to be considerate of respondent limitations that pose barriers to survey participation, including visual acuity, reading literacy, hearing ability, and limited English proficiency. Place a higher priority on tools that enhance the respondent's survey experience, and less importance on making the survey experience more convenient to the research practitioner. Above all, ensure that your survey budget covers the essential elements of the survey research plan.

Tailor the methodology to the target audience. Multicultural studies will require more tailoring than is generally considered by the survey practitioner, including instrument translations, interviewers with the right language skills, survey software that can accommodate the accents and diacritical marks for different languages, attention to biases in the questionnaire design that may lead to response sets, and the appropriate mode choices. Plan on creating a team of talented staff or consultants to remove the guesswork in these areas.

Carefully consider the need to adjust for mode effects. Remember that the main reason for using a mixed mode approach is to improve coverage, which means that you want diverse groups represented in your study. The fact that these diverse groups may show differential responses by mode is not problematic, but rather an expected outcome. Consult an expert who understands the distinction between mode selection effects and measurement effects before making any attempts to make these types of adjustments.

Explore the use of incentives. While the idea of sending $2 bills attached to a mail survey may sound expensive, it pales in comparison to the postage and printing costs associated with multiple contacts by mail. Although not enough is known about the effectiveness of incentives for improving response rates and coverage among Blacks, Latinos and Asians, it would be worth the investment for research practitioners who continue to struggle with engaging these groups.

Resist the temptation to take shortcuts. Faced with a lack of resources to properly design and execute a multicultural study, you may be tempted to take some risky shortcuts, such as (a) using Google to translate a questionnaire, (b) outsourcing the data collection to a research shop that you will not be able to monitor, (c) hiring only monolingual interviewers who cannot provide language choices to the respondents or (d) sending

English-only mail surveys to a heavily Latino or Asian community just to save a few dollars. Taking these shortcuts serves no useful purpose and ultimately lowers the quality of the multicultural study.

In the following chapter, we discuss the special problems one is likely to encounter when conducting focus group research with multicultural consumers, including issues related to recruitment, incentives, project management, screening and invitations, facility location, moderating, translation support, and reporting results.

Chapter 9: Focus Group Research — Special Problems

Although much of the discussion thus far has focused on problems related to survey research with multicultural populations, qualitative research continues to be a popular approach to gathering market intelligence for multicultural populations. Over the past 45 years, I have conducted focus groups and other qualitative research with multicultural populations to explore their experiences on a variety of topics, such as:

- Concept testing for different products or services
- Evaluating advertising messages
- Usability studies to evaluate translated survey instruments
- Taste tests for food products and beverages
- Evaluation of food package design
- Comparing the positioning of political candidates
- Evaluating experiences with healthcare providers
- Understanding perceptions of current treatment therapies for childhood psychiatric disorders among Latino psychiatrists
- Ethnographic observations to evaluate the navigation experiences at airports
- Numerous other topics

Clearly, the participation of multicultural consumers in qualitative research is not only important to the many organizations that sponsor such research, but also to the quality of life that multicultural consumers are likely to experience from the many products or services that they utilize. As a case in point, a recent article in Latino USA pointed to the lack of participation of Latinos in clinical trials: only 5 percent of U.S. Latinos participated in clinical trials even though they represent 18 percent of the U.S. population.[155] According Dr. Eliseo Pérez-Stable of the National Institutes of Minority Health and Health Disparities:

Some drugs may work wonderfully in clinical trials but don't work for a small group of people, and we don't know that unless we study it. These are the kinds of questions where race, ethnicity become an important part of the question on how science, how biology is working.

Similarly, the omission of multicultural persons from qualitative research studies involving products or services benefits no one and underscores the need for qualitative research providers to improve the participation of multicultural persons in qualitative studies, especially in light of the growing presence of this segment in their trade areas. Given the obvious need to include multicultural persons, what are some of the barriers or challenges faced by focus group facilities in addressing this need? In the section that follows, I will share some of our company's experiences in managing and conducting focus group studies and discuss the findings of a limited number of studies that focused on the recruitment of multicultural persons.

Our Qualitative Experience

During the first 15 years of my research practice, our company operated a focus group facility in Dallas, Texas and became acutely aware of the many challenges faced by focus group managers. After those initial 15 years, I continued my qualitative projects by using focus group facilities throughout the U.S. and Puerto Rico, and providing qualitative support for multicultural projects through such services as recruitment, moderating, transcriptions and written reports. This experience provided me valuable insights regarding the readiness of U.S. focus group facilities in meeting the growing demands for qualitative studies of multicultural populations. Thus, the discussion to follow focuses primarily on my past 45 years of experience in conducting qualitative studies and will touch on such topics as missed opportunities, facility location, recruitment, screening and invitations, translation support, facility hostess service, moderating, and reporting of findings.

Missed Opportunities

Much like the survey research industry, U.S. focus group facilities have not kept pace with the dramatic growth of multicultural consumers in the U.S., and sometimes appear indifferent to the opportunities available in their own back yards.

In my opinion, many focus group facilities do not appear particularly eager to attract multicultural projects for various reasons, including the following:

- Absence of multicultural and multilingual staff;
- Use of English-only recruitment literature, websites and maps that offer little or no support for other languages;
- Recruitment databases that include primarily English speakers but few immigrants or non-English speakers;
- Limited access to multicultural moderators, translators, and translation equipment; and
- Locations that are often isolated from multicultural communities, especially immigrants.

Rather than expand these capabilities, some focus group facility managers seem content to allow multicultural qualitative studies to continue their traditional paths to east and west coast facilities that have a long history of facilitating multicultural studies. This apparent lack of readiness can be a source of discouragement to marketers who are evaluating product or service opportunities in geographic areas known to have large numbers of multicultural populations. For example, Tables 18, 19 and 20 on the following pages clearly show the large presence of Blacks, Hispanics and Asians for the top 15 metropolitan areas in the U.S.

Clearly, the east and west coasts are not the only areas with significant numbers of multicultural persons who are available for focus group studies. In fact, marketers are not always looking for the larger markets where competition is more intense, but increasingly show interest in mid-sized markets that offer opportunities for growth. Some of the excuses I have heard over the years from focus group managers regarding their lack of a multicultural capability include: "They are difficult to reach," "It is more costly to hire bilingual staff and translate forms into different languages," and "We are concerned about their low show rates." While each of these excuses may have some merit, it is equally true that the lack of readiness is costly in the long run and encourages marketers to avoid such markets to test their products or services.

Table 18: Top 15 U.S. Metropolitan Areas Ranked by Black Population,*
2018

METRO AREA	BLACK POPULATION	TOTAL POPULATION	PCT. BLACK
New York-Newark-Jersey City, NY-NJ-PA Metro Area	3,131,986	19,990,592	15.7
Atlanta-Sandy Springs-Roswell, GA Metro Area	1,928,984	5,779,463	33.4
Chicago-Naperville-Elgin, IL-IN-WI Metro Area	1,560,816	9,536,428	16.4
Washington-Arlington-Alexandria, DC-VA-MD-WV Metro Area	1,521,416	6,138,382	24.8
Philadelphia-Camden-Wilmington, PA-NJ-DE-MD Metro Area	1,233,368	6,069,448	20.3
Miami-Fort Lauderdale-West Palm Beach, FL Metro Area	1,223,979	6,070,944	20.2
Houston-The Woodlands-Sugar Land, TX Metro Area	1,143,282	6,779,104	16.9
Dallas-Fort Worth-Arlington, TX Metro Area	1,105,876	7,255,028	15.2
Detroit-Warren-Dearborn, MI Metro Area	955,994	4,317,179	22.1
Los Angeles-Long Beach-Anaheim, CA Metro Area	845,917	13,262,234	6.4
Baltimore-Columbia-Towson, MD Metro Area	803,038	2,793,250	28.7
Memphis, TN-MS-AR Metro Area	627,480	1,345,991	46.6
Charlotte-Concord-Gastonia, NC-SC Metro Area	546,419	2,473,125	22.1
Virginia Beach-Norfolk-Newport News, VA-NC Metro Area	515,493	1,722,001	29.9
St. Louis, MO-IL Metro Area	511,016	2,805,551	18.2

Source: American Community Survey 2018 5-Year Estimates

Focus Group Research — Special Problems

Table 19: Top 15 U.S. Metropolitan Areas Ranked by Hispanic Population, 2018

METRO AREA	HISPANIC POPULATION	TOTAL POPULATION	PCT. HISPANIC
Los Angeles-Long Beach-Anaheim, CA Metro Area	5,973,798	13,262,234	45.0
New York-Newark-Jersey City, NY-NJ-PA Metro Area	4,837,457	19,990,592	24.2
Miami-Fort Lauderdale-West Palm Beach, FL Metro Area	2,716,271	6,070,944	44.7
Houston-The Woodlands-Sugar Land, TX Metro Area	2,506,513	6,779,104	37.0
Riverside-San Bernardino-Ontario, CA Metro Area	2,282,330	4,518,699	50.5
San Juan-Carolina-Caguas, PR Metro Area	2,118,734	2,142,392	98.9
Chicago-Naperville-Elgin, IL-IN-WI Metro Area	2,092,989	9,536,428	21.9
Dallas-Fort Worth-Arlington, TX Metro Area	2,077,311	7,255,028	28.6
Phoenix-Mesa-Scottsdale, AZ Metro Area	1,436,464	4,673,634	30.7
San Antonio-New Braunfels, TX Metro Area	1,340,148	2,426,204	55.2
San Diego-Carlsbad, CA Metro Area	1,106,925	3,302,833	33.5
San Francisco-Oakland-Hayward, CA Metro Area	1,020,150	4,673,221	21.8
Washington-Arlington-Alexandria, DC-VA-MD-WV Metro Area	954,071	6,138,382	15.5
McAllen-Edinburg-Mission, TX Metro Area	781,681	849,389	92.0
Orlando-Kissimmee-Sanford, FL Metro Area	731,941	2,450,261	29.9

Source: American Community Survey 2018 5-Year Estimates

Table 20: Top 15 U.S. Metropolitan Areas Ranked by Asian Population,*
2018

METRO AREA	ASIAN POPULATION	TOTAL POPULATION	PCT. ASIAN
New York-Newark-Jersey City, NY-NJ-PA Metro Area	2,148,690	19,990,592	10.7
Los Angeles-Long Beach-Anaheim, CA Metro Area	2,081,197	13,262,234	15.7
San Francisco-Oakland-Hayward, CA Metro Area	1,187,337	4,673,221	25.4
San Jose-Sunnyvale-Santa Clara, CA Metro Area	686,970	1,981,616	34.7
Chicago-Naperville-Elgin, IL-IN-WI Metro Area	617,869	9,536,428	6.5
Washington-Arlington-Alexandria, DC-VA-MD-WV Metro Area	609,062	6,138,382	9.9
Houston-The Woodlands-Sugar Land, TX Metro Area	514,355	6,779,104	7.6
Seattle-Tacoma-Bellevue, WA Metro Area	502,498	3,809,717	13.2
Dallas-Fort Worth-Arlington, TX Metro Area	475,837	7,255,028	6.6
Urban Honolulu, HI Metro Area	409,718	987,638	41.5
San Diego-Carlsbad, CA Metro Area	382,336	3,302,833	11.6
Boston-Cambridge-Newton, MA-NH Metro Area	372,883	4,811,732	7.7
Philadelphia-Camden-Wilmington, PA-NJ-DE-MD Metro Area	351,812	6,069,448	5.8
Atlanta-Sandy Springs-Roswell, GA Metro Area	330,409	5,779,463	5.7
Sacramento--Roseville--Arden-Arcade, CA Metro Area	296,533	2,291,738	12.9

Source: American Community Survey 2018 5-Year Estimates

Project Management

Staff in charge of ensuring the focus group studies are planned and executed properly are especially challenged when the targeted segment includes multicultural consumers. Aside from ensuring that the facility has the staff and other resources to execute a multicultural study, project managers will need to carefully monitor the study to ensure that client expectations are adequately met throughout the study. Difficulties can be expected in several areas, such as screening criteria that produce low incidences; discussion guides that are too lengthy and difficult to follow by the moderator; omission of non-English exhibits to evaluate in the non-English speaking groups; insufficient or inappropriate incentives to ensure good show rates; confusion regarding language usage during focus group discussions; and inadequate accommodations for family members who accompany participants. This is certainly not an exhaustive list of the potential challenges faced by project managers, but rather underscores the importance of assigning a project manager with the knowledge and experience with multicultural consumers to ensure that they have a positive experience at their facility.

Recruitment Issues and Incentives

To identify and invite members of the target audience, focus group facilities generally rely on an in-house database of past focus group participants, although new participants can be added through traditional tools like website recruitment forms, community networks, and word-of-mouth referrals. These traditional tools, however, usually capture English-speaking, more educated and higher-income consumers, and are less successful in capturing non-English speakers who are less educated, lower income and foreign born. And unless a facility has staff who are African American, Latino or Asian that have lived in these communities for some time, the demographic diversity of the facility's database is not likely to change much over time. What is typically absent in many facilities is the development of community networks that serve African Americans, Latinos or Asians — including churches, refugee centers, business groups, sports clubs, retail shops and civic groups. It takes time and trust to establish these networks, but the benefits become obvious once you are tasked with recruiting a multicultural project.

Regarding incentives, experienced recruiters know that multicultural participants are peculiar about the incentives that are provided by the facility, preferring cash over gift cards, checks, or other types of incentives. Checks become an inconvenience because not all multicultural participants maintain a banking relationship and will often pay an extra fee to cash checks at a check cashing retail outlet. The amount of the incentive will likely range from $75 to $150 per person and depends on the expected difficulty or incidence in screening members of the target audience, as well as past facility experience with show rates. Sometimes, however, the social or political climate can unexpectedly influence show rates regardless of the incentive amount offered. For example, one past focus group study I conducted on financial services required native born and foreign-born Latino adults, who were offered a $100 cash incentive for their participation. Only one of the 15 recruited immigrants showed for the study, while all the 15 native-born Latinos showed. In a follow-up telephone call with the immigrant no shows, we learned that concerns about deportation discouraged them from participating in the focus group, although they were willing to conduct a telephone interview on the same topic. We learned that the value of an incentive can change unexpectedly, and suggests the need to modify the recruitment strategy in studies involving hard-to-reach segments like immigrants. For example, a different venue could have been utilized to conduct the group sessions, such as a community church, a local school or local hotel — venues that would be closer to the target segment and perhaps considered "safer." Matching a race or ethnicity and language of the recruiter to the target audience becomes especially important when recruiting immigrants since these attributes increase trust and rapport. When conducting multi-market studies, another successful approach is to train a local community member who is well known by members of the target audience to conduct the recruitment activity. With the proper training, the relevant race-ethnic background and language skills, such community members can increase the likelihood of a successful recruitment outcome.

Screening Criteria and Invitations

An important part of the recruitment process is to finalize the screening criteria that will define the type of respondents who are desired by the client. In defining the criteria, some clients know exactly what they want, and others will need your guidance. Aside from product consumption behavior, criteria will often include race-ethnicity, language skills, use of ethnic media, acculturation scales, gender, age and other characteristics. If the focus group tasks will include reading of documents or exhibits in a specific language, you should also include screening criteria that checks for reading skills and visual acuity. Verbal articulation can also be checked by asking potential participants to discuss their favorite vacation, movie or another topic that generates conversation. You do not want to invite participants who are non-verbal or cannot overcome their shyness in response to a simple question. The invitation letter and map should be provided in English or a native language for persons with limited English-language reading skills. A map prepared in a non-English language is more important than you might realize since immigrants often get lost trying to find a focus group facility in a city they do not know very well. Among other things, the invitation letter should let the participant know that any relatives who accompany the participant will need to wait in the reception area, which will hopefully be family-friendly. Although it is common to invite 10 to 12 participants for 8 shows, you should plan to over-recruit multicultural consumers, especially the foreign born, to compensate for late arrivals and low show rates. Given a choice, I tend to invite native-born participants at 6pm and immigrants at 8pm since immigrants tend to have blue-collar jobs that do not provide much flexibility in their work schedules. Should you rely on emails, telephones or regular mail for your invitations and follow-up contacts? In my experience, cell phones have been more reliable since consumers are increasingly more dependent on these devices for their communications. Multicultural consumers, however, will likely require multiple follow-up contacts to ensure an adequate show rate. Regarding the payment of incentives for late arrivals, my own preference is not to pay participants an incentive if they arrive 10 minutes late. Why? Because this practice rewards the wrong behavior. Exceptions to this policy, however, are made on occasion by clients who believe that all participants who show up, regardless of the time, should be paid the incentive. In the long run, I believe that participants who have a track record of showing up late for focus group studies should be removed from the recruitment database.

Location of Focus Group Facilities

Focus group facilities are not usually located close to communities where multicultural consumers reside, especially those who reside in lower-income and immigrant areas. Most focus group facilities I have visited provide facility maps only in English, which may seem inconsequential to inexperienced recruiters, but which can contribute to low show rates or late arrivals for persons who lack familiarity with the focus group location. On occasion, it makes more sense to consider alternatives to the traditional focus group facility, especially in more isolated communities. I have conducted numerous focus group studies, for example, in communities where no professional focus group facility was available or where the distance that participants would need to travel exceeded 20 minutes. The network of Holiday Inn facilities has been a great asset for conducting focus groups in such communities, which has required our team to set up the audio-video equipment to accommodate clients and participants. In addition, numerous services are now available for conducting online focus groups, which makes sense when travel time and budgets are limited, but may be more challenging for participants who are less accustomed to using the internet for group meetings.

Translation Support

Selecting a simultaneous translator to support a focus group project can be challenging. In my experience, translators fall into three categories: experienced and credentialed, experienced and not credentialed, or not credentialed and not experienced. Ideally, you should seek a translator who is both experienced and credentialed since the risks of an unprofessional translation experience is minimized. A credentialed translator with little or no focus group experience is no guarantee of a positive focus group experience since translators often rely on the skills that they utilize in the courts or conventions; however, after some initial training on the focus group environment, I have found that these translators can quickly adapt to the expectations of a focus group study. A translator who is not credentialed and lacks experience in the focus group environment is a risky option — often an ethnic employee with little formal training in a language — which should be avoided. You should be able to identify a well-trained and experienced translator by asking professional colleagues for referrals. Court-certified translators may not match the ethnicity, country of origin or language nuances of the focus group participants, which may also present some initial challenges in communications.

When possible, I try to match a translator with the focus group participants in terms of ethnicity or country of origin, although one does not always have this option. The matching helps to establish rapport more quickly and facilitates the communicative process. Other investigators who support the matching practice, however, have not always had a successful focus group experience.[156, 157] If you happen to use the translator provided by a facility, it is advisable to spend a little time with the translator to check their language and experience with the target audience. It is also a good practice to provide translators a copy of the English and native-language discussion guides at least one day prior to the study so that they can become familiar with the procedures and terminology that will be utilized during the discussion. The quality of simultaneous translation equipment also varies by facility and needs to be checked out before starting a focus group discussion. Clients sometimes have their own preferences for managing the simultaneous translation experience, so expect to make some last-minute changes to the setup of the equipment and positioning of the translator. Another key thing to keep in mind is that translators will occasionally be asked by clients to provide marketing advice or interpretations of focus group interactions — not something that you want to encourage since translators are not trained marketers. In your initial orientation with the translator, be sure to explain that any questions by the clients related to marketing advice or strategy should be referred to the moderator. The moderator may choose to answer the question or refer the question to the client team.

Facility Hostessing

Most facilities have well trained, courteous staff that know how to manage the focus group experience — from signing in the participants and clients, getting meals ordered, ensuring that clients' needs are attended, distributing incentives, and resolving issues as they occur. Nonetheless, few facilities provide hosts/hostesses that are proficient in languages other than English, especially the Asian languages. Bilingual host/hostesses are real assets when communicating with participants and clients with limited English-language skills. It is a good practice for facilities to maintain native-language staff if not permanently, at least on call. In my experience, focus group clients are not impressed when facilities provide only English-speaking staff for projects that involve native-language participants, and will occasionally choose another market with facilities that provide staff that have the relevant language skills for the project being conducted.

Moderating Groups

In addition to a quality recruitment outcome, clients place considerable importance on the experience and moderating skills of the moderator. The moderator is expected to understand the discussion guide and exhibits that will be utilized in the discussions and clarify any points of ambiguity as well. In my experience, many industry moderators that I have observed or worked with on qualitative projects have not obtained formal training in moderating focus groups — an outcome of the minimal attention that college courses devote to qualitative research skills, and perhaps an outcome of the mistaken assumption that an ethnic moderator who speaks the right language is automatically qualified to moderate a focus group. All things being equal, you should place more importance on excellent moderating skills and training when choosing a moderator. Finding a trained moderator with an ethnicity that matches the focus group participants is icing on the cake. Sometimes, professionals in a related industry have developed excellent communications skills that can transfer to the moderating experience. There are private schools that teach qualitative research skills, such as:

- RIVA Market Research and Training Institute (http://www.rivainc.com)
- Burke Institute (http://www.burkeinstitute.com/SeminarDescription/Detail/Q01)

Even trained and experienced moderators are sometimes challenged in moderating a group of multicultural consumers. Assuming that language is not a barrier, the moderator will need to immediately establish rapport with the participants and de-mystify the focus group experience by explaining the expectations of the study, address concerns about video recording and client observations, and underscore the importance of their opinions. The inexperienced moderator will learn very quickly that multicultural consumers can be difficult to manage even after they become comfortable and rapport has been established. Why? Because they can be very talkative, initiate simultaneous conversations at one time, and begin asking their own questions. On the other hand, some participants will initially appear shy and not expressive, which will require the moderator to occasionally remind them that their opinions are extremely important to the success of the group discussion, and that staying silent is counter-productive. When such interactions are left uncontrolled, it will use up valuable moderating time and make it difficult to understand the conversation when reviewing the video or audio recordings. Care must be taken, however, when interrupting participants or attempting to overly manage the discussion, which can create a "chilling effect" that diminishes the quality and breadth of the discussion. If not interrupted diplomatically, multicultural consumers are likely to feel insulted and decide not to engage in the ongoing discussion. The moderator will need to avoid asking questions that require a yes/no response and focus on questions that require more articulation by the participant. Multicultural consumers will often sit back and allow a dominant speaker to continue a conversation with the moderator; in such instances, the moderator will need to diplomatically shift the conversation to other participants by asking them how they feel about the topic at hand. If evaluating advertising copy with participants with limited English language skills, clients will need to be reminded to also bring advertising copy in the relevant native language for participants to evaluate. A good moderating experience will happen if the moderator manages time well, keeps the participants on task, and covers most if not all the points included in the discussion guide. I often use humor to break the ice with multicultural participants and encourage some discussion about their children or grandchildren to maintain a good flow of conversation. In the event a client wants the participants to complete a questionnaire or some type of evaluation scale, do not be surprised to find participants who cannot read sufficiently well in English or their native language. If the recruiters have not already screened the participants for their reading skills, it is a good idea for the moderator to read the questions on the survey or form out loud to avoid any embarrassing moments for the participants. Of course, participants should always be reminded to bring their reading glasses to the discussion if they will be required to complete written forms. As a general practice, asking participants to complete rating scales or questionnaires during the discussion should be kept to a minimum since valuable time is taken away from the qualitative experience of the focus group — that is, allowing the participants to verbally communicate their experience with the product or service.

To the practitioners who believe that these problems are not unique to multicultural participants but are common with all participants, I would simply add that it is a *difference of degree* — these problems just occur more frequently among multicultural participants.

Reporting the Findings

Clients typically request a top-line summary or a detailed written report. The top-line summary is basically a bullet-point summary of the main findings from the focus group discussions, while a detailed report also incorporates verbatim comments that are integrated into the written report. Budget permitting, it is always great to get a written transcription of the audio recordings in order to more efficiently write your report and resolve differences in perceptions that sometimes emerge from observations of the discussions. However, if the focus group discussion was conducted in a language other than English, you will probably need to use a transcriptionist to translate and transcribe the audio recordings — adding more expense. In the past, I have used Focus Forward (http://www.focusfwd.com/) to obtain transcriptions in different languages, although various other firms can provide this type of support. To avoid this extra cost, however, a native-language moderator can just listen to the audio native-language recordings and write the report based on this review, which can be a slow process.

Clients expect clearly written reports that are accompanied by recommendations from the moderator. However, if your writing skills are not razor sharp, plan to engage another staff member who has good writing skills. Once you submit the report to the client, plan to also submit audio and video recordings and any other exhibits that were part of the study. On rare occasions, you may be provided a video or audio recording by the facility that is damaged and unintelligible. Most facilities have backups of the recordings and should be able to produce a good recording. In one focus group project that I conducted, the facility provided me a damaged video recording and had no backups. The only way I was able to produce a detailed report was by using the audio recordings that the simultaneous translator had produced. In subsequent focus group sessions, I learned to keep my own digital audio recorder in the room as a backup to avoid potential problems with a facility's recording equipment.

It is worth noting that some clients will expect additional multicultural insights in the written report that help explain the findings and form the basis for recommended action. If you find yourself short on these insights, ask another knowledgeable staff member to provide some assistance. To assist in analyzing qualitative data, there are two software products that you might consider: Atlas.ti and WordStat. These products may be worth your time to review if you are looking for a more efficient manner of analyzing qualitative data.

Lessons from Qualitative Studies of Multicultural Consumers

Although limited, some attention has been devoted by past investigators regarding the factors that influence recruitment outcomes for multicultural consumers. For example, a recent study of Spanish-dominant Hispanics provided specific guidance on best practices for recruiting this segment for face-to-face interviews. Although the study did not utilize the most common method used to recruit research participants, i.e., telephone recruiting, it does a good job of demonstrating the resources required to recruit and interview a hard-to-reach segment of consumers.[158]

The goal of this qualitative study was to identify best practices for the recruitment of Spanish-dominant Hispanics with limited English-speaking skills. Once recruited, the participants completed a one-hour face-to-face interview at locations that were generally convenient to the participants and were paid a $40 incentive. The stated purpose of the study was to evaluate a Spanish-language version of a survey that focused on housing and demographics. As is typical in studies of hard-to-reach populations and immigrants, recruiters were faced with challenges that they needed to overcome, including distrust of government, fear and anxiety related to deportation, and limited experience with research studies. Following are some of the lessons that the investigators learned from this study:

- Recruiting in person worked best, which helped to establish trust. Potential participants were intercepted at a variety of venues, such as festivals, Hispanic restaurants, grocery stores, community enters, churches with Spanish services, English learning centers, Hispanic affairs offices, laundromats, and hair salons. Chain referrals, or "snowball sampling," was also useful in identifying potential participants. Advertisements were used --- such as newspaper ads, online ads and flyers --- but attracted the wrong segments, such as more motivated participants and more acculturated and English dominant Hispanics.

- Gaining cooperation was accomplished by building rapport, calming fear and perception of risk, and personalizing the benefits and convenience. Rapport building tactics included recruiters mentioning their own Hispanic origin, ensuring that no sales were involved, emphasizing ties to a Latino community organization, schedule flexibility, and providing a flyer that included contact information. Calming fear and perception of risk, on the other hand, was accomplished by using the word "conversation" or "estudio" instead of "investigation" to describe the study; explaining that there were no right or wrong answers; simplifying the meaning of confidentiality; and providing assurance that the data collected would not be related in any way to immigration. Personalizing benefits and convenience was communicated by describing the potential benefits to the local community; stressing that the interview could be scheduled at a time and location most convenient to the participant; pointing out that the incentive money could be used for groceries or gas; and stressing that their participation would help make the Spanish translation easier to understand for all Spanish speakers.

- Lastly, a profile of the successful recruiter was an important outcome of the study. This profile included such characteristics as formal training in Spanish and English; strong ties to the Hispanic community; a comfort level when approaching strangers and key community figures; past experience with recruiting Hispanic non-English speakers; well trained in study specifications and interviewing in general; ability to adjust the recruitment introduction to the potential participants and convert refusals with a minimum of discomfort; and being flexible in the scheduling and locations of the interview.

The Sha et al. study[159] reinforces the value of language and culturally relevant outreach strategies and serves as a model for designing recruitment strategies with Latinos. Nonetheless, it is important to also note some study methodological issues that may limit its usefulness for traditional focus group practices:

- First, personal face-to-face interviews are not typically used in the recruitment of multicultural consumers — it is very expensive and time consuming. Exceptions, however, are common in the medical industry because special recruitment techniques are required to identify hidden populations like the undocumented, drug users, and others.

- Secondly, a $40 incentive paid for a one-hour interview would be very difficult to implement in current qualitative studies. Current incentive levels for focus group participants range from $75 to $150 and vary with the difficulty of finding the desired participant, travel distance, and the length of the interview.

- Thirdly, with few exceptions, most focus group studies will be conducted in a professional facility that provides the amenities desired by clients and allows a confidential environment for the study. Alternative venues, however, should be considered when it makes better sense to facilitate the recruitment and interviewing of the targeted participants.

An earlier study in 2010 compared two strategies for recruiting Latino and non-Latino families that had children with disabilities into a research study.[160] Active recruitment strategies involved direct contact with potential participants, while passive strategies involved disseminating study information. The study found that active strategies were more successful in recruiting Latino families using such techniques as word-of-mouth through informal networks; collaboration with health service agencies, schools, and community agencies; and use of bilingual research staff and information.

Lastly, two cognitive studies focused on recruitment strategies for Asian participants. One study focused on recruiting limited English-speaking Chinese and Koreans for cognitive interviews with the American Community Survey.[161] The study found that online efforts were more successful in reaching younger, more highly educated bilingual Asians, while word-of-mouth was more successful with older, less educated immigrants. Newspapers and flyers, however, reached overlapping groups by demographic attributes. A second study[162] focused on recruiting Chinese and Koreans found that newspaper ads were best for recruiting non-English speakers; word-of-mouth was better for hard-to-reach persons; emails were more successful in reaching younger, more highly educated persons; and flyers were the least successful.

Regarding the use of media for the recruitment of Latinos, Blacks and Asians, it is important to understand the media environments in each market as well. Our company has conducted syndicated research of multicultural consumers in the Dallas/Ft. Worth metropolitan area over the past 20 years, [163,164] and we have often found that:

- Asians have broad access to Asian-language newspapers but fewer choices in terms of radio and television programs, which partially explains their high readership of newspapers;
- Latinos have had broad access to Spanish-language newspapers, radio and television stations, but use of Spanish-language media has declined in recent years with the decline of foreign-born adults;
- African Americans have access to a limited number of Black-focused newspapers, and broader access to radio and television programs which show strong audiences.

By incorporating some of the findings discussed here, a focus group facility should be in a better position to recruit members of the multicultural communities who reside in their trade area.

Incorporation of Technology

In a white paper about emerging methods in qualitative research technology,[165] L&E Research discusses the utility of several techniques that can enhance the qualitative experience, including:

- **Neuromarketing.** Use of electroencephalography (EEG) and eye tracking;
- **Virtual Reality.** Use of 3D interactive tools to replicate a realistic shopping experience for consumers;
- **360 Degree Streaming.** Provides a super video streaming experience using HD and 360-degree cameras, a major improvement for clients who are unable to attend focus group facilities either domestically or globally;
- **Video Analytics.** Utilizes video capture and intelligence platforms that transcribe and analyze video content so

that it becomes searchable, thus facilitating the time that it takes to tell your story; and

- **In-the-Moment Online Tools.** Provides rapid, real time access to respondent insights by optimizing the use of mobile devices.

QualLink 4.0 is yet another useful innovation introduced recently by 2020 Research.[166] QualLink allows survey participants who meet specified criteria to be immediately transitioned into a moderator of online discussions, saving the time usually required for a recruit and allowing you to directly capture additional insights.

Although the relevance of these emerging technologies for multicultural research is not discussed by these innovators, you are nonetheless encouraged to explore these technologies to evaluate their usefulness for qualitative studies of multicultural consumers. It seems like a good idea to incorporate more innovative strategies into your methodological toolbox with the goal of improving the qualitative experience with multicultural consumers.

Chapter Summary

A well-designed focus group study with multicultural consumers will require considerable resources to implement effectively, especially if a facility is just focused on the typical English-speaking participant. Although a project manager may not be able to recognize and control all the challenges that a multicultural study may present, attention to the points discussed in this chapter may help to ensure a more successful outcome, such as:

- Understanding the presence and composition of the diverse multicultural communities in your trade area;
- Hiring multicultural staff that understand these communities and able to communicate in English as well as languages other than English;
- Employing recruitment strategies that can include hard-to-reach persons like immigrants;
- Making it easier to find a facility location;
- Selecting a trained and experienced translator and moderator that best fits the linguistic behavior and ethnicity of the focus group participants; and

- Provide clients a written report that highlights the key findings of the focus group session and any multicultural insights that may shape the overall conclusions of the study.

In the following chapter, we focus our attention on procurement practices that sometimes undermine the quality of multicultural research studies.

Chapter 10: Procurement Practices That Undermine Research Quality

It may seem unusual to discuss procurement practices in a book about multicultural research, but my past experiences in dealing with purchasing departments compels me to discuss a few experiences I believe directly impact the quality of multicultural research. These insights are derived primarily from my past experiences conducting research studies of procurement practices for several municipal and state agencies, which involved many surveys and in-depth interviews of minority and woman-owned business owners. Based on these studies, I will argue that the traditional procurement process provides too many opportunities for buyers to bend the rules and reward favored vendors with contracts that are often based on factors other than merit or "best value." These experiences — which include public and private contracting at local, statewide and national levels — are discussed anecdotally but nevertheless reflect some of the unpleasant realities of the procurement world.

The Absence of a Research IQ

When buying research services, it should come as no surprise that buyers of research or purchasing agents may lack the technical knowledge and experience related to the complexities of conducting multicultural research studies. Lacking the relevant knowledge, purchasing agents will likely struggle to translate the research needs of a department into a coherent request for bids or proposals. This difficulty is often illustrated in requests for proposals (RFPs) by the inclusion of vague criteria, misguided specifications for sample size, confusion about the sample margin of error, and indifference to incidence levels and weighting. Regarding multicultural research studies, a requirement for non-English language questionnaires and bilingual interviewers is often omitted despite the large presence of Latinos and Asians that often prefer a native-language interview or survey. While experience in conducting studies of multicultural communities may seem like an important asset in surveying a diverse community, purchasing agents are often clueless about its necessity. The budgets allocated for multicultural studies are often inadequate despite the fact that they are typically more expensive to conduct, a trend that compromises the quality of the research study. The combined effect of a limited research IQ and poor funding forces the buyers of research to place less weight on vendor credentials and experience, while placing more weight on the lowest bid. In the long run, the consequences of these missteps are detrimental to the quality of multicultural research studies and decisions based on these studies.

Evaluating Bidders

Buyers of research will occasionally manage competitive bids or proposals in a manner that limits the inclusion of vendors that may be otherwise qualified to conduct a multicultural research study. For example, financial statements are sometimes required as part of a proposal, but it is not clear how financial information about a vendor is utilized — that is, are larger firms with more impressive financial statements rated better than smaller firms? Presumably, if concern about a vendor's financial standing is important to know in the context of research, why not check a vendor's past references to verify their financial performance on a past contract? Another annoying practice is the abrupt cancellation of a competition which is followed closely by initiating a second competition for the same request for proposals. In one competition, a large urban school district requested a large-scale telephone survey study in multiple languages and a survey vendor with experience and facilities to conduct the surveys. Interestingly, only one company submitted a proposal by the required deadline, which was not that surprising since there were not many research vendors with the requested multilingual capabilities in this community. Rather than award the contract to this company, however, the procurement department decided to re-issue the competition because "they had not received a sufficient number of proposals to award the contract." It is perhaps more likely, however, that the procurement department had decided to provide more time for a preferred vendor to submit a proposal, and subsequently awarded the contract to a telemarketing vendor who had minimal experience with survey research.

Another disturbing practice involved a competition for a sizable airport contract. The procurement staff had received a proposal via FedEx which was confirmed by airport staff but was mysteriously "lost." The research team was not successful in obtaining this contract despite a delayed second submission. This practice illustrates the extent to which research buyers will go to limit the competition and award a contract to a preferred vendor.

Evaluation of Proposals

Vendor research proposals are usually rated along several dimensions, such as technical knowledge, proposed budget, credentials, past performance on similar studies, and references. The checking of vendor references would seem to be an extremely important part of the evaluation process, especially as it relates to past performance on similar studies related to multicultural communities. In several competitions when a less qualified research vendor was selected by the evaluation committee, follow-up calls by purchasing staff to check vendor references were not consistently performed. Which begs the question: how is it possible to rate a vendor's past performance without checking their references?

In some competitive bids, procurement staff *created new criteria* that were not part of the original bid specifications for the purpose of disqualifying a low bidder that was likely to be awarded the contract. Although organizations usually provide a process for vendors to protest a bid or contract award, the timely resolution of these protests is not always a priority to purchasing managers. By taking their time, it appears that purchasing staff are hopeful the vendor submitting the protest will simply tire of waiting, become frustrated, and simply go away. In short, bid protests can be dead-end alleys.

Favored Survey Results

In several competitions, it was apparent that some research vendors continued to win competitive research contracts year after year with the same public agency, even when other vendors had proposed lower bids or were technically more competent. The strong bond between such buyers and the favored vendors is difficult to break, even when the favored vendor fails to meet the contract objectives or delivers a sub-standard service. In some cases, the organization may be very satisfied with the survey results produced by the favored vendor, and reluctant to change the conclusions reached by a favored vendor. Such appears to be the case for a local municipality that often boasted about the high citizen satisfaction ratings of city services they have consistently obtained over several years, despite its persistent problems with pot holes, stray dogs, high poverty, crime, police shortages, gas explosions, a poor emergency response system, and other issues. Indeed, how is it possible to achieve such fabulous satisfaction ratings while the city continues to experience such problems in its services? In reviewing the methodology employed by the city's survey vendor that consistently gets this survey contract, it was discovered that specific segments of residents were being systematically excluded from participating in the survey — residents who would be more likely to have negative opinions about city services, such as the lower income, immigrants, renters, less educated persons, non-English speakers, and younger residents. Was the city really doing a great job in delivering its services, or was it just "stacking the deck" by using a survey vendor that would guarantee the positive ratings year after year?

Intellectual Property Concerns

In 2007, the American Association for Public Opinion Research, of which I am a member, issued a memorandum about a practice that was becoming an increasing problem among its members.[167] "RFP Plagiarism" was described in this memorandum as follows:

> In 2006, several AAPOR members brought a troublesome issue to the attention of the Standards Committee. They submitted a proposal to a client. The client did not fund their proposal, but subsequently took some or all of the study design from the proposal and incorporated it into a new "Request for Proposals" [RFP].

This theft of intellectual property comes as somewhat of a shock to research practitioners who are accustomed to disclosing in some detail the methodology that they are proposing for a research study, particularly if they are using an innovative approach that is relatively unknown by other research practitioners. What often happens in these competitive situations is that the research buyer decides to award the contract to a lower bidder and incorporates or "steals" the innovative ideas provided by another bidder without permission or compensation. The process to defend yourself against theft of intellectual property can be lengthy and expensive with much uncertainty about its outcome. The lesson to be learned is that it is probably better to avoid disclosing too much detail to potential research buyers about an innovative methodology in your proposals, and to ensure that your proposal is properly documented with the appropriate copyright and confidentiality statements.

Contract Compliance

Public agencies require a considerable number of documents and certifications in order to qualify for a public contract. Sometimes the documentation serves to discourage qualified research vendors from competing for public contracts, although the intent is to encourage broader participation by all types of vendors and ensure compliance with standards defined by public contracts. Compliance regulations, however, do not always achieve their intended purposes. In one city contract, a subcontractor had to sue a prime contractor because they were not in compliance with the amount of the sub-contract that they had agreed to pay in a local city contract. Despite a defined scope of work for a sub-contract, the prime contractor's staff decided to complete part of the scope of work that was supposed to be conducted by the sub-contractor -— which involved several thousand dollars. When the issue was brought to the attention of the city staff, they felt that it was not their responsibility to decide on contracting issues between a prime and subcontractor, and subsequently forced the subcontractor to sue the prime contractor for breach of contract. Fortunately, the subcontractor was able to recover most of the contract dollars that they were owed but felt that the city staff had literally thrown them under the bus on this issue. It seems ironic that a public entity would require considerable documentation and certifications to ensure that a prime contractor honors a subcontract agreement with a vendor, and yet refuses to get involved when a prime contractor fails to honor their subcontract agreement. Thus, contract compliance in public contracts leaves considerable room for improvement.

Chapter Summary

The procurement process provides many opportunities for buyers of research to undermine the quality of a multicultural research study. The research practitioner who is responsible for submitting proposals or bids should consider incorporating some of the following recommendations in future competitions for multicultural research studies and perhaps research studies in general:

- Do not assume that the research buyer or purchasing agent understands the specifications that they have articulated in a request for proposal or bid. Take the opportunity to request clarifications and details about the work that you will be required to perform if awarded the contract. In addition, it may be helpful to explain some of the more complex research concepts in your proposal in non-technical terms in order to improve its comprehension by procurement staff who will evaluate the merits of the proposals.

- Challenge requests for financial statements in requests for proposals. Sometimes this requirement can be removed if an argument is made that your attorney discourages sharing such information unless it is a tax matter or loan application. It makes more sense to direct such requests to past clients who can vouch for the vendor's financial performance on a particular contract.

- Challenge procurement agents if you discover that the references that you provided were not contacted by procurement staff prior to making a contract award. Evaluation scores that are not based on verified past performance should be subject to challenge.

- Bid protests, especially in public contracting, often fail to bring attention to the poor performance of a favored vendor. It would probably be more useful to focus public attention on the wasted tax dollars that are being spent on survey vendors who continue to obtain contracts despite their poor performance and explore the potential for public corruption.

- To avoid the potential for RFP plagiarism by research buyers, make it a habit to provide a minimum of detail about an innovative methodology that is being proposed. It is not necessary to disclose the details of your magic black box — just explain the required inputs, the results, and its benefits. Thus, if a contract is awarded to another bidder, you can minimize the chances for theft of your innovative ideas. Importantly, you need to file the appropriate copyrights, trademarks or patents to protect your trade secrets.

- When all else fails, be prepared to take legal action if a contractor fails to honor a contract for services or attempts to change the scope of work without your agreement. Contract compliance forms that are intended to discourage contractors from failing to comply with their contractual agreements with other vendors are not consistently enforced by procurement staff and leaves one vulnerable to economic losses.

Research buyers, on the other hand, are likely to improve the quality of multicultural research by expanding their own knowledge of basic research principles, especially regarding multicultural communities, and doing a better job of checking vendor references and capabilities. Importantly, research buyers should avoid the practice of awarding contracts to favored vendors who continue to provide research services that fall below industry standards — a clear misuse of public and private funds. Without a doubt, a well-informed procurement professional can play a critical role in ensuring that the highest standards are applied in multicultural research studies simply by selecting the vendor that is best qualified to conduct the study.

Chapter 11: Expanding Your Analytic Tools with GIS

Studies of multicultural populations in the U.S. have often relied on traditional methodologies — such as surveys, focus groups, and ethnographies — to describe their cognitive, affective and behavioral characteristics. While these approaches are useful for studies of multicultural persons, there are occasions in which other approaches can expand our knowledge regarding their quality of life. One suggested addition to your analytic toolbox is the use of geographic information systems (GIS) that can be used to analyze a broad range of secondary data sources provided by federal agencies.

GIS and Secondary Data Sources

While the Census Bureau provides an abundance of information about the demographic and socioeconomic characteristics of multicultural populations, there are numerous other data sources that will allow you to tell a more complete story about the types of environments in which multicultural populations reside. In recent years, my interest in geographic information systems has increased as the use of maps have been used effectively by news sources to bring public attention to important trends related to health, crime, politics, the environment, disease trends, our infrastructure and various other areas. To the benefit of research practitioners, much of this information is produced by federal agencies and can be analyzed by GIS software to produce maps that display important facts about the quality of life of diverse population segments. An additional benefit is that much of the sources of federal data are available at no cost to the analyst.

Following is a short list of some of these secondary sources of information and a few examples of using location-based analysis to enhance your understanding of multicultural populations beyond traditional research methodologies.

1. **Health and Disease Trends.** CDC Wonder is a web portal provided by the Center for Disease Control that provides access to a wealth of public health data and demographic characteristics. You can access CDC Wonder at https://wonder.cdc.gov/. The website includes datafiles related to the following topics:

- AIDS
- Births
- Cancer statistics
- Environment
- Mortality: causes of death, infant death, fetal deash
- Tuberculosis
- Sexually transmitted disease morbidity
- Vaccine adverse event reporting
- And other topics

2. **Crime.** The Federal Bureau of Investigation provides access to crime statistics throughout the U.S. in their FBI Uniform Crime Reports. You can access their website at https://ucr.fbi.gov/crime-in-the-u.s/2017/preliminary-report/home. The following excerpt taken from this website describes the scope of the crime data that is available:

Today, four annual publications, Crime in the United States, National Incident-Based Reporting System, Law Enforcement Officers Killed and Assaulted, and Hate Crime Statistics are produced from data received from over 18,000 city, university/college, county, state, tribal, and federal law enforcement agencies voluntarily participating in the program. The crime data are submitted either through a state UCR Program or directly to the FBI's UCR Program.

3. **Food Access.** The U.S. Department of Agriculture provides access to the Food Access Research Atlas, which presents a spatial overview of food access indicators for low-income and other census tracts using different measures of supermarket accessibility. It also provides food access data for populations within census tracts and offers census tract level data on food access that can be downloaded for community planning or research purposes. You can access this information at the following website: https://www.ers.usda.gov/data-products/food-access-research-atlas

4. **Public Housing.** HUD administers Federal aid to local Housing Agencies (HAs) that manage housing for low-

Expanding Your Analytic Tools with GIS

income residents at rents they can afford. Likewise, HUD furnishes technical and professional assistance in planning, developing, and managing the buildings that comprise low-income housing developments. This dataset provides the location and resident characteristics of public housing development buildings. You can access this information at http://hudgis-hud.opendata.arcgis.com/

5. **Environmental Hazards and Pollutants.** The Environmental Protection Agency provides the public numerous resources to monitor and analyze the quality of our environment, including such topics as air, chemicals and toxic exposure, health, land, waste, cleanup, and water. You can access this information at the following website: https://www.epa.gov/environmental-topics

   In addition, The Center for Effective Government provides reports and analyses of toxic trends in the U.S. Access to this information is provided at the following website: https://www.foreffectivegov.org/

6. **Civil Rights.** Since 1968, the U.S. Department of Education (ED) has conducted the Civil Rights Data Collection (CRDC) to collect data on key education and civil rights issues in our nation's public schools. The collection was formerly administered as the Elementary and Secondary School Survey (E&S Survey). The CRDC collects a variety of information including student enrollment and educational programs and services, most of which is disaggregated by race/ethnicity, sex, limited English proficiency, and disability. The CRDC is a longstanding and important aspect of the ED Office for Civil Rights (OCR) overall strategy for administering and enforcing the civil rights statutes for which it is responsible. Information collected by the CRDC is also used by other ED offices as well as policymakers and researchers outside of ED. You can access this information at: https://www2.ed.gov/about/offices/list/ocr/data.html

Examples of GIS Applications

On the following pages, we provide some examples of spatial analyses using ArcGIS Pro — a powerful GIS software tool that is commonly used in the federal, academic and private sectors (www.esri.com).

The reader should understand that spatial analysis is not

intended as a substitute for survey research in a community, but rather to complement the survey data. For example, in planning a survey sampling strategy, it is helpful to visualize the distribution of the racial-ethnic diversity in a community in order to evaluate the need for stratification. Also, once a random sample of households or telephone numbers is selected, a map can be used to visualize whether the sample distribution reflects the sample specifications — an important step in multicultural studies since samples are often drawn from high-densities census tracts or zip codes that include higher proportions of lower-income residents. Yet another useful application of spatial analysis would be to visualize the geographic distribution of key subgroups of survey respondents following a segmentation analysis to further analyze their access to key establishments, such as hospital, churches, retailers and other firms.

The examples provided in the following pages display data from federal surveys which can be used by survey practitioners to provide context to their study and perhaps help to better understand the environments in which survey respondents reside. These environments often shape the knowledge, attitudes and behaviors that are captured in surveys of the population.

Race-Ethnic Distribution of Boston City Residents

Figure 19 on the following page presents four distinct maps that illustrate the percentage distribution of whites, Asians, Blacks and Hispanics by census tracts in the City of Boston. For each map, a light blue border identifies the census tracts that include 1,000 or more residents for a particular race-ethnic group. Using American Community Survey data, it is possible to produce a similar map for many communities throughout the U.S. The maps clearly show that whites were clustered in the northern and western census tracts; Asians were highly clustered in a limited number of northern census tracts; Blacks were highly clustered in the central and southern census tracts; and Hispanics were more broadly distributed throughout the city but more concentrated in the central and southern census tracts. This type of spatial analyses would be useful in the planning of a sampling strategy.

Figure 19: Distribution of Race-Ethnic Groups by Boston City Census Tracts, 2016

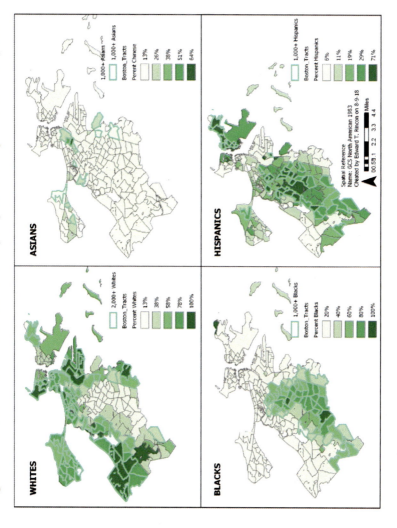

Limited English-Speaking Latinos in the U.S.

Limited English-speaking Latinos were concentrated in the southern and southwestern U.S. counties, although they are expanding into the northeastern part of the U.S. as well (see Figure 20 on the following page). Counties with a higher proportion of limited English-speaking Latinos have a greater need for communications in Spanish and more likely to experience difficulty in understanding and taking action on English-only communications. In planning a national study of Latinos, a survey practitioner could utilize the English-language proficiency data from the American Community Survey to show the counties with the highest concentration of limited English speakers in order to illustrate geographically the need for non-English questionnaires and bilingual interviewing staff.

Figure 20: Percentage Distribution of Limited English-Speaking Latinos by U.S. Counties, 2016

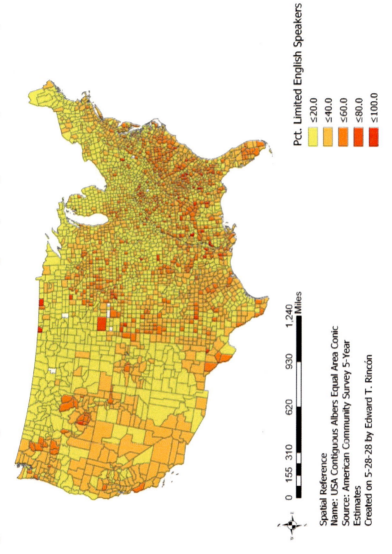

195

Latino Food Expenditures in the U.S.

What is the economic value of food-at-home expenditures for U.S. Latinos, and how is it distributed? In 2016, Latinos spent an estimated $60 billion for food-at-home — an economic benefit for many counties throughout the U.S. (see Figure 21 on the following page). As supermarkets and other food retailers struggle in their competitive industries, Latino food expenditures should provide a good incentive to expand their customer base. Indeed, many food deserts continue to exist in Black and Latino communities in part because supermarket retailers do not bother to analyze the various indicators of economic potential and actual crime data in these communities, opting instead to rely on lingering negative stereotypes. For example, I recently conducted a site location analysis in the City of Dallas to identify food deserts with adequate economic potential to sustain a mainstream supermarket.[168]

Figure 21: Estimated Latino Expenditures for Food at Home by U.S. Counties, 2016

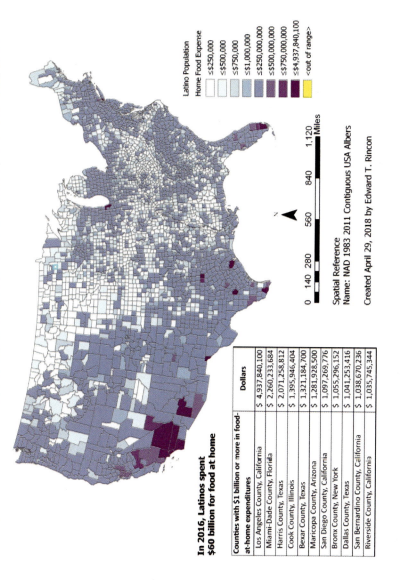

In 2016, Latinos spent $60 billion for food at home

Counties with $1 billion or more in food-at-home expenditures	Dollars
Los Angeles County, California	$ 4,937,840,100
Miami-Dade County, Florida	$ 2,260,233,684
Harris County, Texas	$ 2,071,258,812
Cook County, Illinois	$ 1,395,946,404
Bexar County, Texas	$ 1,321,184,700
Maricopa County, Arizona	$ 1,281,928,500
San Diego County, California	$ 1,097,269,776
Bronx County, New York	$ 1,055,296,152
Dallas County, Texas	$ 1,041,253,416
San Bernardino County, California	$ 1,038,670,236
Riverside County, California	$ 1,035,745,344

The spatial analysis included actual crime data (i.e., robberies, drugs, assaults), aggregate household income, food stamp allocations, and estimates of food expenditures — a broader range of supermarket potential than is typically included in retail site location analyses. The study identified three food deserts or census tracts that could sustain average U.S. supermarket sales of $18 million annually and revealed crime rate patterns that were similar to other parts of the city. Despite the evidence of economic potential for a mainstream supermarket, however, mainstream supermarket retailers continue to avoid these communities — even with a $3 million incentive program that was initiated by the city to encourage investment in these communities. Ironically, what has clearly been missing in these communities is a survey of residents that measures market demand for a mainstream supermarket — a study that would likely provide supermarket decision makers the information that they need to make a smart business decision.

Environmental Hazards

Is there an association between the racial-ethnic composition of Dallas County schools and their proximity to toxic waste sites? According to Figure 22 on the following page, schools with higher proportions of minority populations show greater proximity and exposure to toxic sites. How does this affect the health and learning abilities of these students?

Figure 22: Dallas County Schools by Level of Exposure to Toxic Waste Sites

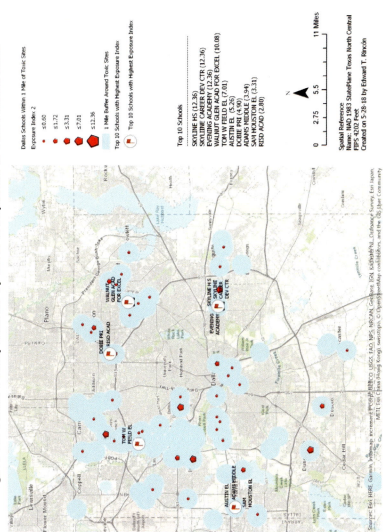

As schools and communities continue the trend toward becoming more segregated by race and income, concern should be devoted to the environmental hazards that are often in close proximity to poor Hispanic and Black schools and neighborhoods. A survey practitioner who is only focused on gathering public opinion and analyzing disparities in academic achievement would obtain an incomplete picture of the challenges that Blacks and Hispanics face in the communities where they reside, such as proximity to liquor stores, food deserts, toxic waste sites and crime hotspots.

Redlining by Coffee Shops

Does Starbucks avoid Dallas County communities where Blacks are concentrated? Without considering any other factors, Figure 23 on the following page would suggest that the answer is "yes." As discussed in a blog that I wrote entitled "Starbucks and unconscious bias? I don't think so," a spatial analysis revealed that few Starbucks coffee shops were located in lower-income Black communities, while higher-income Black communities had better access to Starbucks coffee shops.[169] Similar patterns were observed for Latinos.

Figure 23: Distribution of Blacks in Dallas County and Proximity to Starbucks and Competitive Coffee Stores by Census Tract, 2016

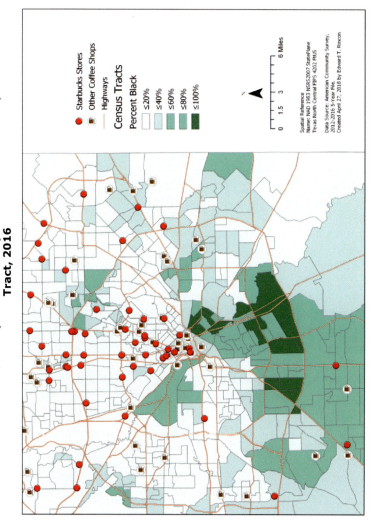

The analysis was prompted by recent attention received by a Starbucks shop in Pennsylvania regarding the mistreatment of two Black men, who were asked to leave the premises even though they were just waiting for a meeting to take place. Although Starbucks required all employees to attend an unconscious bias workshop, it was ironic, it my opinion, that while Starbucks perceived the need to train their employees on the negative impact of unconscious bias, that Starbucks executives were practicing a site location strategy that "consciously" placed their coffee shops in communities that avoided lower-income Blacks and Latinos.

Crime

Are robberies concentrated in specific neighborhoods? Are multicultural communities victimized more often than other communities? Believing that crime is concentrated in communities of color, many retailers and real estate developers will refer to high crime rates as a basis for not doing business in these communities. These perceptions of high crime rates, however, are not necessarily supported by analyses of actual crime rates. The City of Dallas, for example, was recently engulfed in news headlines related to the surge in homicide rates between 2018 and 2019, which prompted Chief of Police Hall to request that Governor Gregg Abbott send state troopers to assist the under-staffed Dallas Police Department to help control the alarming rise in homicides. Curiously, however, the state troopers were directed to monitor the South Dallas community — a segment of the city populated primarily by Blacks and Hispanics and often associated in the news and social science publications with higher crime rates than other sectors of the city. In a more detailed analysis of city crime rates in 2016 from Police Department crime files, however, our research team discovered that the crime rates in South Dallas were not substantially different from other sectors of the city as illustrated by Figure 24 on the following page.[170]

Figure 24: Point Densities of Robberies, Assaults and Narcotics/Drug Incidents in City of Dallas by City Service Areas, 2016

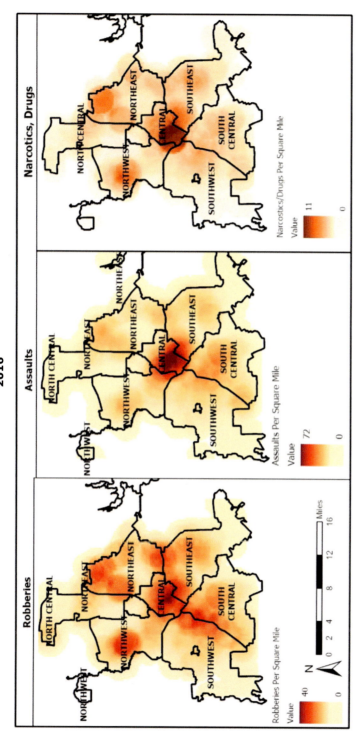

In addition, we discovered that the recent surge in homicide rates between 2018 and 2019 was not properly reported. The actual share of homicides in South Dallas districts *declined* from 66.5 percent in 2018 to 58.0 percent in 2019, while the share of homicides in non-South Dallas districts *increased* from 39.0 percent in 2018 to 47.0 percent in 2019. Thus, it appears that crime incidences that are not properly analyzed and lack geographic detail are likely to lead to misguided interventions, such as the state troopers who were sent to the South Dallas community that perhaps should have been directed to other non-South Dallas council districts experiencing relatively more increases in the number of homicides since 2018. Moreover, the inflated crime rates in South Dallas reported by other social scientists may have also contributed to the crime hysteria at the time.[171]

The survey practitioner who is asked to conduct a survey of community residents regarding perceptions of crime would be well advised to conduct a spatial analysis of actual crime rates to evaluate disparities between perceptions of crime and the geographic distribution of different types of crime. Such an analysis may help to identify census tracts in poor communities where crime rates are not that different from other census tracts, and thus not deserving of the stigma in the real estate industry that discourages interest in economic development.

Public Housing and Social Services

Social services are important to all persons living in a community, especially those with fewer financial resources. The goal of public housing sites is to be located near essential social services, such as childhood education, food assistance, support for seniors, families living in poverty, and childcare services. Figure 25 on the following page displays the various public housing sites throughout Los Angeles County, and their proximity to social services agencies using a 0.25, 0.50 and 1.0-mile distance rings or buffers. It appears that some public housing sites have access to numerous social services agencies, while this access is more limited for other public housing sites — an issue that clearly merits more attention. A survey practitioner who is responsible for conducting a survey that evaluates access and satisfaction with social service agencies may consider it useful to compare the survey results with indicators of physical access to these agencies.

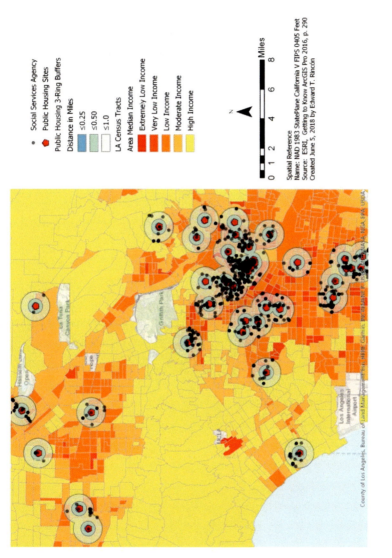

Figure 25: Access to Social Service Agencies for Public Housing Sites in Central Los Angeles County, by Median Household Income

Chapter Summary

Geographic information systems show great promise for expanding a survey practitioner's understanding of the environments in which multicultural persons reside. These environments are often associated with poverty, high crime, over exposure to toxic chemicals, limited shopping choices, and declining infrastructure. By analyzing these environments, perhaps we can enhance our understanding of the knowledge, attitudes and behaviors that research practitioners capture in the more traditional forms of research. The datasets that are available for a GIS analysis are extensive and often publicly available at no cost. Moreover, many of these datasets can be spatially joined by a common geographic unit that allows a more intensive analysis of a broad range of human and environmental characteristics that are often interconnected.

Chapter 12: Future Outlook for Multicultural Research

What does the future hold for research practitioners conducting studies in U.S. multicultural communities? Unquestionably, the challenges are likely to be daunting if industry research practitioners and academic institutions fail to adapt traditional practices and instruction to the changing demographic composition of the U.S. population. Here are five reasons that bring me to this conclusion.

First, Census Bureau projections and other federal surveys confirm that the transformation of the U.S. population will continue well into the future, fueled by the growing numbers of multicultural persons, an increasing number of elderly persons, technological changes that shape the modes of collecting data, and a political climate that is shaping immigration flows and trade with the global community. The changing composition of the U.S. population points to a clear need for research practitioners to place a higher priority on adapting their research tools to ensure that the opinions and behaviors of all segments of the population are not inadvertently excluded. Indeed, it makes little sense to exclude residents of the U.S. population who are unable to speak English very well; who have difficulty seeing and hearing; who cannot read very well; and those who feel uncomfortable sharing their opinions with online surveys. These residents are taxpayers and consumers whose opinions merit the additional effort and expense required to include them in the many research studies conducted in the U.S. In my opinion, the multi-modal, multilingual methodology offers the best promise for achieving this goal since research respondents are not forced to share their opinions in only one language or one mode of data collection. Indeed, research practitioners should be more concerned with optimizing the research experience for study respondents and less concerned with making it more convenient for themselves.

Second, it is incumbent upon research practitioners to expand their knowledge and skill set beyond the traditional curriculum provided in college research methods courses. Having taught at four universities, I have observed minimal attention devoted in academic departments to the methodological problems that a research practitioner is likely to encounter in studies of multicultural populations. Not surprisingly, college textbooks show a similar pattern. For example, following are four textbooks used in U.S. college courses that devote little or no attention to U.S. multicultural methodological issues:

- Don A. Dillman, Jolene D. Smyth and Leah Melani Christian. *Internet, Mail and Mixed-Mode Survey — The Total Design Method*, Third Edition. John Wiley & Sons, Inc., 2009.
- Joel J. Davis. *Advertising Research: Theory and Practice*, Second Edition. Prentiss Hall, 2012.
- Peter R. Stopher and Arnim H. Meyburg. *Survey Sampling and Multivariate Analysis for Social Scientists and Engineers*. Lexington Books, 1979.
- Roger O. Wimmer and Joseph R. Dominick. *Mass Media Research: An Introduction*, 8th Edition, Wadsworth Cengage Learning, 2006.

Until institutions of higher education address this shortcoming, research practitioners will need to explore other resources to expand their "cultural IQ" in the research area. This book is perhaps a starting point toward this goal. In the meantime, research practitioners and students of research should put pressure on academic departments to include a course on multicultural research methods that would complement traditional research methods courses. Online courses would be a suitable option if academic institutions lack the faculty with the requisite training, experiences or desire to teach a course on multicultural research methods. In an earlier chapter, I discussed an excellent model for an online course that is offered by Dr. Felipe Korzenny at Florida International University. The course is focused on Hispanic marketing topics with some attention to research methods. Institutions of higher education would be well advised to study Korzenny's online instructional model and implement a similar approach to teach multicultural research methods. The dramatic growth and composition of the U.S. population will require research professionals who will be able to meet higher standards in conducting multicultural research studies than are currently practiced. A professional certificate in multicultural research methods would be a reasonable way of certifying the achievement of the relevant knowledge and skills in our research industry. Being Hispanic, Black or Asian would be icing on the cake, but not sufficient as a single criterion.

Future Outlook for Multicultural Research

Third, organizations that sponsor or fund studies of multicultural populations should re-evaluate the level of funding allocated for such studies and the criteria for selecting vendors chosen to conduct the research. The complexities associated with multicultural research underscores the need to provide a level of funding that exceeds the level of funding that traditional research studies typically receive. Without this additional level of funding, research vendors are forced to "cut corners" by providing English-only options, reducing sample sizes below statistically recommended levels, and shorten the length of surveys — actions that are known to lower the quality of statistical indicators. The selection of vendors who lack the credentials and experience with multicultural research is another persistent problem that contributes to lower quality studies. In my experience, procurement staff often lack the research acumen and training to properly evaluate the credentials and experience of research vendors and show more serious shortcomings in evaluating the technical elements of research proposals. With limited research knowledge and inadequate funding, purchasing agents sometimes have little choice other than taking the path of least resistance by selecting the lowest bidder, and skipping a thorough review of vendor references. The future outlook for raising the quality of multicultural research will continue to suffer unless concerted changes are made in the areas of funding levels and the evaluation practices of purchasing agents.

Fourth, the addition of GIS tools to analyze the numerous sources of federal secondary data sources would greatly enhance our understanding of the quality of life of multicultural persons beyond the information that is typically generated from smaller scale research studies. The environments in which multicultural persons reside often influence the attitudes and behaviors that are captured in surveys. Consequently, it makes sense to evaluate community factors such as crime, exposure to toxic chemicals, proximity to retail establishments, and other community attributes. Indeed, GIS analyses can also identify the need for further research in our communities. The Pew Research Center exemplifies one of the best models for the integration of survey research and geographic information systems to describe the nation's quality of life.

Lastly, even the most experienced research organizations will need to adapt their strategies to the new reality. Institutions that we hold sacred, like the U.S. Census Bureau, are under siege by government officials who seek to limit their funding and undermine the quality of the information products that our industry utilizes. The Supreme Court's decision to exclude the citizenship question in the 2020 Census was a great sigh of relief to the research industry, although its widespread publicity was successful in raising anxiety levels and still likely to diminish response rates among immigrants. Response rates to general surveys are also likely to suffer in this political climate, underscoring the need for research practitioners to adapt their methodological approaches to the new reality. To underscore this point, we downloaded the self-response rates (dated 7-28-20) provided by the Census Bureau for Dallas County, Texas and produced the following map by census tracts (see Figure 26 below).

As illustrated by this map, the U.S. Census Bureau has achieved a cumulative self-response rate of 62.7 percent to the 2020 Census across the nation, while the response rate was lower for Texas (57.7%) and Dallas County (58.4%). Interestingly, 60 percent of the 644 census tracts in Dallas County revealed self-response rates that were *lower* than the U.S. self-response rate of 62.7 percent. Importantly, most of the "struggling" census tracts, highlighted in yellow, were located in areas where Blacks and Hispanics were concentrated. Assuming a similar pattern emerges in communities throughout the U.S., the Census Bureau will have a greater burden of completing its goals by household in-person interviews. During the current pandemic, the completion of in-person interviews will indeed be a greater challenge.

Figure 26: Dallas County Census 2020 Self-Response Rates by Census Tracts and City Service Areas

387 (60.0%) of the 644 census tracts in Dallas County revealed cumulative self-response rates less than the U.S. rate of 62.7%. As shown by the yellow highlighted areas, most of these tracts were located in the central, southern and northwest sectors where Black and Hispanic residents were concentrated.

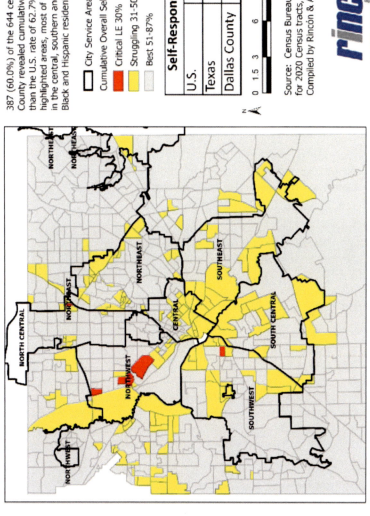

Legend:
- City Service Areas
- Cumulative Overall Self-Response Rate
  - Critical LE 30%
  - Struggling 31-50%
  - Best 51-87%

Self-Response Rate	
U.S.	62.7
Texas	57.7
Dallas County	58.4

Source: Census Bureau Self-Response Rates File for 2020 Census tracts, File accessed on 7-29-20. Compiled by Rincón & Associates LLC.

The adverse political climate and the human misery caused by COVID-19 have required research practitioners to adapt their tools to improve the outcome of their studies. For example, following are some of the practices that I predict are likely to increase in studies of multicultural populations:

- Increased use of wireless telephones for delivering online surveys, already a practice that is being used by the Census Bureau in conducting its Household Pulse Surveys, as well as by Latino Decisions in conducting political polls of U.S. Latinos. Wireless penetration in U.S. households is widespread and captures a broad demographic diversity of respondents.

- Expanded use of remote interviewers to minimize exposure to the virus. With the proper training and monitoring, the transition to remote interviewing has proven to be economical and productive.

- Increased use of consumer panels despite their recognized coverage bias and lower data quality with multicultural populations. More confidence can be expected with the use of panels that employ address-based samples in the recruitment of panel members.

- Larger sample sizes will likely follow to compensate for the expected lower response rates of hard-to-reach segments. However, the expected benefit from larger sample sizes will be diminished unless the research study incorporates other techniques, such as language and mode choices, to capture the hard-to-reach segments of the population.

- Although outsourcing of survey data collection to foreign companies has been a solution for U.S. research firms that lack the multicultural talent and resources, it is likely to increase as restrictive immigration policies reduce the linguistic talent available to U.S. research firms. Unless the appropriate training and monitoring is in place to evaluate the performance of out-sourced studies, it is likely the quality of multicultural studies will be compromised.

In conclusion, our research industry appears to be at a crossroads in choosing between the one path that focuses on the most economic and efficient approach for improving survey quality and response rates, and a second path that aspires for the same objectives by also employing procedures that expand the diversity of the study respondents. I remain optimistic that our research industry will meet the challenge of raising the standards in multicultural research and move in a direction that will ensure the inclusion of all segments of the U.S. population. In my opinion, this can only be achieved by making the research experience more convenient for the many research participants who are willing to take the time to complete the multitude of research studies we send their way. In the meantime, research practitioners would do well to utilize some of the recommended practices, summarized below, that have been discussed throughout this book in planning their next multicultural study.

Project management (Chapter 2): Does your research team have the cultural competence and the needed resources? Ensure that you have team members with multicultural knowledge and expertise, software that supports different language features, sampling experts, and experienced translators. The added complexities in conducting multicultural studies means more time and budget than expected of traditional research studies.

Identifying multicultural persons (Chapter 3): Physical appearance and zip codes with high concentrations of multicultural persons may be easy tools for identifying these segments, but there are better ways. Use current Census or ACS to identify the size and geographic distribution of the multicultural communities, their language characteristics, and obtain feedback from community members regarding commonly used race-ethnic labels, local issues or events that could pose a barrier to study progress.

Sampling multicultural persons (Chapter 4): If you cannot decide which sampling strategy is best, consult a sampling expert. Clear decisions are needed regarding a probability vs. non-probability sampling strategy, the sampling frame with best coverage and access to the target audience, and sample size. The sample design is a task that deserves high priority in the planning process.

Adapting Survey Instrument (Chapter 5): It is wishful thinking to believe that one survey instrument will adequately capture the sentiments of a linguistically and culturally diverse community. Remove the uncertainties by using Census data to understand a community — its racial-ethnic composition, number and types of immigrants, and languages spoken. Conduct pilot or usability studies to check for offensive or outdated terms, evaluate the cultural relevance of key constructs, and identify problems with survey length, grammar, response sets, visual acuity, literacy rates, use of accent or diacritical marks, or placement of skip instructions.

Limitations of traditional data collection methods (Chapter 6): All traditional data collection modes have distinct limitations, but online surveys pose more challenges in capturing multicultural populations. It is easy to understand industry preoccupation with online surveys: they are less costly, easier to implement, and can be deployed on a global scale. However, panels that are often used to select respondents for online surveys generally provide poor coverage of multicultural persons, especially immigrants, non-English speakers, the less educated and older persons. When provided a choice of modes, multicultural respondents tend to favor mail over online modes, but respond very favorably to follow-up telephone interviews. Proceed with caution if you are considering online surveys with multicultural persons and ensure that the panel sampling frame meets your sampling needs.

Use of Incentives (Chapter 6): Yes, money talks, but in surveys it matters when incentives are paid. Incentives generally provide a lift to survey response rates, especially if they are pre-paid rather than promised. Little research is available, however, to guide the best use of incentives in surveys with multicultural populations. There is a great need for our research community to explore incentive options among multicultural persons, including pre-paid vs. promised incentives, sweepstakes, cash vs. non-cash incentives, and perhaps other ideas. Past research shows that Latinos and Asians respond favorably to games of chance. So, there is room for optimism here.

Analysis (Chapter 7): Resist using simple solutions in handling data analytic problems. For example, mean substitution of missing values is easy to implement, but follow-up contacts to survey respondents and imputation from other survey data are preferable techniques, especially when key variables are missing. If most of your surveys by Latinos or Asians are completed in English, this may point to a potential interviewing bias that leads to biased statistical indicators. Other potential problems that will require your analytic attention are response sets, and the appropriate use of current Census data in adjustments to survey data.

Multi-Modal, Multilingual Method (Chapter 8): With a U.S. population that is linguistically and culturally diverse, the traditional practice of using one language and one mode of data collection is hard to justify in the survey industry. Reviews of traditional mixed mode research show excellent potential for improving survey coverage in general populations but offer little guidance regarding its relevance or usefulness for multicultural persons. Multi-modal, multilingual surveys have the best potential for expanding coverage of multicultural persons since they are most likely to experience problems related to lower literacy levels, limited English-language proficiency, visual acuity and hearing impairments.

GIS analysis (Chapter 11): A survey respondent may not be satisfied with the healthcare that they are receiving, but do they have access to a healthcare provider that meets their needs? A GIS analysis could easily address the issue of access by illustrating the location of healthcare providers and patients in a geographic area. Adding environmental information to survey data has the potential of expanding our understanding of multicultural persons and the structural challenges that they face in their communities.

Focus Group Research (Chapter 9): With few exceptions, many U.S. focus group facilities are not extending the needed welcome mat to multicultural qualitative projects. This lack of readiness and interest in implementing multicultural focus group studies stems from such factors as a lack of understanding of the multicultural communities in their own backyards and minimal multicultural resources such as staffing, literature, and language support. The recruitment strategies of multicultural persons often result in more acculturated, English speakers and fewer unacculturated immigrants who are more comfortable communicating in their native languages. Moderators and translators are generally available but not always formally trained or experienced. Asian moderators are especially more challenging to coordinate in qualitative projects. There is usually a need to enhance the visibility of the facility location using bilingual maps to avoid no shows or late shows. Bilingual hostess support is not always present but necessary for non-English speaking groups.

Procurement Practices (Chapter 10): Procurement practices are sometimes at odds with the goal of funding high-quality multicultural research studies. Procurement personnel who write specifications for proposals and evaluate vendor submissions often lack the research acumen to evaluate the technical merit of proposals related to multicultural research. Procurement staff are inconsistent in checking vendor references, fail to include minimum eligibility criteria for past vendor training and experience, and often choose the proposal with the lowest bid regardless of past performance. To address these challenges, proposers should consider adding explanations of key concepts about research and its multicultural complexities so that proposal evaluators can better understand how the proposed study will address the desired objectives. The practice by purchasing staff of placing a high value on the lowest bid, however, should not unduly influence your ability to submit a realistic budget for the study. Importantly, proposers should limit the amount of proprietary information provided on proposals to avoid the potential for theft of their intellectual property and mark their proposals accordingly.

Future Outlook for Multicultural Research (Chapter 12): Academics and research practitioners: Are you listening? Knowledge about the special problems associated with multicultural research studies is missing in traditional research methods textbooks and college courses, a reality that continues to threaten the quality of multicultural research. Members of the research industry should show some leadership by including adequate sample sizes of key U.S. multicultural segments — such as Latinos, Blacks and Asians — in studies that analyze the influence of race-ethnicity and language factors on key study indicators. The emerging body of knowledge from the research should be integrated into traditional academic textbooks and courses so that future generations of research practitioners will be better positioned to design and implement high-quality research studies of multicultural populations.

About the Author

Edward T. Rincón is President of Rincón & Associates LLC, a research firm that has been dedicated to improving the cultural intelligence of organizations using sound research practices, publications, and speaking engagements. In addition to his research practice, Dr. Rincón has taught various courses at academic institutions on such topics as mass communications research, statistics, Hispanic marketing and survey research methods. He received his master's and doctorate degrees from The University of Texas at Austin with a concentration in psychological quantitative methods. More recently, he completed a Master's Certificate in Geographic Information Systems from The University of Texas at Dallas. He has consulted as an expert witness to members of the legal community on such topics as demographic trends, advertising practices, methodological soundness of opinion polls, trademark confusion, and the composition of jury pools. His research interests have focused on measurement biases that are embedded in societal systems and organizations that impact the quality of life for U.S. residents, including aptitude testing in secondary and higher education institutions, environmental hazards, public contracting, food insecurity, media usage and healthcare practices. He is an Associate with the SMU Tower Center for Political Studies and a member of the American Association for Public Opinion Research. Dr. Rincón can be contacted as follows:

Rincón & Associates LLC
6060 N. Central Expressway, Suite 500
Dallas, Texas 75206
Email: edward@rinconassoc.com
Website: www.rinconassoc.com
Telephone: 214-750-3800

Appendix

List of Selected U.S. Multicultural Research Firms

- Rincón & Associates LLC - http://www.rinconassoc.com
- American Dimensions - http://www.newamericandimensions.com/
- Hunter & Miller Group - http://www.peppermiller.net/
- 361 Degrees Consulting - http://www.361degrees.net/
- Interviewing Services of America - http://www.isacorp.com/

List of White Papers by Rincón & Associates

Access these white papers at: http://www.rinconassoc.com/category/publications

- Texas: Quality of Life at the Crossroads
- New Test Reveals Your Latino IQ
- Are Latinos Over-Estimating Their Language Abilities with Self-Reported Measures?
- A Research Primer for Spanish-Language Newspapers
- The Dream Act: A Win-Win Situation
- Measurement Bias: The Value of a Second Opinion

Viewpoints in Selected Publications

- A tight Texas Senate race exposes the true meaning of political 'Hispandering' 10/15/18 Available at http://latinalista.com/palabrafinal/politics/guest-voz-a-tight-texas-senate-race-exposes-the-true-meaning-of-political-hispandering
- Texas lawmakers have turned our state into a Wild West show with campus carry, *Dallas Morning News*, Available at https://www.dallasnews.com/opinion/commentary/2016/03/18/edward-t.-rincon-texas-lawmakers-have-turned-our-state-into-a-wild-west-show-with-campus-carry

- Sanctuary City Politics: Wolves in Sheep's Clothing, *Trib Talk*, Available at https://www.tribtalk.org/2017/02/13/sanctuary-city-politics-wolves-in-sheeps-clothing/
- Supermarkets Shouldn't Overlook Native-Born Latino Consumers, *Progressive Grocer*, 8/7/18, Available at https://progressivegrocer.com/supermarkets-shouldnt-overlook-native-born-latino-consumers

List of Blogposts by Rincón & Associates

Access these blogposts at:
http://thecultureofresearch.blogspot.com

- CDC Blunders in Excluding Communities of Color Among High Risk Groups for COVID-19 (7/30/20)
- Governor Greg Abbott Fumbles the Ball on COVID-19 (6/30/20)
- Does Unconscious Bias Explain Police Brutality? (6/14/20)
- Texas GOP Reveals Cowardice on Mail-In Ballot Issue (5/28/20)
- Missing Race-Ethnicity Data Complicates COVID-19 Mortality Counts, But the Solution is Simple (4/16/20)
- Undermining the 2020 Census: Trump's Toxic Brew of Crime, Hysteria and Immigrants (2/17/20)
- What Hurts South Dallas More — Crime or the Hasty Reporting of Crime? (1/10/20)
- Unconscious Bias at Starbucks? I Don't Think so. (4/18/18)
- Amazon's Investment in U.S. Immigrants (1/16/18)
- Takata Recall Campaign: Consumer Safety Threatened by Corporate Greed and Government Missteps (1/9/17)
- Texas Rangers Stadium: Questionable Polling Practices in a High-Stakes Competition (10/24/16)
- Journalistic Blind Spots (9/12/16)
- UNT Dallas School of Law: A Work in Progress (8/19/16)
- Latino Voter Turnout: Time to Re-fresh Our (8/3/16)

- Political Leaders Often Embrace Positive Satisfaction Ratings, But Should They? (6/8/16)
- Latino Leadership Development in Dallas: Some Room for Optimism (5/16/16)
- Donald Trump: The New Chicken Little (8/21/15
- Is Your Multicultural Research Misleading Marketing Decisions? (8/6/15)
- Some Simple Truths About Language Usage Among U.S. Latinos (6/24/15)
- Latinos and the Dallas Legal Community: A Case of Two-Way Myopia (5/28/15)
- Politicians' Reckless Disregard for Our Quality of Life (4/22/15)
- Is Mayor Rawlings Hiding Behind Inflated Satisfaction Ratings of Dallas Residents? (4/2/15)
- Does Dallas Need a Mayoral Election This Year? (2/26/15
- The Texas Recipe for Muting the Hispanic Voice in Public Opinion Polls (4/29/13)
- National Poll on Arizona's Immigration Law May Be Misleading (5/13/10)
- Segmenting Multicultural Consumers: Old Dinosaurs Die Slowly (7/21/09)
- Multicultural Research in Need of a Facelift (7/16/09)

List of Multicultural Marketing Publications with Some Attention to Research

- David Morse. *Multicultural Intelligence: Eight Make-or-Break Rules for Marketing to Race, Ethnicity and Sexual Orientation*, Updated and Revised 2nd Edition, Paramount Marketing Publishing, Inc., 2009.
- Felipe Korzenny, Sindy Chapa, and Betty Ann Korzenny. *Hispanic Marketing: The Power of the New Latino Consumer*, 3rd Edition, Routledge, 2017.
- Pepper Miller and Herb Kemp. *What's Black About It?* Paramount Publishing, 2006.

- Pepper Miller. *Black Still Matters in Marketing*, Paramount Publishing, 2012.

News Source About Multicultural Marketing Trends and Events

- Multicultural News: http://multicultural.com/

References

1. U.S. Census Bureau (March 2011). Overview of Race and Hispanic Origin (2010 Census Briefs), Washington, DC.

2. Weeks, M. (2017, March 2). UGA report: Minority groups driving U.S. economy. *USA Today*.

3. U.S. Census Bureau (2018, March). Population Estimates and Projections, Demographic Turning Points for the United States: Population Projections for 2020 to 2060.

4. Chishti, M. and Hipsman. F. (2015, May 21). *In historic shift, new migration flows from Mexico fall below those from China and India.* Migration Policy Institute. Retrieved from https://www.migrationpolicy.org/article/historic-shift-new-migration-flows-mexico-fall-below-those-china-and-india.

5. ETC Institute (2016). *2016 City of Dallas Direction Finder Survey Final Report*.

6. Rincón, E. T. (2004). *The Latino Television Study*. Sponsored by the National Latino Media Coalition with funding by ABC and CBS Television. Retrieved from http://www.rinconassoc.com/wp-content/uploads/2014/01/p9_tvstudy.pdf.

7. Rincón, E. T. (2016, January). How DPS can improve its system of recording race/ethnicity during traffic stops. *Dallas News*. Retrieved from https://www.dallasnews.com/opinion/commentary/2016/01/27/edward-t.-rincon-how-dps-can-improve-its-system-of-recording-raceethnicity-during-traffic-stops.

8. Ibid.

9. Holland, A.T. & Palaniappan, L.P. (2012, June 22). Problems in the collection and interpretation of Asian-American health data: Omission, aggregation, and extrapolation. *Ann. Epidemiol*. 2(6).

10 Ang, S. and Vann Dyne, L. (2015). *Handbook of cultural intelligence: Theory measurement and application.* New York: Routledge.

11 Ibid.

12 Williams, Ph.D., R.L. (2006). *Black Intelligence Test of Cultural Homogeneity (B.I.T.C.H).* Retrieved from https://eric.ed.gov/?id=ED070799.

13 Aiken, Jr., L.R. (1971) Chitling Test. Available at http://psychlotron.org.uk/resources/issues/A2_AQA_issues_chitlingtest.pdf.

14 Morse, David R. (2009). *Multicultural Intelligence.* New York: Paramount Market Publishing, Inc.

15 Hoffman, K.M., Trawalter, S., Axt, J.R., and Oliver, M.N.(2016, April 19). Racial bias in pain assessment and treatment recommendations, and false beliefs about biological differences between blacks and whites. *PNAS* Vol. 113 No. 16.

16 Dallas Morning News (1999, August 14). Pepper spray remarks backfire on department. Cited from *Los Angeles Times*.

17 Rincón, E. T. (2013, November 4). *New test reveals your Latino IQ.* White Paper Series. Dallas: Rincón & Associates.

18 Rincón, E. T. (2012, July 31). Want to fix the diversity problem? Start with colleges. *Advertising Age.* Retrieved from www.adage.com.

19 Ibid. Rincón, E. T. (2016). How DPS can improve its system of recording race-ethnicity during traffic stops.

20 Ibid. Holland, A.T. & Palaniappan, L.P.

21 Marín, G. & B.V. Marín. (1991). *Research with Hispanic Populations. Applied Social Research Methods*, Volume 23. Newbury Park CA: Sage Publications.

22 Livingston, G, and Brown, A. (2017, May 18). *Intermarriage in the U.S. 40 years after Loving v. Virginia.* Pew Research Center.

23 Ethnic Technologies. Retrieved from http://www.ethnictechnologies.com/product/e-tech/.

References

24 Fiscella, K. and Fremont, A.M. (2006). Use of geocoding and surname analysis to estimate race and ethnicity. *Health Services Research*, 41-4, Part I. Retrieved from https://www.ncbi.nlm.nih.gov/pmc/articles/PMC1797082.

25 Taylor, P., Lopez, M.H., Martinez, J., and Velasco, G. (2012, April 4). *When labels don't fit: Hispanics and their views of identity*. Pew Research Center. Retrieved from www.pewhispanic.org.

26 Sanchez, G. R. (2012). *A closer look at Latino pan-ethnic identity*. Available at http://hispanicad.com/blog/news-article/had/business/taking-closer-look-latino-pan-ethnic-identity. Seattle WA: Latino Decisions.

27 Census Bureau. (2012, August 8). *Results from the 2010 Census race and Hispanic origin alternative questionnaire experiment*. Press conference, U.S. Census Bureau, Washington, D.C.

28 Fontenot, Jr, A. E. (2018, January 26). *Using two separate questions for race and ethnicity in 2018 end-to-end Census test and 2020 Census*. U.S. Census Bureau.

29 Miller, P. and Kemp, H. (2005). *What's Black About It?* New York: Paramount Market Publishing, Inc.

30 Newport, F. (2007, September 28). *Black or African American?* The Gallup Organization. Retrieved from http://www.gallup.com /poll/28816/black-african-american.aspx.

31 Advertising Age Supplement (2012, April 23). *In plain sight: The black consumer opportunity*.

32 Forson, T.S. (2018, February 21). Who is an 'African American'? Definition evolves as USA does. *USA Today*. Retrieved from http://www.usatoday.com.

33 Pew Research Center (2013, April 4). *The Rise of Asian Americans*.

34 Ibid. Holland, A.T. & Palaniappan, L.P.

35 Dutwin, D. & Trent, Buskirk, T.D. (2017). Apples to Oranges or Gala versus Golden Delicious? Comparing

data quality of non-probability Internet samples to low response rate probability samples. *Public Opinion Quarterly*, Vol. 81, Special Issue 2017, pp. 213-240.

36 Kennedy, C., Mercer, A., Keeter, S., Hatley, N., McGeeney, K. and Gimenez, A. (2016, May 2). *Evaluating online non-probability surveys*. Pew Research Center.

37 U.S. Census Bureau (2017, November 15). *Declining mover rate driven by renters*, Census BureauPress release, U.S. Census Bureau, Washington, D.C.

38 Dataman Group, Available at http://www.datamangroup.com.

39 Kennedy, C. and Hartig, H. (2019, February 27). *Response rates in telephone surveys have resumed their decline.* Pew Research Center. Retrieved from http://www.pewresearch.org/fact-tank/2019/02/27/response-rates-in-telephone-surveys-have-resumed-their-decline/.

40 Seltzer, J.A. (2017, December 6). Selzer: *Study on data quality*. Retrieved from www.Huffington Post.com.

41 Keeter, S., Doherty, C., Dimock, M., and Christian, L. (2012, May 12). *Assessing the representativeness of public opinion surveys*. The Pew Research Center for The People & the Press.

42 Keeter, S., Hatley, N., Kennedy,C. and Lau, A. (2017, May 15). *What low response rates mean for telephone surveys*. Pew Research Center.

43 Sanborn, J. (2017, July 20). *Why the death of malls is about more than shopping*. Retrieved from www.time.com.

44 Heckathorn, D.D. (1997, May). Respondent-driven sampling: A new approach to the study of hidden populations. *Social Problems*, Vol. 44, No.2.

45 Goela, S. and Salganik, M.J. (2010, April 13). *Assessing respondent driven sampling*. Vol. 107 No. 15. Proceedings of the National Academy of Sciences of the United States of America. Retrieved at http://www.pnas.org/content/107/15/6743.full.

References

46 Brickman-Bhutta, C. (2009, October 7). Not by the books: Facebook as sampling frame. *Sociological Methods and Research*, Vol. 41, Issue 1, pp. 57-88.

47 Valdez, R.S., Guterbock, T.M., Thompson, M.J., Reilly, J.D., Menefee, H.K., Bennici, M.S., Williams, I.C. and Rexrode, D.L. (2014, October 27). *Beyond traditional advertisements: leveraging Facebook's social structures for research recruitment*. Retrieved from https://www.ncbi.nlm.nih.gov/pmc/articles/PMC4259909/.

48 McGeeney, K. (2016, January 5). *Pew will call 75% cell phones for surveys in 2016*. Pew Research Center.

49 Guterbock, T. (2018, October 25). Communication received via email.

50 Heimlich, R. (2012, May 24). *Pollsters face challenges in getting survey respondents*. FactTank News in the Numbers. Pew Research Center. Retrieved from http://www.pewresearch.org/fact-tank/2012/05/24/pollsters-face-challenges-in-getting-survey-respondents/.

51 Cohn, D. and Passel, J.S. (2016, August 8). *A record 60.6 million Americans live in multigenerational households*. Pew Research Center, Factank News in the Numbers.

52 Rincon, E.T. (2011, May 1). *Are Latinos over-estimating their language abilities on self-reported measures?* (White Paper Series, No. 2011-01). Dallas: Rincón & Associates.

53 Ibid. Marín, G. & Marín, B.V. (1991).

54 Taras, V. (2008, August 19). *Instruments for measuring acculturation*. Retrieved from http://ucalgary.ca/~taras/_private/Acculturation_Survey_Catalogue.pdf.

55 Wallace, P.M., Pomery, E.A., Latimer, A.E., Martinez, J.L. and Salovey, P. (2010, Feb 1). A review of acculturation measures and their utility in studies promoting Latino health. *Hispanic Journal of Behavioral Sciences*, 32(1): 37—54.

56 Coyle, E. (2020). Accessing race, ethnicity, foreign born and ancestry data. U.S. Census Bureau. Retrieved from https://www2.census.gov/about/training-workshops/2020/2020-01-29-clmso-presentation.pdf?#.

57 New American Dimensions and interTrend Communications (2009, March). *Asian Indians in the U.S.*

58 Perez, B. (2020 June 11). *A data driven approach to language determination*. Presentation at the American Association for Public Opinion Research Virtual Conference.

59 Ibid., Rincon, E. T. *Are Latinos over-estimating their language abilities on self-reported measures?*

60 Ibid. New American Dimensions and interTrend Communications.

61 Interviewing Service of America (2002, July). *TFC Subscriber Study*.

62 Pew Research Center (2013, April 4). *The Rise of Asian Americans*.

63 Guterbock, T. (2018, October 25). Communications via email.

64 Wang, L., Sha, M. and Yuan, M. (2017). Cultural fitness in the usability of U.S. Census Internet survey. Survey Practice, Vol. 10, No. 3, 2017. Available at www.surveypractice.org.

65 Elliott, J. (2017, December 29). Trump Justice Department pushes for citizenship question on Census, alarming experts. *ProPublica*. Retrieved from https://www.propublica.org/article/trump-justice-department-pushes-for-citizenship-question-on-census-alarming-experts.

66 Lind, D. (2019, February 15). The census lawsuit headed straight to the Supreme Court, explained." *Vox*. Retrieved from https://www.vox.com/policy-and-politics/2019/2/15/18226578/census-supreme-court-lawsuit-citizenship-question.

67 Manuel, O. (2020, February 20). Majority of U.S. adults incorrectly believe 2020 census will ask about

References

citizenship, survey finds. *Dallas Morning News*. Retrieved from https://www.dallasnews.com/news/2020/02/20/majority-of-us-adults-incorrectly-believe-2020-census-will-ask-about-citizenship-survey-finds/.

68 Wang, H.L. (2018, May 11). Many noncitizens plan to avoid the 2020 Census, test run indicates. *National Public Radio*. Retrieved from www.npr.org.

69 Kissam, E., Mines, R. Quezada, C., Intili, J.A., and Wadsworth, G. (2019, January). *San Joaquin Valley Latino Immigrants: Implications for survey findings for Census 2020 — Executive summary*. Retrieved from https://cviic.org/san-joaquin-valley-latino-immigrants-and-the-2020-census/.

70 Hyer, V. (2019, January 24). *New study examines barriers, attitudes and motivators toward participating in the upcoming 2020 Census*. Census Bureau Public Information Office. Retrieved from https://www.census.gov/newsroom/press-releases/2019/2020-census-cbams.html.

71 Rincon, E. T. (2020). Undermining the 2020 Census: Trump's toxic brew of crime, hysteria and immigrants. *The Culture of Research Blog*, retrieved from https://thecultureofresearch.blogspot.com/2020/02/undermining-2020-census-trumps-toxic.html.

72 Nowrasteh, A. (2018). *Criminal immigrants in Texas: Illegal immigrant conviction and arrest rates for homicide, sex crimes, larceny, and other crimes*. Immigration Research and Policy Brief No. 4, The Cato Institute. Retrieved from https://www.cato.org/publications/immigration-research-policy-brief/criminal-immigrants-texas-illegal-immigrant.

73 Wines, M. (2019). 2020 Census won't have citizenship question as Trump administration drops effort. *New York Times*. Accessed at https://www.nytimes.com/2019/07/02/us/trump-census-citizenship-question.html.

74 Korzenny, F. and Korzenny, B.A. (2005). *Hispanic marketing: A cultural perspective*. New York: Elsevier, Inc.

75 Vital and Health Statistics (2014, February). *Summary of Health Statistics for U.S. Adults: National Health Survey*. Series 10 Number 260. U.S. Department of Health and Human Services, Center for Disease Control, National Center for Health Statistics. Retrieved from https://www.cdc.gov/nchs/data/series/sr_10/sr10_260.pdf.

76 National Center for Education Statistics, *A First Look at the Literacy of American's Adults in the 21st Century*. U.S. Department of Education, Institute of Education Sciences, NCES 2006-470.

77 Dotson, V.M., Kitner-Triolo, M.H., Evans, M.K., and Zonderman, A.B. (2009, July). Effects of race and socioeconomic status on the relative influence of education and literacy on cognitive functioning. *J Int Neuropsychol Soc*. 15(4); pp.580-589.

78 Wang, K. and Sha, M. (2013). A comparison of results from a Spanish and English mail survey: Effects of instruction placement on item missingness. *Survey Methods: Insights from the Field*. Accessed at http://surveyinsights.org/?p=1741.

79 Martin,E., Childs, J.H., DeMaio,T., Hill, J., Reiser,C., Gerber, E., Styles, K., and Dillman, D. (2007, June). *Guidelines for designing questionnaires for administration in different modes*. Retrieved from https://www.census.gov/srd/mode-guidelines.pdf.

80 Survey Research Center. (2016). Guidelines for best practice in cross-cultural surveys. Ann Arbor, MI: Survey Research Center, Institute for Social Research, University of Michigan. Retrieved from http://www.ccsg.isr.umich.edu/.

81 Lavrakas, P.J. (1993). *Telephone survey methods: Sampling, selection and supervision*, Second Edition.

82 Dillman, D.A., Smith, J.D., and Christian, L.M. (2009). Internet, mail, and mixed-mode surveys: The Tailored Design Method. Third Edition. New Jersey: John Wiley & Sons, Inc.

References

83 Ibid.

84 Lavrakas, P.J., Dirksz, G., Lusskin, L. and Ponce, B. Experimenting with the addressee line in a mail survey of Hispanic households. *Survey Practice*, Vol. 9, No.4, 2016. Available at www.surveypractice.com.

85 Kennedy,C. and Hartig, H. (2019, February 27). *Response rates in telephone surveys have resumed their decline*. Pew Research Center. Retrieved from http://www.pewresearch.org/fact-tank/2019/02/27/response-rates-in-telephone-surveys-have-resumed-their-decline/.

86 Retrieved from https://en.wikipedia.org/wiki/Telephone_Consumer_Protection_Act_of_1991.

87 TCPA Rules, Retrieved from https://transition.fcc.gov/cgb/policy/TCPA-Rules.pdf.

88 Ibid, Dillman, D.A., et al.

89 Rincón, E. T. (2008). *Dallas/Fort Worth Multicultural Study*. Dallas: Rincón & Associates.

90 Ibid. Rincon, E. T. (2011, May 1).

91 Cohn, D., and Passell, J.S. (2016, August 11). *A record 60.6 million Americans live in multigenerational households*. Pew Research Center.

92 Kohut, A., Keeter, S., Doherty, C. Dimock, M. and Christian, L. (2012, May 5). *Assessing the representativeness of public opinion surveys*. Pew Research Center for the People and the Press.

93 Kennedy, C., McGeeney, K. and Keeter, S. (2016, August 1). *The twilight of landline interviewing*. Pew Research Center.

94 Rincon, E. T. (2016). *Texas Rangers Stadium: Questionable polling practices in a high-stakes competition*. Retrieved from http://thecultureofresearch.blogspot.com/2016/10/texas-rangers-stadium-questionable.html.

95 Ibid.

96 Federal Trade Commission (2014, April). *Consumer fraud in the United States, 2011, The Third Survey.*

97 AARP (2018, January). *AAPI 50-plus fraud research brief.* Retrieved from https://www.aarp.org/research/topics/economics/info-2017/aapi-fraud-survey.html.

98 GFK Knowledge Network, retrieved from http://www.gfk.com/products-a-z/us/knowledgepanel-united-states/.

99 YouGov, Retrieved from https://today.yougov.com/.

100 YouGov, Retrieved from https://today.yougov.com/find-solutions/sectors/academic-and-scientific/.

101 Kennedy,C. Mercer, A., Keeter, S., Hatley,N., McGeeney, K., and Gimenez, A. (2016, May 2). *Evaluating online nonprobability surveys.* Pew Research Center.

102 Meyers, E. (2016, July 20). Why the digital divide between Latinos, whites is almost closed. *Dallas Morning News.* Retrieved from https://www.dallasnews.com/business/technology/2016/07/20/digital-divide-latinos-whites-narrows-immigrants-spanish-speakers-go-online.

103 Tourangeau, R., Maitland, A., Rivero, G., Sun, H., Williams, D, and Yan, T. (2017). Web surveys by smartphone and tablets: Effects on survey responses. *Public Opinion Quarterly*, Vol. 81, Number 4, Winter.

104 FocusVision (2018, October 8). *Five steps to getting the most out of mobile surveys.* Retrieved from https://www.focusvision.com/resources/five-steps-to-getting-the-most-out-of-mobile-surveys/.

105 Edison Research, National Election Pool. Retrieved from http://www.edisonresearch.com/election-polling/.

106 Barreto, M. (2016, November 10). *Lies, damn lies and exit polls.* Latino Decisions. Retrieved from http://www.latinodecisions.com/blog/2016/11/10/lies-damn-lies-and-exit-polls/.

107 Czajka, J.L., and Beyler, A. (2016, June 15). *Declining response rates in federal surveys: Trends and*

References

implications. *Final Report*, Volume 1, Mathematica Policy Research.

108 Ibid, Dillman et al.

109 Riedman, P. (2008, May 27). Details make the difference in Harrah's multiethnic marketing efforts. Ethnic Technologies. Available at http://www.ethnictechnologies.com/details-make-the-difference-in-harrahs/.

110 Medina, J. (2011, August 29). Casino town puts its money on Hispanic market. *The New York Times.*

111 Kulzick, R., Kail, L., Mullenax, S., Shang, H., Kriz, B., Walejko, G., Vines, M., Bates, N., Scheid, S. and Trejo, Y.G. (2019). *2020 Census Predictive Models and Audience Segmentation Report: A New Design for the 21st Century.* U.S. Department of Commerce, Economics and Statistics Administration, U.S. Census Bureau. www.census.gov.

112 Ibid. Korzenny, F. and Korzenny, B.A.

113 Ibid. Marín, G. & Marín, B.V.

114 Morren, M., Gelissen, J.P.T.M, Vermunt, J.K. (2012). Response strategies and response styles in cross-cultural surveys. *Cross-Cultural Research*, 46(3) 255–279.

115 Pew Research Center (2018, February 3). Sampling. Retrieved fromww.pewresearch.org.

116 Wikipedia (2018, Feb 12). The Literary Digest. Retrieved from https://en.wikipedia.org/wiki/The_Literary_Digest

117 Rincon, E. T. (2004, June 3). *Measurement bias: The value of a second opinion.* Dallas: Rincón & Associates. Retrieved from http://www.rinconassoc.com/wp-content/uploads/2014/01/p8_measurement_bias_white_paper.pdf.

118 U.S. Department of Education, Institute of Education Sciences (2006). *A first look at the literacy of America's adults in the 21st century.* National Center for Education Statistics.

119 Ibid. Vital and Health Statistics.

120 U.S. Census Bureau, American Community Survey 1-Year Estimates, 2016. Table B1005D, *Nativity by language spoken at home by ability to speak English for the population 5 years and over (Asian alone),* and Table B16005I, *Nativity by language spoken at home by ability to speak English for the population 5 years and over (Hispanic or Latino).*

121 Ibid. Czajka, J. L. and Beyler, A.

122 Ibid, Dillman et al

123 De Leeuw, E. (2005). To mix or not to mix data collection modes in surveys. *Journal of Official Statistics,* Vol. 21, No. 2, pp. 233-255.

124 U.S. Census Bureau (2014, Jan 30. *American Community Survey Design and Methodology,* Version 2.0. Retrieved from https://www2.census.gov/programs-surveys/acs/methodology/design_and_methodology/acs_design_methodology_ch04_2014.pdf.

125 Ibid, De Leeuw, E.

126 Fowler, F.J., Roman, A.M., Mahmood, R. and Cosenza, C.A. (2016). Reducing nonresponse and nonresponse error in a telephone survey: An informative case study. *Journal of Survey Statistics and Methodology,* (4), 246-262.

127 Link, M. and Mokdad, A. (2006). Can web and mail survey modes improve participation in an RDD-based National Health Surveillance? *Journal of Official Statistics,* Vol. 22, No. 2, pp. 293-312.

128 Dillman, D.A. et al.

129 Ibid.

130 Ibid. De Leeuw, E.

131 Ibid. Dillman, D.A. et al.

132 Santos, R. Personal email communication, May 2, 2017.

133 Ibid. Martin, E. et al.

134 Ansolabehere, S and Schaffner, B.F. (2014). Does survey mode still matter? Findings from a 2010 multi-mode comparison. *Political Analysis,* Vol. 22, Issue 3,

References

Summer. Available at http://people.umass.edu/schaffne/ansolabehere_schaffner_mode2.pdf.

135 Sanders, D., Clarke, H.D., Stewart, M.C. and Whitely, P. (2007). Does mode matter for modeling political choice? *Political Analysis*, Vol.15, No. 3 (Summer 2007), pp. 257-285.

136 Convers, P.D., Wolfe, E.W., Huang, X., and Oswald, F.L. Response rates for mixed-mode surveys using mail and e-mail/web. *American Journal of Evaluation*, January 8, 2008.

137 Guterbock, T. Personal email communication, October 24, 2018.

138 Hox, J., De Leeuw, E., Klausch, T. (2015, September). *Mixed mode research: Issues in design and analysis*. Retrieved from https://www.researchgate.net/publication/313585673_Mixed-Mode_Research_Issues_in_Design_and_Analysis.

139 De Leeuw, E. Personal email communication. September 20, 2018.

140 Hospital Consumer Assessment of Healthcare Providers and Systems (2008, April 30). Mode and Patient-Mix Adjustment of the CAHPS Hospital Survey (HCAHPS). Retrieved from https://hcahpsonline.org/.

141 Mockovak, B. (2008). *Challenging research issues in statistics and survey methodology at the BLS: Mixed-mode survey designs. What are the effects on data quality?* July 19, 2008. Bureau of Labor Statistics. Available at https://www.bls.gov/osmr/challenging_issues/mixedmode.htm.

142 Ibid. Santos, R.

143 Ibid., De Leeuw, E.

144 T.J., Davern, M.E., McAlpine, D.D., Call, K.T. and Rockwood, T.H. (2005, April). Increasing response rates in a survey of Medicaid enrollees: The effect of a prepaid monetary incentive and mixed modes (mail and telephone). *Medical Care* Vol. 43, No. 4, pp. 411-414.

145 Ibid., Dillman, D.A. et al.

146 Ibid., Korzenny, F. and Korzenny, B.A.

147 Ibid., Wang, L., et al.

148 Ibid.

149 Trejo, Y. and Schoua-Glusberg, A. (2017). Device and Internet use among Spanish-dominant Hispanics: Implications for web survey design and testing. *Survey Practice*, Vol. 10 No. 3, 2017. Retrieved from www.surveypractice.org.

150 Census Bureau (2018). *What people and households are represented in each American Community Survey data collection mode*. Retrieved from https://www.census.gov/library/visualizations/interactive/acs-collection.html.

151 Santos, R. Personal email communication. June 15, 2018.

152 Kleiner, B., Lipps, O. and Ferrez, E. (2015). Language ability and motivation among foreigners in survey responding, *Journal of Survey Statistics and Methodology*, (2015) 3, pp. 339-360.

153 Ibid, Santos, R.

154 Paniagua, F. A. (2005). *Assessing and treating Culturally Diverse Clients — A Practical Guide*. Third Edition. SAGE Publications.

155 Guadalupe, P. (2019, March 8). Lack of Latino participation in health studies and clinical trials could have negative impacts, advocates say. LatinoUSA.org, Retrieved from https://latinousa.org/2019/03/18/latinosclinicaltrials/.

156 Leong, F.T.L., Ebreo, A., Kinoshita, L., Inman, A.G., Yang, L.H., and Fu, M. (2007). *Handbook of Asian American Psychology*. Thousand Oaks, CA: Sage Publications. Page 52.

157 Halcomb, E.J., Gholizadeh, L., DiGiacomo, M., Phillips, J., and Davidson, P.M. (2007). Literature review. Considerations in undertaking focus group research with culturally and linguistically diverse groups. *Journal of Clinical Nursing*. Retrieved from

References

https://onlinelibrary.wiley.com/doi/abs/10.1111/j.1365-2702.2006.01760.x.

158 Sha, M., McAvinchey, G., Quiroz, R., and Moncada, J. (2017). Successful techniques to recruit Hispanic and Latino research participants. *Survey Practice*, Vol. 10, Issue 3.

159 Ibid.

160 Kao, B., Lobato, D., Grullon, E., Cheas, L., Plante, W., Seifer, R., and Canino, G. (2010, November 17). *Recruiting Latino and non-Latino families in pediatric research: Considerations from a study on childhood disability*. Retrieved from https://www.ncbi.nlm.nih.gov/pmc/articles/PMC3199442/.

161 Park, H. and Sha, M.M. (2015). Do different recruitment methods reach different Asian demographics? *Survey Practice*, Vol. 8, Issue 4.

162 Sha, M.M., Park, H. and Liu, L. (2013). Exploring the efficiency and utility of methods to recruit non-English speaking qualitative research participants. *Survey Practice*, Vol. 6, Issue 3.

163 Rincon, E. T. (2008). *Dallas/Ft. Worth Multicultural Trendline Study*. Syndicated Research by Rincón & Associates.

164 Rincon, E. T. (2016). *Dallas/Ft. Worth Latino Trendline Study*. Syndicated Research by Rincón & Associates.

165 L&E Research (2018, June 6). *Emerging methods in qualitative research*. Retrieved from http://www.leresearch.com/resources/publications/emerging-methods-in-qualitative-research-technology.

166 20/20 Research (2019). *Introducing QualLink 4.0*. Shared via email dated July 23, 2019.

167 American Association of Public Opinion Research (2007, January). *Protecting against RFP plagiarism*. Retrieved from https://www.aapor.org/Standards-Ethics/Resources/Protecting-against-RFP-Plagarism.aspx.

168 Rincon, E.T. and Tiwari, C. (2020 March 23). Demand metric for supermarket site selection: A case study. *Papers in Applied Geography*. Retrieved from https://doi.org/10.1080/23754931.2020.1712555.

169 Rincon, E.T. (2018, April 18). *Unconscious bias at Starbucks? I don't think so*. Retrieved from https://thecultureofresearch.blogspot.com/2018/04/unconscious-bias-at-starbucks-i-dont.html.

170 Rincon, E.T. (2020, January 10). What hurts South Dallas more — crime or the hasty reporting of crime? *The Culture of Research Blog*, Retrieved from https://thecultureofresearch.blogspot.com/2020/01/what-hurts-south-dallas-more-crime-or.html.

171 Crowe, J., Lacy, C., and Columbus, Y. (2019). Barriers to food security and community stress in an urban food desert. *Urban Science*. Retrieved from https://www.mdpi.com/2413-8851/2/2/46.

Made in the USA
Columbia, SC
30 January 2021